D0675601

Paying For It

SCARLETT O'KELLY

Northumberland County Council	
3 0132 02122150 7	
Askews & Holts	Aug-2012
B/OKE	£7.99

PENGUIN BOOKS

PENGUIN BOOKS

Published by the Penguin Group
Penguin Books Ltd, 80 Strand, London WC2R ORL, England
Penguin Group (USA) Inc., 375 Hudson Street, New York, New York 10014, USA
Penguin Group (Canada), 90 Eglinton Avenue East, Suite 700, Toronto, Ontario, Canada M4P 2Y3
(a division of Pearson Penguin Canada Inc.)
Penguin Ireland, 25 St Stephen's Green, Dublin 2, Ireland
(a division of Penguin Books Ltd)
Penguin Group (Australia), 250 Camberwell Road,
Camberwell, Victoria 3124, Australia (a division of Pearson Australia Group Pty Ltd)
Penguin Books India Pvt Ltd, 11 Community Centre,
Panchsheel Park, New Delhi – 110 017, India
Penguin Group (NZ), 67 Apollo Drive, Rosedale, Auckland 0632, New Zealand
(a division of Pearson New Zealand Ltd)
Penguin Books (South Africa) (Pty) Ltd, Block D, Rosebank Office Park, 181 Jan Smuts Avenue, Parktown North,
Gauteng 2193, South Africa

Penguin Books Ltd, Registered Offices: 80 Strand, London WC2R ORL, England

www.penguin.com

First published as *Between the Sheets* by Penguin Ireland 2012
Published as *Paying For It* in Penguin Books 2012
001

Copyright © Scarlett O'Kelly, 2012

All rights reserved

The moral right of the author has been asserted

Typeset by Palimpsest Book Production Limited, Falkirk, Stirlingshire
Printed in England by Clays Ltd, St Ives plc

Except in the United States of America, this book is sold subject
to the condition that it shall not, by way of trade or otherwise, be lent,
re-sold, hired out, or otherwise circulated without the publisher's
prior consent in any form of binding or cover other than that in
which it is published and without a similar condition including this
condition being imposed on the subsequent purchaser

ISBN: 978-0-241-96323-4

www.greenpenguin.co.uk

MIX
Paper from
responsible sources
FSC www.fsc.org FSC™ C018179

Penguin Books is committed to a sustainable
future for our business, our readers and our planet.
This book is made from Forest Stewardship
Council™ certified paper.

ALWAYS LEARNING   **PEARSON**

A Note about Fact and Fiction

Scarlett O'Kelly is obviously not my real name. When you're reading this account of my year spent having sex with strangers for money, you should be aware that, while everything told here is true, the details have been broken down and reconstructed so that my identity, my children's identities and the identities of my extended family and clients are safe. This element of 'fictionalizing' is essential because if anyone ever found out my secret, it would be utterly devastating. Therefore I have changed details about my background and family circumstances to keep us hidden from view.

I have given my clients false names, too. If you're reading attentively, you'll notice that they are in alphabetical order – Aidan, followed by Brian, then Colin, Derek, Eddie, etc. These names are fictional and I've been careful to omit any identifying details about my clients. So if, as you're reading, you think you recognize someone, you don't. No man mentioned in this book – whether client or lover – corresponds exactly to a real man out there.

The key to my success as an escort was discretion: the men required it, I demanded it, and my whole life is dependent on the thin veil of obscurity that separates escort me from real me. (Though the book is written in the present tense, my escort work is largely in the past. However, I still think of myself as having two selves – 'escort' me and 'real' me.) If that veil were to be torn down, I would have to relocate along with my children outside the country. I live in small-town Ireland; I am a respectable middle-class woman and mother; I am supposed to keep my 'normal' sex life safely behind curtains and doors. If it ever got out that I am in fact an experienced sex worker who has slept with more than one hundred men, my life here would be over. That's why this account of my secret life has been carefully constructed to give the truth, but in veiled form. Everything in this book is real: my story, the stories of the men and the sex. It all happened.

Contents

Prologue

I open my eyes and look up. The branches hanging over my head are laden with soft, just-fallen snow. Small flakes are landing on my face. I open my mouth to catch one on my tongue. Everything is so white, so pure, so beautiful. I don't notice the cold any more, only the stillness and silence around me, and the feeling of deep, rhythmic thrusts getting faster and faster. I zone out a little, overcome by the pleasure. He reaches his hand under my coat and upwards, under my red lace bra – cold fingers against my warm skin. He strokes my breast, his thumb rubbing the nipple until it's hard and sensitive. His other hand pushes down between my legs, stroking my clit with the same rhythm as his thrusts grow deeper and faster. We're both groaning as the feeling builds. I give myself over to a delicious slow orgasm and my client starts to come the moment he feels me clench his cock inside me.

We lie there for a minute, as breathing returns to normal, then he whispers to me to get up and back to the car before we're spotted. I could happily lie there longer, but he takes my hand and pulls me up. Once back in the car, we sit in silence for a while, regaining our composure.

'Well,' I smile at him, 'I learn something new every day on this job.'

'And what's that?' he said.

'I never knew sex outdoors, even in the snow, could be so enjoyable.'

He grins at me. 'I haven't done that in years. It's much more of a turn-on than regular sex. Thank you.'

Sadly, this was to be our last encounter. In the year I had been working as a full-time escort, this man had become a regular client and we had got to know each other well. Now his wife had been made redundant and they were going to have to manage on one income. This was our farewell shag. I gave him a discount.

That little vignette explains this book in a nutshell: there's a lot of sex in it but, as much as sex, this is a story about money. There are fantastic books out there by financial journalists and economists and all kinds of experts about the global financial crash and how the Irish economy turned to dust almost overnight. I haven't read them. I've been too broke to buy them and too busy trying to survive. But I'd like to think that this book complements those others because it gives a vivid account of what happens when you become a statistic – jobless, hopeless and mired in debt. Granted, the way in which I decided to tackle my predicament was a bit extreme. If, twelve months earlier, anyone had told me that during the coldest December for decades I would be earning my living sprawled under a tree having sex in the snow, I would have been horrified and incredulous. It's strange how your understanding of your limitations changes when you've spent nearly a year having paid sex with strangers.

I am a hooker, a prostitute, a whore or an escort – whatever you like to call me, I'm it. I'm also an ordinary mum getting on with life. You may have seen me in the supermarket with my children doing the weekly shop, or popping into the pharmacy to pick up a kiddie's cough bottle, or at Sunday Mass in my local town. I'm someone you would comfortably chat to at the school gates – maybe you have – or in the doctor's surgery or while queuing at the post office, and you would probably think I was a lovely lady. I am basically anyone who looks like a well-groomed, attractive, educated woman hitting forty. How I pay my mortgage, fund the children's hobbies and interests and put food on the table may make me unusual, but I hope it doesn't change who I am.

There is nothing extraordinary in my background. I am a 'respectable' separated mother of three, a refugee from middle-class Ireland. I am the daughter of a comfortable farming family and my siblings are all successful in the professions. My parents would be seen – rightly – as good, decent Catholics and pillars of their community. I went to a convent boarding school and university and had a successful professional career, during which I gained a number of further qualifications. Like many Irish women who came out of university in the early 1990s, I had the confidence, drive and ambition to believe I could and must succeed and have it all. In the course of my career

I travelled extensively, worked in responsible positions in corporate environments and was comfortable dealing with top-level management in large companies and government departments.

I got married and for many years my husband and I enjoyed the typical Celtic Tiger lifestyle of the moderate middle classes: we worked hard and we enjoyed the rewards work gave us – nights out fairly regularly, two holidays a year, good-quality clothes, nice food, a spacious home. On our joint income we could comfortably afford it and there were no crazy excesses – no drugs (nice people with an ounce of cop-on who value their lives don't do drugs), no benders (responsible parents know that hangovers and children do not mix) and no living on credit (my parents often warned us about the recession of the 1980s and advised that dealing with cash only was the best way to stay solvent and sane). Then life's demands and pressures took their toll, the marriage waned and we parted nearly a decade ago. We have a reasonably amicable relationship.

It never occurred to either of us that there was anything unstable about what we had built our lives upon or that there could be drastic consequences if circumstances changed. I am sure we are not alone. Now I live in the kind of place that features in newspaper articles about 'ghost estates', where businesses are closing on a daily basis and where people like us, who were used to good lifestyles, find themselves on the St Vincent de Paul circulation list. The housing estates around mine were marketed as 'up and coming' a few years ago; the only thing up and coming about them now is the level of fear.

I accept that I am unusual in how I have responded to that fear. I guess I am unusual in another respect, too: although I went into the sex industry because of economic necessity, and although the double life I lead is sometimes extremely stressful, I have to admit that I often enjoy the work. Sometimes I even find it therapeutic. I think most people want to run away and hide from the real world from time to time, and the good sexual encounters I have are my experience of getting away from it all. Sex with strangers can be exciting: it's always unpredictable and it allows me to zone out for a bit – in much the same way as yoga or meditation. I can get very aroused when I just live in the moment. A sexual encounter is brief and reality is always waiting when it's over, so why not enjoy it for as long as it lasts?

It's an odd thing to have discovered, and it was the last thing I would have expected when I decided to become a sex worker, but some of the encounters I've had with my clients are among the most honest, intimate sexual experiences of my life. There are no expectations, no waiting for the phone to ring, no 'Will he? Won't he?' dilemmas, no flapping about what he thought of me, my sexual expertise, my personality, looks, figure, dress sense, intellect. There's nothing but a simple moment, a moment when two adults can put aside the world and enjoy each other, enjoy that moment for what it is. It's just sex.

1. Life Before Sex Work

Money. I could start and end this book with that one word. It has dictated my life in many ways – paying for the good times, defining the bad times and driving my decision-making all the while. As a middle-class person, you don't ever think you'll be without money. It's not that you can't imagine tough times, but you don't really factor in the idea that a time could come when you have twenty euro in your purse and nothing else whatsoever – no back-up in the bank and no savings salted away. Nothing. When you've lived with the safety net of money all your life, it's a huge shock when that net is suddenly taken away and you're allowed to crash to earth.

When I first got married, my husband and I easily kept up with the Joneses and thoroughly enjoyed our lifestyle. Then a baby came along, but that wasn't a problem and we still had the holidays, the two cars and the safety net. Life was rosy. We were delighted when I got pregnant again quickly and we immediately decided we needed a bigger house. Like everyone else around us, we got a huge mortgage to buy our 'for ever' family home – a big, spacious, light-filled house with a garden, on the edge of town. Being a country girl, I didn't want to settle in the middle of a built-up area, so living in a detached house on a small estate was the best of both worlds. Glowing with the joys of young motherhood, I had been considering giving up work and staying at home with the children, but paying for our beautiful new house would require both incomes, so I put that daydream aside. I had plenty of qualifications and experience in my field, which was a growth area in the booming Celtic Tiger economy, so securing a suitable job with a bit of flexibility in terms of childcare wouldn't be a problem.

That was all well and good for a bit. We were busy, but we were managing. I worked for a company for a while, then opted to go freelance so that I could be my own boss and pick my hours to suit. If one of the children was sick, I didn't have to work; if I needed more money for a holiday or Christmas, I worked a little extra. There was a nice crèche near our house that didn't mind me dropping the kids off at short notice if I got work unexpectedly. Plus I only had to pay for the times my kids were there, unlike a lot of places where you pay regardless of whether or not your child attends.

Then along came pregnancy number three. I felt wretched throughout, so I didn't work very much. It was hard with two other young children to mind, and I was struggling to keep everything going, including my relationship with my husband. By month eight of the pregnancy the house had become a millstone around our necks and we were only just keeping our heads above water. By the time the baby was born I was exhausted and stressed out, and my husband, although there in person, had checked out emotionally. I didn't know it then, but it was the beginning of the end for us as a couple. Eventually someone had to call it a day. I couldn't bear the feeling that I was sharing my life with a man who was continually making it clear he wanted to be elsewhere. I asked my husband to leave.

Roll on two years and the picture isn't so nice: shitty separation, three kids under eight and financial commitments that didn't add up. I kept the house after the separation, but I hated it now. I went back into full-time employment to make ends meet, fitting a demanding job around crèche times, school runs, laundry, meals, single parenting and the seemingly non-stop school breaks and holidays. I was a shell of my former self, on autopilot from day to day, month to month.

Naturally, my top priority was to provide and care for my children. My job was difficult to keep up and a source of stress, but it did give me an excellent salary and benefits, so I reckoned that as long as I dedicated myself exclusively to work and my children for a couple of hard years, all would come good in the end. I didn't think in any great depth about how I would manage – I figured the details would work themselves out along the way. In my naïvety, I believed that, as long as there was money coming in and the children were healthy and happy, I could live this crazy 24/7 lifestyle for the next two years. By then, the children would all be in school and the seriously hard slog of raising toddlers would be over. I promised myself that I would then give some attention to myself and my needs, and live a little. I fantasized about the *Sex and the City*-style social life I would have. I wondered what evening courses I would do. I imagined that some weekends I would just relax, read and have mammoth lie-ins. What fabulous dates would I be asked on? What would my knight in shining armour look like? Would I have more children with him, the man I had concocted in my mind who would eventually come to my rescue? That was the fantasy life: real life was an agreement with myself to do without personal wants or needs and put my entire focus on work and raising the children. I had no option. If I was to keep all the balls in the air, this was the only way I could do it.

That system of non-living was fine for a while, but after about ten months of working eighteen-hour days, between my career and home-making, I started to get very, very tired. My initial enthusiasm for my new single life was waning and I was finding it harder and harder to make it through the week. The fantasy life of my future didn't sustain me any more. I felt bored, irritable and utterly exhausted. I looked pale and drawn, my skin was dull and spotty for the first time since my teenage years and I started to put on weight. I didn't have the time to plan sensible meals for myself. I'd stop at a garage on the commute home from work and buy sugary drinks and chocolate to keep me awake and alert at the wheel. I would go to bed praying that the kids would sleep through the night and that I'd get more than my usual three or four hours' sleep. I'd visualize waking up in the morning feeling rested and invigorated, leaving the house with a spring in my step. It never happened.

The tiredness wouldn't go away, so I arranged to see my GP. She listened to my description of my life, asked some leading questions and finally diagnosed depression. She prescribed medication, told me I had to slow down, that I was burned out, and asked me to check in with her regularly. I was horrified. Depression? How could I, a strong and capable person, not be coping? I felt ashamed and embarrassed. I felt like 'depression' was a euphemism for weak, incapable, vulnerable. I also felt like I had brought this on myself – that by asking my husband to leave I had set in motion the dominoes that had knocked over my free time, my disposable income, my sense of self and self-worth and now, it seemed, my sanity. Was this my fault? How could I have been so naïve as not to see this coming and to think I could get away with burning the candle at both ends without it having an impact on my health?

After the initial shock of that diagnosis, I tried to clear my head by writing lists and being the super-organizer I had always prided myself on being. I rejigged the childcare arrangements to give myself the odd hour here and there to have a walk, a rest or even the occasional nap. I rearranged the access agreement with my husband so that I'd get a break every other weekend and on some weekdays, too. I approached my employers and proposed a part-time contract, which they accepted. I examined the household budget and reorganized that too, trimming my spending in line with my reduced salary. It was nothing dramatic – just being a bit more careful and selective. I had to add my own health to the list of priorities now because I had to remain well enough to look after the children properly.

A few months later it was all working out fine: my health was recovering, the kids were happy and we were all actually enjoying the slower, less frazzled pace of life. Then the recession hit. Like most ordinary people getting on with everyday life, I never saw it coming. Even if I had been paying attention to the economists who were saying it would all end in tears, I don't think I could have got my head around just how devastating it was going to be. Within a matter of a few months, it seemed, work dried up in my sector and part-time contracts weren't renewed. My qualifications and extensive experience didn't matter. I was out of a job. It was a crippling blow, both personally and financially. Then came the nail in the coffin: my husband's hours were cut and his finances hit the rocks. There were no more maintenance payments coming from him.

There was nothing else for it – I had to sign on for social welfare for the first time in my life. When I was told how much I would get per week, I went home and cried. It wasn't nearly enough – it wouldn't even make a teeny dent in my monthly mortgage repayment. I cut back everything to the bone, but the bills still mounted. Only people who are in or have been in this position know how terrifying it is to sit down with the calculator and the bills every night and see the awful truth staring back at you. Doing that as a single parent is even worse because there's no one to hold your hand and say it will be okay. There's just you, the bills, the unrelenting responsibility and the misery of feeling that you're failing your children. I hated not being able to pay my way when I had been contributing all my life. And I really hated having to say no to my children all the time, no matter how reasonable or modest their requests. It was very difficult to come to terms with the life I was now giving them, one that was so far removed from what I had envisaged when I set out on married life.

I needed cash . . . now. I racked my brains for ideas to make a few euro. What were other people doing to manage? I looked around, but I didn't have any gold to sell, no antiques or paintings. I had no investments, risky or otherwise, to fall back on to cushion the blow. I didn't have any bonds to cash in. My savings were long gone. I was just another jobless worker without reserves – there was an idle army of us, apparently. But what could I do – swoon and bemoan my bad luck? Lose my home? Watch my children live miserable, colourless lives? No fucking way! Shit happens . . . and then some, but you have to fight and fight and do whatever it takes to make a living. Well, that was my approach anyway.

2. Thinking the Unthinkable

You would think that with debts, stresses and a recession, I wouldn't have had any energy for a love life, but the loneliness really started to get to me after a while. I found myself wondering if everything would be easier to handle if I had a partner to confide in and have fun with. Even if he couldn't help me out financially, he could at least make me feel attractive, make me laugh and feel less alone. I was so busy with daily living that I knew it was unlikely I would just happen to bump into Mr Right now, so I decided to get out there and be proactive in trying to fill the gap in my life.

I signed up with a reputable Internet dating site, but after a while I had to admit to myself that I was making zero progress. When I say zero progress, I mean I was getting very few dates from the site and the men I did meet left a lot to be desired. I spent a lot of time ensuring my profile was detailed and accurate and included a true-to-life photograph of myself. I wanted to meet a nice gentleman to share meals and nights out with, someone with whom I could have a friendship or a relationship that would take my mind off reality for a bit, but men of that sort remained elusive, at least on that dating site.

I went on a number of dates, but they were all one-offs. I don't think I'm fussy, but those guys made it so blatantly obvious that they were just after a quick shag that I found it irritating and downright disheartening. Were there no men out there who wanted to engage in conversation and decide after that if there was any mutual attraction? The ideas some of those guys had were incredible. I arranged a coffee date with one guy and he had the cheek to book a hotel room in advance, obviously interpreting 'coffee' as 'shag'. Then there were the ones – and, yes, it happened more than once – who'd meet me, shake my hand, say hello-and-isn't-the-weather-terrible, then ask my sexual preferences! They didn't even pretend to be interested in me as a person. Their arrogance and forwardness guaranteed them a cold shoulder and absolutely no chance of getting laid – even when they were good-looking.

I was at home one day, having checked my dating messages only to find, yet again, a slew of transparent 'shag contacts'. I was bored and a bit down about everything. The doorbell rang and it was a close friend, popping in for tea and sympathy. Her husband had been made redundant and she was now in the same boat as me – budgeting like crazy, but never having enough money. We sat down for a coffee and chatted about the difficulties we were facing, then tried to come up with money-making ideas. We started to get a bit giggly at the sheer frustrating hopelessness of it all.

'At this stage,' my friend said, shaking her head, 'I'd feckin' sell my body – money's that tight.'

'Yeah, me too,' I laughed, 'but who the hell would pay for it when we're hitting forty and trying our damnedest to hold back the ravages of time?'

We howled with laughter as we pictured parading ourselves on a sexual catwalk for selection by potential punters: 'And this is Destiny, gentlemen, late thirties, several owners, only given birth to three children, a few pounds overweight, but sure ye like something to grab on to, don't ye, lads? Destiny describes herself as being very low maintenance – she only gets a chance to shave her legs once a month. Now that there's no money coming in, she can't send the kids to childcare and go off to the spa any more, so ye'll have to ignore the few pimples as well. She's very versatile and can go from dominant (like when she's dealing with the kids) to submissive (like when she's with the bank manager) in a split second. She's very fit and flexible thanks to scrubbing the house and doing a million things at once, and she doesn't mind a bit of pain either if that's what yer into, lads – to be honest, she'll probably just fall asleep on ye if she gets half a chance cos she's bolloxed tired. With Destiny, you can be guaranteed you're getting an honest-to-goodness real woman. Now, any takers here, lads?'

We laughed ourselves silly, then came back to reality, sighed and got on with our day.

We had, of course, been joking, but I found that I couldn't stop thinking about the idea of selling my body. Was it so crazy? I had been planning to delete my profile from the dating site because I was so sick of the sex-hungry chancers who were contacting me, but now I began to wonder if there was something in it. The guys on the site were obviously eager for no-strings sex, but how many women out there would fulfil that wish? Probably not many, I reckoned, and especially not the ones, like myself, who were on dating sites for genuine reasons. What did those guys do once they had been turned down by a number of dates? When I thought about it logically, it would make much more sense for them to admit to themselves what they wanted, ask for it and pay for it. So why didn't they do that? I suddenly realized why not: they might want no-strings sex, but they wanted to have it with someone of a certain standard, someone they would actually date. They just weren't so much into the dating part of it.

I laughed at myself for even thinking like that, telling myself it was just an experimental line of thought. The truth was, though, that the idea was starting to take hold. Could I sell sex for cash? I was on the slippery slope to my forties and far from *Pretty Woman* proportions so, for starters, would anyone buy my body? I thought about the eagerness of the dates I'd met and thought, Actually, yes. I'd say men would like to have sex with a normal woman like me – it had certainly never been a problem in the past. But then, could I actually lie down with a stranger and let him penetrate me? I thought about my sexual experiences over the years – my ex-husband, all the ex-boyfriends, the odd one-night stand – and again found myself thinking, Actually, yes, I think I could do it. I enjoyed sex, I had a strong sense of my own identity, and surely I could use some kind of screening process to weed out the gobshites and protect myself. It's money for old rope after all, and the oldest profession in the world. I knew that I could have done it years ago, but could I do it now, as a mother with responsibilities? The answer was easy: it was precisely because I was a mother with responsibilities that I could do it.

I decided to do a little research and see if I was thinking like a mad woman or whether there was a market out there for what I could provide: a high-end escort service that would be a million miles away from the grisly reality of the black-market sex industry reported in the newspapers. First, I invented a fake profile on a legitimate dating site to test the waters. The profile gave no details apart from my age (minus a few years), location, gender and that my occupation was 'masseuse'.

Well, I was blown away by the reaction. This nameless, faceless 'profile', devoid of personality, got tons of attention. I couldn't believe it when my inbox filled up rapidly. As I started opening the emails, I realized I had found an untapped, readily available but under-serviced market – an entrepreneur's wet dream! Although my profile on the dating site said hardly anything about me, it gave just enough details to reel in the guys who were only interested in sex. The initial emails I received coyly asked what sort of massage service I provided, what my rates were and if any 'extras' were on offer. The men could sense a mile off that what I was suggesting was a sexual service for sale, and they took the bait. Eureka! I had finally uncovered a chink of light at the end of the long, dark tunnel I had been trudging through for so long. It looked like I had struck a potential goldmine.

I expanded my research to find out what the escort experience was generally like in Ireland and also to try to ascertain what exactly the men were looking for. I discovered through the Internet, via web forums and Irish escort directory sites, that the majority of the women were under time pressure to fit in a given number of clients every day/night and therefore were always clock-watching when they were with the men. This tallied with what the men replying to my profile were saying in their emails. My respondents were chiefly older, married and attached men, who repeatedly emphasized the importance of discretion, safety and good sex. Some mentioned negative experiences with foreign girls, when they had felt like 'just another punter', and said they were looking for an encounter that felt special and unrushed. They were interested in being with an Irish woman, with the emphasis on 'woman' – curves, stretch-marks and all. Email after email stated that the escorts they had previously tried were too rushed and impersonal in their approach. These guys were looking for the Girlfriend Experience – sex with frills! The value they put on this was, of course, reflected in what they were willing to pay.

By now, I had moved away from being shocked at myself and was simply fascinated by the world I was uncovering, which I had been largely unaware of until now. There was clearly no safety guarantee in this area of work, but as I read the emails and assessed what the men were saying, I realized that, with a bit of preparation and common sense, it would be possible to have rigid selection rules that would identify the men most suited to me and my situation – in other words, the ones that had as much to lose as I did if word of their exploits ever got out. The other thing that struck me was that those guys weren't looking for a porn-star fantasy fuck: they wanted fairly straightforward sex in a warm, open environment and some rapport with their escort. That didn't sound too difficult. Now I seriously began to wonder, Would I do this in the right circumstances?

In my former working life, I had been a follower of 'the six Ps' – *prior preparation prevents piss-poor performance* – and I decided to treat this 'venture' like any other business plan and do the groundwork. I realized that my qualifications and training would stand to me in this sphere as much as any other: sales training, dealing with the public, presentation skills, time management and marketing. Finally, the 'Death by PowerPoint' in-service training I had both received and delivered in other jobs would also pay dividends. (A note of thanks to all previous employers for those training days – it was worth it, after all!) I put my business acumen to devising a marketing strategy that I could apply to the sex industry as a professional service provider. I drew up a rough business plan, setting out my goals, priorities and time-management aims. I included the pros and cons, listing the legal, health and safety implications of selling sex. If I was going to do this, it had to be as safe as possible.

A very basic rule of sales is to find out what the customer wants and give it to them. I read and re-read the emails from the men interested in the 'masseuse' service, extracting the key points to create a profile of what they most wanted in paid lady company. Their top priorities were: complete anonymity; no chance of being caught, by either spouses or the gardaí; safe sex practices to ensure the health of their own wives and lovers; and enthusiastic expert sex – vaginal, oral and anal. When it came to rates of pay, I didn't have much to go on. However, I knew there were two standard models: price low and generate a high turnover of customers to make a profit; or secure a low turnover with a high price tag per customer. I decided that, from what the initial contacts were telling me, I could price high and have a low turnover. These men seemed educated and were available during the day, which implied they were either self-employed or travelled as part of their work. I drew up a 'price list': four hundred euro for the first session, which I reckoned at ninety minutes, and three hundred for each session thereafter, which I reckoned at sixty minutes or thereabouts. I wasn't going to clock-watch as that was one of the things the men said they hated, but I figured about an hour and fifteen minutes max would see the job through to its natural conclusion.

It was becoming more and more real as I worked through the research and plans. Looking at it objectively, as a business proposal, it seemed worth a try. So I took the final steps. On the Internet I found a full and current risk assessment for sex workers, courtesy of the New Zealand government; sex work is legal there. It spelt out the specific risks of the work relating to security and safe sex practices and how best to safeguard against them. It also had several nuggets of information that I wouldn't have thought of myself, such as: carry a torch in case you need to check a penis to ensure it looks healthy; don't let body fluids near *any* orifice; and don't shave or wax for twenty-four hours prior to seeing a client as the skin may be more susceptible to infection. I bought a cheap, unregistered mobile phone. I ordered a credit card with a humble credit limit – my first credit card ever. I created a work name and an alias email account. Then I put the mobile phone number online with my masseuse profile, and waited to see what would happen.

3. First Call

It was a Tuesday afternoon in early February when I took my first call from a potential client. I remember it clearly: I was peeling potatoes in the kitchen sink when the 'work mobile' lit up. I rushed to grab a towel to dry my hands. My heart started to beat faster and I had butterflies in my stomach bordering on nausea – similar to the way you feel when you get a shock. I picked up the phone and paused to steady myself. I took a deep breath, then pressed the green button. In my head, a voice was saying, 'Are you mad?' On the phone I heard my voice say, 'Hello, this is Scarlett speaking.'

Luckily for me, the caller was more nervous than I was – he had a country accent and was hesitant, unsure how to express himself. My managerial instincts kicked in and I immediately felt calmer and in control. My plan was to ask him as much about himself as I could, to ascertain if he was the right client for me – especially for my first time. We talked for ten minutes or so and I was surprised at how quickly he relaxed into the conversation and opened up to me.

Aidan described himself as a 'regular guy' in his mid-thirties. His partner had been under the weather for some time and, although it wasn't a serious illness, her libido had taken a nose-dive. He had talked with her about finding a solution to their non-existent sex life, but nothing was happening. He had decided to visit an escort because he couldn't tolerate the frustration any longer, but didn't want an affair or a one-night stand. He thought an escort was the best option to release his frustration while ensuring he wouldn't be found out. He said he just wanted 'normal' sex – 'nothing kinky or outrageous'. Wearing my non-escort hat, he didn't sound my type at all – I like men who are confident and well able to express themselves. In the circumstances, though, I decided that his lack of experience and low expectations made him an excellent candidate for a trial run. I told him the price and he didn't comment, which I took to mean he had no objection. We discussed and agreed a location. The date was set for two days later.

When I'd been mulling things over, I hadn't been able to decide if I'd be better off having my first encounter with a virgin client or a seasoned user. On the one hand, if I made any mistakes or looked like I hadn't a clue what I was doing, a first-timer wouldn't be any the wiser. On the other, someone more familiar with the business could give me valuable feedback, directly and indirectly. But what were the chances of meeting an experienced guy who would understand if I found I couldn't go through with it, or if it was rubbish sex and he thought I wasn't worth the money?

I hadn't had sex for several months, and even then it had been with plenty of vodka tonics on board to loosen my inhibitions. In my sex life I wasn't much of a leader – good sex in the past was where we had fed off each other's responses – and of course the guys hadn't been strangers, didn't expect me to be some *über*-experienced shag of a lifetime and weren't forking out for it. The normal precursor to sex for me was drinks and/or dinner, good conversation, slow music, flirting, kissing: the usual. Meeting my first client, however, I would be stone-cold sober (not even a sip of alcohol on board for Dutch courage – I would be driving before and after the meeting) and full sex would be expected without much of a lead-in. It could be a disaster and I didn't fancy being on the receiving end of abuse. Nor did I think I could handle it if a guy thought I was useless. No, I was definitely better off with a first-timer, I decided. I needed my first experience to be positive to give me the confidence to continue.

I applied a lesson from my previous professional life: perception is reality. If you appear confident and competent, people will believe that that is what you are, even before you do anything. I knew that to pull off this new role successfully, I had to take on a persona and make that perception my client's reality. I had to imagine what an experienced sex worker would do, how she would think, how she would behave, how she would control and direct the client without being overbearing, and how she would manage the time during the session. This needed to be the best performance of my life if I was to have any chance of making money out of it in the future. And I badly needed the money.

It didn't really bother me how it would work physically, even though I'd never had sex where I wasn't at all aroused. Does a vagina even accept a penis when it isn't in the least bit lubricated? I wondered. Of course it must, I told myself – it would be impossible for sex workers to be aroused with every client. The mechanics shouldn't be a problem. It was the acting I was worried about. How good would I be at all the pretend moaning, groaning and dirty talk that clients would expect? Talking dirty on the phone was one thing, but how would it work when there was a naked body in front of me – a naked body that mightn't turn me on in the slightest, that might even repel me? Could I appear in control and subtly manage the client, tell him when he overstepped the mark or had an unsheathed cock too close to me? Yes, I knew his penis was going to touch me, but I didn't want it going anywhere near my genitals – there's no room for compromise in safe sex: it's either safe or it's not, and if he got too close to any orifices, I'd have to let him know. What if he was rough and wanted to hurt me? What if I came away with bruises where he had held me down when I asked him to stop? What if I felt so used and degraded that no money seemed worth it? I did worry about these things, but then, if you lived life by studiously avoiding the what-ifs, you'd never have any experiences at all.

We had arranged to meet at a three-star hotel we were both familiar with and which was within reasonable driving distance for both of us. I'd had lunch there a few times and it had always seemed quiet and clean. I hoped the rooms were decent. On the day of the appointment I felt nervous, but up for the challenge. We were to meet at nine p.m., which gave me plenty of time to prepare. I telephoned the hotel and made the booking, sounding confident and courteous on the phone and securing the room with my new credit card. I dropped the children to their father, as usual on a Thursday, then tried to think through all the scenarios for the meeting ahead.

It was hard to know what I'd need. Obviously, condoms, lubricant and massage oil were essential, I'd worked out that much. Since I would be waiting for him in the room all hot to trot, I'd have to look the part. I scrambled through my bedroom drawers. I had lovely negligees and silk undies I'd worn for my ex-husband, but they seemed too subtle for this situation: something a bit racier was required. I drove into town and picked up a red and black satin basque in Penney's. The bodice had black criss-cross detailing leading to an underwired balcony bra. It gave me plenty of cleavage and support – essential for boobs that had breast-fed three babies. A short red chemise and a red lacy G-string finished off the outfit. It was tight, tacky and tarty – perfect. I also found a bargain pair of red patent stilettos that were so uncomfortable they could only have been intended for bedroom wear. It didn't matter – once the client was in the room and I'd strutted around enough to impress him, I'd be kicking them off. I felt incredibly self-conscious standing in line for the checkout with my basket of tat, but thankfully I didn't see anyone I knew.

Okay, now for the more technical stuff. A few doors up from Penney's there was an old-fashioned pharmacy. It wasn't somewhere I would normally shop, so I hoped my luck would hold and that I wouldn't spot any friends or mums from school there. I strolled in and looked for the section that would have the lubricants. I quickly found it and browsed through the various products, eventually settling on plain old KY jelly – it seemed more clinical than Durex Tingle and a bit less embarrassing to approach the tills with. If my bits completely shut down on me, I'd have this stuff for back-up. I went to look at the many different types of condom on offer. I knew what type my ex liked, but what did men generally prefer? In the end I bought a twelve-pack of Durex Fetherlite. The blurb on the packet told me they increased sensitivity, were better shaped and therefore a better fit and easier to apply: that all sounded fine to me.

Finally, I headed to the innocent safety of the homeopathy aisle and bought lavender oil and a base oil for massaging. I had advertised myself as a masseuse, after all. My ex had loved a good massage, especially in our early years together, and I, eager to please him then, had learned how to give a sensual, relaxing one and knew which oils were best to use. I felt massage was an easier progression from introduction to full sex: it would act as a buffer for me and for the client.

I arrived home with my new work gear and set about planning how to organize myself. Was I going to arrive at the hotel in a regular outfit and change into my 'uniform' in the room? What if I got delayed or he arrived early and saw me in regular clothes? That would destroy the illusion. Right, I'd have to arrive half ready. I showered, did my hair and makeup and got into the new underwear, then put on a long black skirt, a nice blouse and a smart jacket. I looked perfectly respectable. The hooker heels and other paraphernalia went into a trendy, oversized leather bag along with my wallet, from which I'd removed anything of a personal nature – photos of the kids, receipts, anything with my real name and address on it. I put my credit card into a pocket in my jacket, where it wouldn't be seen. I didn't mind that it had my real name on it – I would appear to be just another travelling businesswoman booking into a hotel room and I would make sure I hid it from the client. I didn't see it as a problem.

When I was done, I stepped in front of the mirror. The overall look was fashionably understated.

I was ready, with loads of time to spare. My head had been spinning all day with all the possible outcomes of tonight's meeting. I had cramps in my stomach and felt nauseous, but I still wanted to do it. Time dragged and I just wanted it over with. I needed something in my tummy as it would be a good few hours before I was home again, so I forced myself to have tea and toast. I phoned the kids to say goodnight so they wouldn't be looking for me later. Hopefully, that would prevent them calling my normal mobile phone and wondering why I wasn't answering. If they did call, I'd just have to make up some excuse.

During the forty-minute drive to the hotel I thought of how I would manage things there. I had brought some folders with me to create the impression that I was in the area on business. I was confident that I looked the part and nothing about me screamed 'sex'. If there was no one at Reception when I left, the room would be charged to my credit card and that would be easy. If there was someone on the desk, I'd make up a story about a relative being ill and having to get home in a hurry. I turned on some music to relax myself as I drove, but my stomach was doing cartwheels.

I parked in a far corner of the main car park, where I was sure my registration couldn't be seen from the hotel entrance. If things went very wrong and I needed to get out fast, I didn't want anyone to be able to identify my car. I walked through the front doors of the hotel. One half of my brain was concentrating on looking as normal as possible, while the other was urgently telling me I could turn around and walk away right now and it would be okay. I went up to the reception desk and told the girl I had a reservation for one night. She was very friendly and chatty – too chatty. In the state I was in, I couldn't handle small-talk and sounded abrupt, even a bit rude. I excused myself by saying I'd had a long drive and was very tired. *Lesson One*: If I ever did this again, I would approach Reception in a crisp, businesslike fashion and not make eye contact or smile. They were not going to be chatty with someone who clearly wasn't the chatty type. I grabbed the key-card off the desk and made my way to the lift, taking it to the fifth floor. I stepped out into a long corridor of closed doors. What was going on behind them all? God only knew. I walked slowly, watching the numbers until I reached mine.

From the moment I stepped into the room, I wanted to get out of it. It was small, poky, and reeked of stale tobacco and air freshener. The rust-coloured carpet looked miserable against the bare magnolia walls. A stained, shabby throw was laid at the end of the bed. I rolled it up and shoved it into the wardrobe. The bed sheets were thin from laundering, but at least they were clean. The overhead lighting was very bright and I looked for a lamp, but there wasn't one. In the bathroom there was soap, a few clean towels and two plastic cups covered with paper hygiene seals. God, this was basic – so different from any hotel I would have chosen for recreation. There was no ambience and no way of creating any. It occurred to me that a couple of scented candles would have made a huge difference. If the bathroom light was left on, the main bedroom lights were off and a few candles flickered around the room, it would have disguised the shabbiness of the place, softened any flaws in my appearance and created a more inviting atmosphere. *Lesson Two*: Be prepared to dress the room appropriately.

When I had stripped down to my escort attire and stored my clothes in the rickety MDF wardrobe, I texted Aidan the room number and details of how to get to it without asking at Reception. My mouth was dry and my heart was pounding. I got myself some tap water and sat on the armchair, waiting. I saw my reflection in the full-length mirror on the wall opposite: I hardly recognized myself in the garish lingerie and the ridiculously high shiny heels.

'What the fuck are you doing?' I said out loud. I sounded like someone else. 'Move away from the mirror,' I told myself sternly. 'You know why you're here.' The only thing breaking the silence was the occasional sound of traffic from the car park below. I tried the television to see if it had any radio channels, but there was nothing. I turned it off. *Lesson Three*: Bring your own source of music.

I got up, paced and twitched with nervousness. Seriously, what the fuck was I doing? What if he was horrible or rough or wanted to harm me? This was just too dodgy – what had I been thinking? It flashed through my mind that I should get the hell out of there, but as I started to bolt, there was a gentle knock on the door. I composed myself, took a deep breath, pulled back my shoulders, tried to relax my face into what I hoped was a pleasant – or at least non-terrified – expression and opened the door a few inches. I saw a pair of grey-blue eyes and a face with an open, kind expression. He looked normal.

'Aidan?' I said.

'Yep, that's me,' he whispered. I let him in and locked the door behind us. The time had arrived.

I was doing it.

4. First Encounter

Aidan looked me up and down, from teased shiny hair to tarty shiny shoes. 'Sexy,' he said. I was glad someone thought so – he clearly had no taste. Mind you, if he was as nervous as I was, he had probably just said the first thing that came into his head.

'Thank you. It's lovely to meet you,' I said, trying to sound sincere. I told him to make himself comfortable as I got him a glass of water.

He was about six feet tall with a fairly muscular build. His coarse red hair could have done with the attention of a good barber. His clothes were old-fashioned for a man in his thirties. I couldn't help but notice his dark brown loafers, the kind my father had started wearing for comfort in his sixties. He wore a sweater over jeans and both looked like they could do with a wash. He was neither attractive nor unattractive to me – just not my type.

'Okay then. If you'd like to get started, you can undress and lie on the bed,' I said, in an upbeat voice, in keeping with the illusion of control I wanted to create.

He started to strip in silence. I knew from how he was doing everything I suggested that he was happy for me to take the lead. There was only so much I could prepare for and I didn't have a plan of what I would do with him during the next ninety minutes. I was just playing it by ear, hoping to pick up cues from him. One thing comforted me: he clearly didn't have any expectations.

With great relief, I kicked off the fuck-me shoes. As he lay on the bed, I picked my bottle of massage oil from my bag and told him that, if he'd like to lie face down, I'd start with a gentle massage. I couldn't believe how steady my voice sounded. My heart was still pounding and my stomach was still in bits – I hoped to God I wouldn't throw up. I had forgotten to arrange my stuff on the locker and had to apologize for rooting around in my bag to find things. I had also forgotten to put out my watch and phone – the watch for time-keeping and the phone in case I needed to make an emergency 999 call. *Lesson Four*: Have your stuff organized before the client gets to the room. Aidan didn't seem to notice that things were not going too smoothly. I hadn't told him I was new to this – I wanted to see if I could pull it off without any hand-holding and I didn't want him looking for a discount because I was a beginner.

He was naked, lying face down on the bed. I stood beside it, leaning over him, and poured some massage oil on to my palms. I warmed it up and then started massaging his back. It was so strange touching him – his skin was unfamiliar and unlike any skin I had been close to in the past. I cringed at the feel of his flesh. When my arms started to ache, I knew I had to get closer to massage him properly and that I had to get over my hang-ups about him. If I was going to pull it off, I had to go for it.

I climbed on to the bed and knelt between his legs, which was much more comfortable. But I was still wondering how the hell I was going to spend the next hour with him. He was so quiet – was he thinking of walking out? Had he sussed me as an amateur?

'That feels good,' he said softly.

His words were a reality check. I *could* do this. He was enjoying it already, even if I was dying inside. If I just stopped thinking about how bad I was at this and focused on his enjoyment, I'd get through it, I told myself. I knew at that point that I would go through with full sex. If I'd got this far, I was going to see it out and get my money – that was what it was all about.

The atmosphere was awkward. Indeed, with no music and neither of us talking, it was downright horrible. I started to talk quietly, nothing too taxing, but enough to break the silence and put us at our ease. I discovered he was a manager in a factory and a part-time farmer, so I had been right about the country accent.

'Things are bad for farmers at the minute, aren't they?' I said, knowing that things were always bad for farmers, or at least they always thought they were. That got him going for a bit, sounding off about the agriculture sector and the stresses.

'Tell me if you'd like me to go harder or if the pressure is okay now,' I said, sounding quite the old hand.

'It's lovely the way it is, thanks,' he said, and I continued, happy that now it was all running smoothly. I moved down to his legs and back up to his bottom. I took a quick peek at my watch. Bloody hell! Only fifteen minutes gone, and already both the G-string and the underwire in the basque were digging into me, driving me mad. I gritted my teeth – it wasn't yet the right time to get out of them.

I asked him to turn over and massaged his chest. He smelt of soap and deodorant, but he hadn't shaved and had a distinct five o'clock shadow. I wasn't impressed by that, but then, what the hell had I expected? That he would make an effort to meet an escort? I'd better get real – this was not a date and he was not trying to impress me.

He lay there with his hands behind his head, staring appreciatively at my breasts. He looked quite comfortable. By now he had an erection, so it was time to move things up a gear.

'You're allowed to touch me,' I said, giving him an encouraging smile, and I hopped off the bed to peel off the horrible 'sexy' outfit. God, what a relief! I wouldn't be wearing cheap tat like that again – it wasn't worth the discomfort. *Lesson Five*: Invest in decent work wear for my own sake, as much as theirs. If I was going to use the sexed-up look successfully, I had to find gear in my price range that was a bit more comfortable and a bit more me; I was too long in the tooth for cheap and cheerful.

It seems the old saying about women losing all inhibitions in the labour ward is true: it didn't cost me a thought to get naked in front of him.

'Lovely body,' he said, as I sat back on him and he started to caress my breasts.

'Thanks,' I said, genuinely delighted. At the back of my mind I'd been a bit concerned about whether I had the body for the job, particularly if I was pitching myself to the upper end of the market. I have a good shape – I go in and out in the right places – but in the last few years I'd put on weight and wear size sixteen clothes. I'm certainly far from being a stereotypical pin-up girl with perky tits and a tight arse, but my reservations seemed to be unfounded. And since he had an erection before he saw me naked, he was probably past being picky about my physical shortcomings.

It felt contrived for me, sitting on him and gyrating my hips, but I could feel him stiffen and I was pleased that I was doing okay so far.

'Will you lie back so I can kiss your body?' he said.

'Sure.'

I was glad he'd suggested something. If I was doing what he wanted, that was good. He spent ages kissing and caressing me – my legs, abdomen, breasts and arms, then on to my pussy. Just when he had his head between my legs and was about to go down on me, he suddenly asked if it was okay to do so.

'Yes, please do,' I said. It felt like it was taking for ever, but so long as he was doing something, then time must be passing and the nearer it was to the end. As I was lying there, I was thinking how inexperienced he seemed: his touch was too rough, he kissed my body, even my pussy, with his lips – no tongue – and he didn't appear to have any technique. Since it was a bit tedious, my mind wandered: did his partner let him go down on her? Was she too shy to tell him what to do, or didn't she know? That must have been the case because his approach was so basic. I'd have found a way of instructing him if it was for my pleasure, but it wasn't, so I lay there and took it.

He stuck his head up from between my legs. 'Are you enjoying this?'

'Hmm, it's lovely,' I drawled. I was surprised that he cared. I closed my eyes and tried to enjoy the bits that were reasonably pleasurable. His cock was really hard now and it was thick and heavy-looking. This I liked. I've always enjoyed the feeling of fullness in my vagina during sex. If I imagined I was with someone else, I'd be able to enjoy it when he was inside me.

'I think it's time for a condom,' I whispered, stretching over the bed to pick one up from where I'd left them on the floor. I'd used condoms for a long time as my main form of contraception so I was very good at putting them on. I preferred to do it myself, so I knew it was on properly. I rolled the condom down over his cock and he positioned himself at the entrance to my pussy, looked straight at me and paused.

'What's up?' I said.

'I'd like you to enjoy this. It's been a long time for me.'

'I'm sure I will,' I said, trying to sound hot and eager.

He held himself upright on his arms so he wasn't putting his body weight on me and thrust slowly, deeply into me. It did feel lovely. I closed my eyes to avoid looking at him – that would be too intimate for this type of encounter and it just didn't feel right. With my eyes closed, I could focus on the great sensations I was feeling as he continued to push himself in and out of me. I'd almost forgotten how much I liked sex and that I'd missed it. This went on for a while until I thought he surely must be ready to speed up his thrusting and come. I had been wet, mainly because he had gone down on me, however badly, but as he thrust on I started to get a bit dry and sore. Plus, his time was nearly up and he needed to get to the finish line.

'Would you like to come?' I said, as if giving him permission to go ahead.

'I'm all right,' he said. 'I can go on like this for hours.'

From the way he said it, I guessed I was supposed to be impressed that he could sustain an erection for so long, and maybe if he was a boyfriend I would have been, but I just wanted him to finish up and get the hell out.

'I'm really sorry, but your time is up shortly, so I'm letting you know you need to be out of here soon.'

'God, sorry, I didn't realize the time,' he said, pulling out of me and hopping out of the bed without climaxing.

'Eh, do you want me to finish this off?' I said awkwardly, motioning to his still-hard penis.

'No, no, it's okay,' he said, as if he felt bad for having forgotten the time. 'It will settle in a minute,' he said, as he started to get dressed. For some reason, he didn't seem fussed about climaxing.

I threw on the red chemise as he dressed. Then he took out his wallet and started counting out notes. I was glad I didn't have to ask.

'One, two, three hundred,' he said, putting six fifty-euro notes on the coffee-table.

'Em, it's four hundred for the first visit. I was quite clear about that on the phone.'

He seemed genuinely taken aback and embarrassed. 'Jesus, I'm so sorry, that's all I have on me, but I have my bank cards. Let me fly down to the nearest ATM and I'll be straight back.'

He shut the door behind him as he left and I thought, Well, that's the last I see of him. I'd been pleased enough that it had gone smoothly, but this had taken the good out of it. He had cheated me and I was kicking myself, trying to figure out what I could have done differently and how I would handle this if it happened again.

The room smelt of sex, latex and bodies. I opened the window to let in some fresh air. He had left the condom on the floor and I picked it up with a tissue and put it in a little rubbish bag I had brought. It seemed silly to pick it up with a tissue when moments earlier it had been inside me, but it was as if I had now switched off my escort persona and was back to being me. I washed my hands well with the cheap soap and cleaned the smudged mascara from under my eyes with some tissue paper. I threw the tissue into the bin over the bagged condom. I could have done with a shower there and then to wash him off me and to take off my work makeup, but I hadn't thought to bring my toiletries. I went to tidy up the bed and then clocked something else I hadn't considered: the state I'd be leaving the sheets in. This hadn't been the type of sex to leave a big mess, so I didn't think Housekeeping would notice anything. I made up the bed, put the old throw back in position and made it look like I had just maybe lain down on the outside covers. *Lesson Six*: Be ready to freshen up afterwards and cover your tracks – bring a spare sheet.

I was just pulling on my skirt when there was a knock at the door. Before opening it, I glanced around quickly to make sure nothing looked suspicious. No, everything was in order. I opened the door and was amazed to see Aidan standing there. He handed me a hundred-euro note, apologized again and said goodnight. I stood there, staring at the money in my hand, pretty much gobsmacked: it hadn't occurred to me that he would come back and settle up with me. I smiled to myself and shook my head. Life was full of surprises.

I was a different woman approaching Reception than I had been a couple of hours earlier. The nerves were nearly gone and I felt like I had burned a bridge to my old life. I was still me, but now I was me with a mighty big secret and a new understanding of my own inner resources. The receptionist from earlier was still on duty. Damn, she would naturally ask why I was leaving so soon. I launched into my prepared story about having to get home quickly because of a sick child and needing to pay my bill.

'Oh, it's okay, madam, you were hardly there and you're missing breakfast, so there's no charge.'

Shit. Housekeeping wouldn't service the room and that would be gross for the next person checking into it.

'I did have a wee lie-down though because I was so tired when I arrived, so you better charge me something for linen.'

'No, really, it's okay, there's no charge. I hope your baby is better soon,' she said kindly.

As I walked towards my car, I was incredibly relieved that it was all over. That thing with Reception bothered me, though. I just hoped the sheets would get changed in the morning. At any rate, Housekeeping wouldn't make any connection to what I was up to and I wouldn't be staying there again either: the rooms were too shabby.

I threw my bag into the boot and lowered myself into the driver's seat. I sat there for a moment, feeling exhausted and slightly pumped up, both amazed and relieved that I had done it. Yes, I felt a bit manky and wanted to steep in the bath but, Jesus Christ, I had got the money for the outstanding heating bill in just over an hour's work. That first encounter had been the crucial last step in the research process and I now knew I could and would do it again. Apart from the nervous anticipation of doing something I had never done before – which I'd never have to go through again – the actual meeting wasn't half as bad as I had thought it would be. It was just very boring sex with someone I never needed to clap eyes on again. It would be relatively easy money – there was nothing too scary about having sex with a stranger in a hotel room, I knew that now. It just needed a bit more planning based on the lessons I had taken away with me from that dingy room.

On the drive home, it occurred to me that Aidan wasn't by any means wealthy: part-time farmers are not known for their large incomes. If he could come up with my fee without quibble, I felt confident I could get that amount consistently. He had been a bit rough and ready, though – the unshaven face, the grubby jeans, the overgrown hair – and he'd had no dress sense. I love decent conversation and meeting new people: Aidan had been too much of a quiet country fellow and had had nothing to talk about. But I missed sex more than I'd thought, so if I could aim for a different calibre of man, there was a good chance I'd get to really enjoy it while still making plenty of money. Win-win. I decided to fine-tune my 'admission criteria' and be super-selective about the men I agreed to see. My type – a worldly, well-presented man – was likely to be enjoyable company, and enjoyable company meant more enjoyable sex. Conversation, after all, is where arousal starts.

I don't suppose personal enjoyment is to the forefront of most escorts' minds, but I felt it would help. So, what should I look for in sussing out potential clients on the phone? I decided to see only those who spoke well, sounded smart and described themselves as clean-shaven. I would stay with the basic criteria of married or attached men because they had something to lose, just like me. I would vet them carefully by phone beforehand, looking for my key boxes to be ticked and listening for any clues that warned me against getting involved.

As I pulled into my driveway, my work phone lit up with a text message. It was from Aidan: Thanks for the meeting. Hope you got home safely. The irony struck me: I had got a thank-you and a follow-up text from a guy I had just charged for sex. How many times do you get that when you give it away for free?

That night I soaked in the bath for hours, still giddy with the adrenalin rush of the day. I was delighted I had got through it, and now I felt confident that my new job wasn't going to be half as bad as I had feared. Far from the outrageous porn-star stuff I'd imagined men buying sex would demand, it had been very tame indeed. I presumed the client had enjoyed it because otherwise he could have refused to pay me – and certainly wouldn't have bothered to come back with the last bit he owed me. It also showed he had integrity, something I wouldn't have expected in a man who paid an escort for sex. Maybe I had skewed notions of the sex industry and the men it serviced – was that possible? I supposed there were many situations when men needed sex outside their relationships, and it didn't necessarily make them weirdos or sex fiends. The whole thing had been shockingly straightforward.

5. Human Contact

Once I'd had that first encounter, I felt like a full-fledged sex worker. It was all about the persona, the character, the acting, and as I had done it successfully once, I knew I could do it again. I had fine-tuned my client criteria and now I put the lessons from the first encounter to good use. I acquired a portable music system, some chill-out CDs, scented candles and comfortable but sexy underwear. My good lingerie, given to me by my ex-husband, would have to suffice until I could invest in some specific work wear.

From the moment the ad appeared online for my 'masseuse' service, my work mobile rang pretty much constantly, albeit with some obvious peak times. Evenings and weekends there were non-stop calls, but the early mornings were busy too as men would take advantage of the daily commute and phone me while en route to work. I was getting very comfortable with talking about sex on the phone and taking charge of the conversation. This was no ordinary escort service and I knew that, in order to stick to my admission criteria, I'd have to turn down the majority of callers. However, the calls broadened my knowledge of male sexual preferences.

I knew I couldn't expect the second time to be like the first – every time would be different – but from our conversation on the phone, I had a feeling I would get on with Brian. He seemed like a nice, personable man, although I could tell he was very stressed by his current situation. As we talked, he mentioned that he was going through a rough time: he had lost his job and things weren't good at home. He didn't elaborate on the difficulties, except to say that he couldn't talk to his wife about them, was feeling under pressure and needed to switch off temporarily. That was why he had called me. To be honest, I expected him to hang up when he heard the price, especially as he'd said he wasn't working, but it didn't deter him. I agreed to see him and we arranged to mee... following day. I made the booking in a confident, p...

This time I dressed in a pretty bra and matching undies, with tiny embroidered roses over a sheer base. I was instantly n... comfortable than I had been in the tacky ensemble I'd worn with my first client. I packed my oversized bag with the massage oil, lubricant, condoms and disposal bags. I added some fresh undies, a toothbrush and toothpaste, a couple of scented candles, a lighter and the music system. I threw in a packet of baby wipes as well, which would do for removing my makeup and having a quick freshen-up after the main event.

I got to the hotel twenty minutes before him, which gave me plenty of time to set up the music and all my things. The room was much bigger and better decorated than the last one. It was broken up into a bed area and a separate lounge / sofa section, which would act as a nice introduction spot when the client arrived. This time the massage oil, watch and phone were all in easy reach of the bed. Surveying the room after I'd lit the candles, I smiled to myself – anyone would think I'd been doing this for years! A quick text to Brian to let him know the room number, then I sat and waited, feeling a million times more confident than I'd done with the previous client.

There was a knock at the door. I ran my hands through my hair, threw back my shoulders and opened it.

There was nothing in the demeanour of the man outside to suggest he was meeting an escort. He looked like someone presenting himself for a counselling or psychotherapy session: his breathing was heavy and his speech was quick and agitated. Brian had all the trademarks of someone who had long since forgotten to look after himself. He was overweight, had a ruddy complexion and his eyes were shadowed by dark circles, telling of worries that kept him from sleep. At first, I wasn't sure if it was just nerves that had him worked up, so I offered him a cup of tea and started to chit-chat as a prelude to what he was going to pay me for.

Even though he was sitting on the sofa next to me, as we talked and sipped our tea, he was actually breathless. It flashed across my

.ind that I'd have some amount of explaining to do if he keeled over with a heart attack. From my experience working in healthcare years previously, I knew he was an ideal candidate for a stroke or cardiac episode, and I sure as hell wasn't going to let him collapse in my company.

'Hey, you need to chill out for me, Brian. I'm going to get you a glass of water.' I went to the bathroom tap, then brought it over to him. 'Is there anything physically wrong with you? You don't look so well,' I said, as I handed him the glass.

'I'll be okay in a moment,' he said tiredly. 'I've just been running round like a headless chicken all day – and trying to keep the wife off my case while I got here has been a nightmare.' He paused and took a sip of the water. Just then his phone rang. 'Speak of the devil.' He sighed and took the call. He told his wife he was meeting a mate to talk about a job and would be home in a couple of hours. Clearly there was a problem with the electrics in the house and she needed him to sort it out. He told her he would call the electrician when he had a minute and would have a look at the problem himself when he got home. He hung up and apologized for the interruption. His mobile rang again and he looked at the screen and threw his eyes to heaven. It was his wife again: she needed him home by a particular time as she was meeting friends later and he had to mind the children. He confirmed a time with her, rang off and apologized again.

'Jesus, there's always feckin' something to do. I'm bloody knackered.'

'What has you so worked up?' I asked.

It was an all too familiar story in recession Ireland: he had lost his job some months back and this was the first time in his adult life that he had been unemployed. He had taken the usual steps – rescheduled his mortgage and other loans – but he could not find another job and was coming under increasing pressure from the banks. He had always worked and provided for his family, while his wife was the homemaker and mother to their two children. She seemed oblivious to their financial predicament and continued with the lifestyle she had enjoyed when he was earning. He felt she didn't give a shit and couldn't care less about him, that he was there only to bring home the bacon. I asked if he had told her this – had he sat her down and explained how isolated and under pressure he was feeling? He said their relationship had been this way for years and that he had given up trying to talk to her about his feelings.

'I take it nothing's happening in the bedroom then, if you can't even communicate about the basics,' I said.

'Well, actually, nothing's been happening in the bedroom since the birth of my youngest child,' he replied, taking another sip of water. The chat seemed to be calming him down and I noticed that his breathing was less shallow and he appeared more relaxed now he was talking openly. 'It's been so long since I had any sexual contact with my wife, I can barely remember what it's like. You may think I'm exaggerating and you may hear this all the time in your line of work, but it's literally been years since anything happened between the wife and myself.'

I felt genuinely sorry for him. He seemed like a decent sort and it struck me that he was hurting inside. He had soft blue eyes that were honest but sad and I found myself overlooking his lack of physical attractiveness and liking the person I was getting to know. With all the stress, he added, he hadn't had an erection in six months and was worried that he wouldn't even be able to get one now, never mind sustain it and proceed to sex. I reassured him that the objective was not an erection or climaxing: this was about relaxing, enjoying the chat and having some time out for himself.

He took a deep breath and sighed. 'God, it's even good to talk openly about what I'm going through. I've been bottling this up for ages and thought I'd just explode with the pressure.' I asked him if he would mind if I took over and directed him into what would happen between us, asking him to trust me that I knew what I was doing. He agreed wholeheartedly, seeming relieved that all he had to do was follow my instructions and just switch off.

I asked him to strip and sit cross-legged in front of me on the floor. He did so, showing little inhibition. I peeled off my clothes, down to my stylish feminine undies, still feeling very in control. I scattered some cushions on the floor. The room was warm, the lights were dimmed and the candles flickered. I turned on some relaxing music. This was not about arousal, it was simply about being in the moment and finding some inner peace and calm. I knew that arousal would naturally follow relaxation, but first I wanted to help Brian find peace. I told him to take a yoga breath, demonstrating the technique to him; it is the simplest de-stressor in the world. I was a little surprised at how calm and steady my voice was when entering into this unorthodox territory – it sure wasn't what anyone would expect an escort to ask them to do. I was also surprised to be using my knowledge of relaxation techniques in such a setting – it certainly wasn't a use I'd ever thought of for all those yoga classes I'd attended!

Brian closed his eyes and followed my directions. With yoga breathing, you're so focused on getting the technique right that the mind empties of all other thoughts. It engages the correct chest and abdominal muscles, which allows maximum delivery of oxygen body-wide. I did a little guided imagery with him, asking him to put his hand on his body where he felt the physical hurt that was going on in his life. He placed his open hand to his chest, saying that he felt a weight there, in his heart. It was no wonder he looked like the perfect candidate for a coronary when he could locate the manifestation of his stresses to his chest. There is a concept that all illnesses are the body's attempt to say what we cannot express freely in words. It's known as the 'intention of illness' and is slowly becoming more widely accepted among psychologists and the medical profession, particularly in the fields of chronic pain and psychosomatic illness. It's not by accident expressions such as 'a heavy heart', 'heartache', 'having the weight of the world on one's shoulders' and 'feeling something in the pit of one's stomach' have emerged. Our bodies are affected by everything we think and feel, so it makes sense that stress would be interpreted physically as pain or discomfort.

At this point, I still hadn't touched Brian – he was sitting opposite me, totally absorbed in his breathing and my quiet words. I told him that this was his time, he was in a safe place and that, for this moment, nothing mattered except staying with the relaxation he was feeling. Gradually his breathing became regular, deep and slow. We stayed like that for a while. As I looked at the person across from me, I felt such a sense of empathy because I knew what it was like to feel alone and yet be in a relationship. It's remarkable how you can be living with someone, sharing your bed with them, and yet they have no clue how isolated and hurt you're feeling inside. I found myself also living in that moment with Brian and instinctively leaned over and very gently kissed him. His lips were slightly parted and he didn't move them. It seemed he was just enjoying the pure sensation of a moment of affection, something he hadn't experienced in a very long time. I kissed him tenderly, as if in some way to kiss away his hurt, and he started to respond tentatively. He opened his eyes as the kiss came to its natural end. 'Oh, my God, that was beautiful,' he whispered.

I asked him to lie comfortably on the floor so that I could massage him. I instructed him again not to worry about the sexual side of things but, rather, to focus on the physical sensations and relaxation. I used the lightest touch to tingle the skin on his back. I kneaded his neck and shoulders, easing out the knots in his muscles and ligaments. I got into a rhythm of stroking his back lengthways in time with the music. After about fifteen minutes, I noticed that he was sleeping. I felt a sense of satisfaction that this man, who had arrived only a short while ago in a tense and agitated state, was now so relaxed that he was snoozing. I had felt something similar when I was working in healthcare – the satisfaction in acknowledging someone's discomfort and having the skills and ability to alleviate it for them. I was surprised – I couldn't help wondering whether other working girls had had the same experience or if this was down to my personality and how I had managed my work thus far. It was certainly nowhere in the job description, that was for sure.

I let Brian have a little power snooze as I continued to stroke him with the gentlest butterfly touch, then softly asked him if he'd like to turn over. He roused from his half-sleep and rubbed his eyes, then turned over and lay on his back. 'God, I'm so sorry I dozed off,' he apologized. 'This is weirdly fantastic. I haven't felt so chilled out in as long as I can remember.' He mumbled that he'd like to say one other thing to me, still not fully alert. 'If nothing else happens with you, I just want to thank you for all you've done for me so far and for showing me that I can actually find some headspace,' he said.

I was a bit taken aback. Brian had come to me solely for sex: nothing of what I would consider a sexual nature had happened yet but he seemed genuinely grateful. This was just so not what I would have expected in the sex industry and it forced me to question the narrow-mindedness that had led me to believe that all punters were sad, sex-starved pervs who couldn't get it without paying.

I continued my session with Brian and, much to his delight and relief, not only did he have a very decent sustained erection but also a very enjoyable climax. He couldn't stop thanking me. God love him, I thought, here is a man who's lost his livelihood and had thought he'd lost the ability to be a man. That's a tough blow for any guy and it's easy to see how self-esteem could be weakened and undermined. I've always believed that the two most important contributions to a man's self-esteem are his ability to work and provide for his family and his sexual prowess. Work and self-worth are so intrinsically linked for men, as are self-worth and sexual ability. I could understand why Brian was so grateful: he thought I'd given him some sort of a lifeline in helping him have an orgasm. Of course, I had only facilitated his orgasm – all he had needed was some attention and the right environment to make it happen. It was sad he wasn't getting this at home. When I asked him did he masturbate to get some relief, he said he couldn't do it to orgasm because his home environment was too stressful and, anyway, he hadn't the inclination or concentration for it. He was just racing through life, stressed and unhappy, with no outlet for his anxiety.

Brian stayed way over his time, but I didn't mind. To be honest, I got as much out of the interaction as he did. I love open, direct personalities, and our meeting was real and sincere.

After showering and dressing, Brian paid me, thanked me again and hugged me, saying he'd be in touch. I wondered how he could afford my fee, but figured he had a bit put by that his wife didn't know about. I closed the door behind him and caught myself smiling: I was happy I'd made someone else happy, not on a sexual level but on a deeper, more meaningful plane. I showered and snuggled down into the clean sheets. I was glad we hadn't used the bed: the entire meeting had taken place on the floor. The kids were with their dad and I had decided to stay over at the hotel, mainly to divert any suspicion but also to enjoy the peace and quiet without the distraction of the chores I would find to do if I was at home.

The following morning when I was checking out, the receptionist handed me a card with my room number written on it. I briskly put it into my bag, wondering what the hell it could be and who could have known I was staying there. Once I had settled my bill and got into my car, I ripped open the envelope. It was from Brian. He must have dropped into the hotel early that morning. Inside he had written: 'Thank you so much for last night. I slept like a baby and feel fantastic today. I'm very grateful and will be in touch soon.'

I was moved by the thoughtful gesture and, again, amazed by how wrong my preconceived notions of users of the sex industry had been. When you've reached a certain age, you think you have a fair idea of what's what. When something happens that makes you question the validity of your beliefs, you begin to wonder what else you may have got wrong. I had expected a very particular type of man to call me and have sex with me but, based on my first two experiences, I'd had it all wrong. These weren't predatory men, casually cheating on their wives and treating me badly. If anything, they were lonely individuals who needed far more than a shag: they needed to connect with someone on a human level, to know they were still alive. After seeing Aidan and Brian, I was convinced that I was doing the right thing – the bills were paid, the men were happy and I was helping people in a way I would never have thought possible.

6. Learning How to Talk the Talk . . .

As a solo sex worker, without the back-up of a brothel, a pimp or security to ensure clients behaved themselves, I relied completely on my ability to choose the right clients from all the men who rang my number. The initial contact was all-important. How I marketed myself and how I responded to enquiries were – as in any business – the cornerstones on which the whole enterprise would stand or fall.

In terms of marketing, I placed just one ad – a free online one in the Personals category – and I didn't need to do anything more than that. It carried a very simple message of my services, accompanied by my work name, mobile number and email address. My catchline was: 'I'm probably the only escort in the world who gives a satisfaction/money-back guarantee.' This cheeky promise set me apart from others and tapped into one of the main things men wanted: a more leisurely approach that valued personal interaction as much as sex. I'd heard what my clients were telling me: they had visited girls before and hated being thrown out of the door as soon as the deed was done, meeting the next punter on his way in. That sort of sex left them feeling empty and lonely, and was nothing to do with the reason they had sought out an escort in the first place. Men wanted value for money and they wanted to feel individual. That was why I never had a 'routine'; I was happy to go with the flow.

For the men, the first contact was every bit as important because they were trying to find out if I could deliver what they wanted. It was one of the things that surprised me about my work in the sex industry. I had expected men to want all kinds of strange things no one else would let them do – but again and again what it came down to was the Girlfriend Experience, which I now knew was referred to as GFE in the sex industry. They didn't want a quick shag – no matter how athletic. They wanted a woman they could talk to, be comfortable and relaxed with, have sex with, and then go away feeling good about themselves. It really hadn't occurred to me that this would be the case, especially at the higher end of the scale, but there you are: men's needs are not seedy and odd – they just want good, no-judgements sex with a fanciable woman who can talk the talk as well as she can walk the walk.

Given that the first contact was so important, I planned my side of it very carefully. I researched a lot of sex and escort websites and learned that when I picked up the phone I had to sound confident, professional, upfront and up for it. I needed to be able to use some pretty graphic language, if that was what the caller wanted to hear. That wasn't too bad – I'm naturally direct and was well aware that anyone phoning me on that particular number was calling for one reason only. It was my job to put him at his ease, find out if he was the right client for me and to seal the deal. I generally switched on the phone at times that were convenient for me so I could get into my escort character. I was becoming more and more comfortable with my new pursuit, so the character was becoming easier and easier to play.

I always told them the fee early on in the call, to weed out the serious takers from the chancers. Some reacted with shock, some with incredulity, some with curiosity – I could tell they were intrigued to know what they'd get for that kind of payout. The ones who didn't flinch when they heard the price were invariably the older, attached men who cited safe sex as a priority – they appreciated the value of the service I offered and didn't quibble about the bottom line. I must admit, when I started talking to the guys who called, I was astounded by how ill-informed so many were about safe sexual practices. I would explain carefully that I provided a full service, so long as everything was safe practice. If a caller didn't understand what discretion and safe sex meant, I simply cut the conversation short and hung up. There were so many idiots out there, asking me would I perform oral sex without a condom (or OWO, in the new shorthand I was fast learning) for an extra few quid and could I text or email a picture of myself. I was horrified by the number of men who would pay to have unprotected sex with a stranger.

I'd ask questions about their current sex life, their sexual likes and dislikes, and if they had any preferred underwear style/colour or particular music they enjoyed. I would explain that the visit would be individually tailored to whatever they wanted. One thing's for sure, men have no problem talking about themselves, and with the anonymity of the telephone, I was able to get lots of information out of them. Men like to talk about sex, that's no big revelation. I found all the callers very direct when talking about their preferences and about how to be discreet to ensure we weren't caught. Their main concerns, I quickly discovered, were confidentiality and discretion.

I was able to apply the advance sales techniques I'd learned in my former professional career to sell my service to the callers. Once I knew what a man wanted, I would tell him what I was going to do with him – basically using different language and paraphrasing in order to let him know I had been listening, had understood him and was able to supply what he needed. So, for example, if the client said he would like some pampering before sex, where he could just lie back and enjoy an erotic massage, then in my best phone-sex voice I would say, 'So, what I will do is have flickering candles, dim lights, soft music, aromatherapy oils, and we will start with a long, relaxing massage where you can totally switch off and get back in touch with your self. I will undress myself slowly throughout the massage as I read your body language, sense when your body is moving from relaxed to aroused, and we will take it from there. Do you like the sound of that?' By doing so, I was painting a very real picture for him, invoking all his senses so he could clearly visualize what would happen. That's the first step in getting someone to buy what you're selling – convincing them they want it. And, of course, once the client had started picturing it, he could begin to 'feel' it happening, so the arousal and the teasing kicked off before he ever set eyes on me.

The majority of queries I received were by phone, but I also had a certain amount by email, to my work address. Some men preferred this 'non-contact contact' to test the waters and find out what I was like. This seemed to be particularly the case for first-timers. If their typing was grammatically correct, they'd used correct punctuation and could spell, I'd reply. If the email was sloppily written, I didn't bother. A standard 'copy and paste' reply to someone looking for information generally went something like this:

Dear A. N. Other,

Thank you for your mail. I'll start by telling you a little bit about myself so you can have a think about it. Feel free to ask me any questions you may still have.

I run a very discreet service for discerning gentlemen who respect privacy, safety and confidentiality. I'm considered a very attractive woman and easy to talk to – I guess it's not all about the sex, it's about being comfortable with the person you're with, feeling relaxed and knowing you can walk away with just a happy memory. I'm not a perfect size with supermodel looks, but I am sexually confident and open to ideas/suggestions. I'm comfortable in my own skin and with bodies in general, so I can pretty much say I have no sexual hang-ups. My two rules are that no unsafe sexual practices are requested, and that absolute discretion is a must.

Rates-wise, it all depends on what you want. I usually charge 400 euro for the first visit, which tends to last an hour and a half, and 300 for repeat clients: this allows enough time for a shower and a coffee before/after, as needed. The reason I charge this amount is that I only want to see a certain type of client: one who appreciates and values the standard of service I provide. If there is travel involved, then we can discuss the details as this has to be factored into my costs.

I don't work from home, but I'm happy to visit clients at their homes. What usually happens is that I book a hotel at a mutually convenient place or I can visit the client at their hotel if they are away with work, etc.

I don't rush things and I ensure the client is happy with whatever happens so that the arrangement continues, as that keeps both parties content. I'm available weekdays and some evenings/ weekends by prior arrangement. I prefer to have a good chat on the phone first because I think that gives us both a better idea if we are happy to meet. I see a select number of clients and work independently, so ultimately I decide if I will see you or not based on what we discuss and if I feel you appreciate and understand what the service is all about. I tend to dress pretty classy and I stick with this unless requested to dress otherwise.

If there is anything in particular you want to know, just ask – and be direct as it saves a lot of time. After all, we're all adults, so don't hold back! Feel free to give me a call if you'd like to chat further.

I disliked the admin side of dealing with emails – it took up a lot of time staying on top of them – but it had the benefit of giving a potential client the chance to mull things over in his own time and assured him that what I offered was no bargain-basement hooker service. The phone calls and emails were my background checks. I had to decide, based on what the men told me, whether I was going to see them or not. I had to use intuition and gut instinct and, thankfully, they worked well for me.

7. Running the Gamut

It was just over six weeks since my first time and I was getting more familiar and comfortable with the escort scene. I'd met guys in hotels and at their homes, some who had wanted a good old-fashioned shag, some who had needed something more intimate and relaxing, and some who were downright boring and unremarkable. I'd learned that being confident and in control was of key importance for me and I'd also learned not to judge men or make assumptions. Nothing shocked me any more. I could still be surprised, though, especially by the unexpectedly great sex and by the fetishes some men confessed to.

On a wet late March evening I was sitting at the kitchen table helping the kids with their homework. I hadn't worked that day because I couldn't get any clients who fitted in around my other commitments. We were just reciting the nine times table when my work phone rang. I looked at the number before answering it. I didn't have it among my contacts, but the caller hadn't withheld it – always a good sign. 'Sorry, kids, I just have to take this call. I'll be back in one minute, continue on.'

I slipped into the hall and pressed the Accept button. 'Hello,' I said, in a bright, friendly manner.

'Hello there, I'm calling about your services.'

'Yes, and what would you like to know?' This was always the first question I asked and I always left it open-ended so I could suss out the caller. I'd get a feel for him within a couple of moments of him speaking, then decide if I'd proceed with the call.

'Well, I presume it's a full service?'

'Yes, indeed it is.'

'And where are you based?'

'It depends on where and when you were thinking of, but I'm

pretty flexible. Can you tell me a bit about yourself, please?' I'm not sure if other escorts ask clients a few preliminary questions, but certainly no man ever objected, so maybe it's common enough.

'Well, I'm married, forty-six, professional and living in the City . . . What else do you need to know?'

'Nothing really, except what you'd like.'

'Well, do you do bareback sex, and what are your rates?'

'I never do anything unsafe, so sex without protection is not on, and my rates –'

'No, that's grand. I actually want someone really safe so I'm glad to hear that. Sorry, carry on.'

Thankfully, Colin was not fazed by my fees and asked if I was free the next day, on the outskirts of the city. It was a bit of a trek, but I could make it there and back if I continued straight on after the school drop-off and kept an eye on the time. He was staying at a hotel on a work trip, so that was one less thing for me to organize and pay for. We agreed a time and he gave me directions to the hotel, which I didn't know. I made a mental note to check the route on the AA website later.

'You didn't say what you would like,' I said, as the call was coming to an end.

'Pretty straightforward, really. Generally I like a bit of kissing, but if you don't kiss clients I understand. I absolutely love giving oral sex and receiving it, my balls sucked a little, and just take it from there, really. Just a real woman and a real experience is what I'm after.'

'Sounds good. Just text me your room number beforehand.'

'Will do. Thanks very much. See you then.'

I hung up, switched back into Mum mode and opened the door into the kitchen. 'Sorry, kids, just had to take that call from the bank. Now, where were we?'

When the evening routine was finished and the kids settled in bed, I checked the route to the hotel. Once I'd seen it on the map, I had my bearings and knew where I was headed. I went upstairs and laid out my work clothes for the morning: smart trousers and a simple fine-knit jumper would work well. The jumper was V-neck, taupe, a colour that brings out the blue of my eyes, and with my cerise push-up bra underneath, it was sexy enough without being 'in your face'. I rooted in my undies drawer for the matching knickers. Feck it, they were in the laundry. I had several other pairs that would do fine. At the start, I had been obsessed with wearing matching stuff, but I'd learned that once a man was aroused, he couldn't have cared less if I was wearing a cut-up bin liner as underwear. A man with an erection has tunnel vision – he simply doesn't see what's covering your body.

I pulled my hotel bag out from under the bed and checked that all the essentials were there: condoms, lube, baby wipes, small plastic bags, music system, clean knickers, toothbrush, toothpaste and massage oil. All present and correct. While the bath was filling, I popped outside to leave my bag in the boot of the car. Whenever I was going straight to an appointment after the school run, I always had my bag ready and in the car the night before so the kids didn't ask any awkward questions. I hurried back inside and headed up to the bathroom. I had a long soak with lavender oil and mentally walked myself through the arrangements for tomorrow. The guy had sounded nice on the phone, confident and relaxed. I tried to imagine what he looked like from his voice. Would it be one of those meetings where I was just willing him to come so it was over and done with, or would he be one of the enjoyable types? Fuck it, either way it was money, but I hoped he'd be the enjoyable type all the same.

I washed my hair, shaved my underarms, bikini line and legs, stepped out of the bath and wrapped a hot towel around me. As I was drying myself, I took a closer look at my bits to see if I'd left any stray hairs on display. I was sort of short back and sides because I didn't like it totally bare – there's something too pre-pubescent about it for my taste. I find that well-trimmed is enough to enhance sensation without the childlike look. It was fine until I spotted, horror of horrors, a grey pube. I rushed into my bedroom to inspect the area more closely with my bright reading lamp.

Damn! A couple of them were lurking down there. How dare my pubic hair remind me of my age? Surely it couldn't be time for my fanny to start ageing? I grabbed a pair of tweezers from my bedside locker and attempted to pluck one of the grey little shits from its roots. Ouch! That was way too sore. Right then, if it had to be either the bald look or the ageing fanny look, I chose the former. I hopped back into the bath, lathered up the area and, hey presto, in a few painless minutes those greys had met their maker and I was all bare. Being clean-shaven showed up my Caesarean scars a hell of a lot more, but that didn't bother me as my client wouldn't mind – most of the men I saw were fathers and knew what real women looked like.

Satisfied, I smothered myself in perfumed body lotion and picked out my minimalist makeup for the morning. I wouldn't have time to shower again before meeting the client, so this bath and a quick top and tail in the morning would have to do. I was all set.

The next morning I was woken by my littlest one snuggling into me. I do love mornings when I'm woken by the kids with cuddles. They're so gorgeous and good-humoured in the morning – until I mention it's time to get ready for school.

After a bit of whingeing, they were dressed and seated at the table for breakfast. I dished out the cereal and put on some porridge for myself. Once we'd finished, I ran upstairs to dress while the kids brushed their teeth. As I put on my long coat over the smart trousers and jumper, to cover my cleavage, my boy said, 'You look nice, Mummy. Where are you off to?'

I mumbled something about meeting my bank manager and hurried them out to the car.

'You're meeting your bank manager a lot these days,' my observant boy said, as he buckled up.

God, don't I know it, I thought.

I drove out to the main road and immediately met the school traffic. None of the other mums looked like they were on their way to shag strangers after dropping off their darlings. Did I look like them, I wondered, or subtly different? I pulled up at the school set-down area and the kids blew me goodbye kisses. 'Have a good day, everyone.' I smiled as they scrambled out of the car.

'You too, Mum. Good luck with the bank manager,' my boy called, and a pang of guilt stopped my smile. They slammed the car doors and were gone. I took a deep breath and focused on the next job of the day – my paid work.

Colin texted me with his room number when I was half an hour from his hotel. I was making good time and the drive wasn't as long as I had thought. Nonetheless, I'd have to clock-watch on this one. I had to be on the road home by one fifteen p.m. at the latest, to pick up the kids from school at three.

I pulled into the hotel car park shortly after eleven, pulled my bag of essentials out of the boot and quickly scanned the car park: it was almost full, with lots of new cars. Recession or no recession, there's always pockets of money in certain areas. From my car I could see the entrance and the reception area. It looked quiet, which wasn't good for me as it would make it harder to pass unnoticed. I sat back into the car, topped up my makeup and tousled my chin-length bobbed hair. I might let it grow out, though shorter hair is so easy to manage. Funnily enough, men say they love it – that it's soft, feminine and different from the usual longer hair that I'd have presumed they all preferred.

Colin phoned to see if I'd arrived. 'Hey, I'm glad you phoned,' I said. 'You've just given me an idea. Reception is dead quiet, so stay on the phone to me and I'll walk in as I chat to you. No one's going to interrupt me if I'm on the phone and look like I know where I'm going.' I kept the phone to my ear, locked the car and walked into Reception.

Colin had been quiet at the other end. 'I'm looking forward to seeing what you look like,' he said, in a low tone.

I was just in front of Reception and spotted the sign for the lifts straight ahead. 'Yes, I'm looking forward to our meeting too. I hope it will be very productive,' I said formally, while giving a raised eyebrow of recognition to the receptionists as I walked ahead. 'We've a lot to get through,' I continued. I reached the lifts and jabbed the button. 'Great, I'm past Reception. I'll be there in a moment. I'll knock once, okay?'

'Grand. See you in a minute.' His upbeat tone told me he was not nervous and, from his call the previous night, I'd have said he was a regular user. I knew I had to be good because I reckoned he'd be comparing me to other girls. As I approached his room, I took a deep breath, licked my lips and gave one firm knock on the dark wood door. He opened it immediately and greeted me warmly, but quietly, by my working name. He shook my hand and kissed me on both cheeks as the door swung closed behind me – very European for an Irish man. He was wearing suit trousers and a pale lemon shirt with a couple of buttons loosened. I could see his jacket and tie on the back of the dressing-table chair. He had kicked off his shoes as well. 'How was your journey up?' he asked pleasantly.

'Fine, all very straightforward.' I started to ramble a bit, the way I do when I'm nervous. He sat on the bed as I looked for somewhere to arrange myself. This was the one drawback of going to their hotel rooms – I didn't have time to set the scene to my liking.

'I'm just going to use the bathroom – excuse me a moment,' I said. In there, I took off my boots and jacket and threw them under the sink. I pulled up my boobs in my bra cups to accentuate my cleavage, tugged the front of my sweater down a bit more and walked back out with my bag of essentials. 'That's better.' I smiled, putting my bag on the floor and sitting on the bed beside him. 'You're here with work, I take it?' I asked, in a friendly manner that let him know I was going to make small-talk first.

'Well, it's actually a team-building exercise – work is a bit mental at the minute so the big boys at the top decided this might improve morale.'

'And is it working?'

'It is now,' he said, giving me a cheeky grin, 'but it's been a drag keeping on my work persona for forty-eight hours on the trot.' He threw his eyes up to heaven.

'How did you manage to get away in the middle of the morning?' I asked.

'We're supposed to be brainstorming and go back with a list of ideas. I reckoned yesterday when I phoned you that my brain would work a lot better after some time out. I've my ideas done already, so this is me-time.'

'And how often does one manage to have me-time? I mean me-time your other half doesn't know about.'

'God, it hasn't been for a while now, but certainly once or twice a year,' he replied matter-of-factly. 'Oh, that reminds me, your money is there.' He pointed to a wad of notes on the dressing-table.

'Thanks,' I said casually. 'I'll get it after.' I was no longer embarrassed or awkward about the transfer of money. For a while I was: I never knew whether to count it, put it in my bag or leave it until the end of the meeting. By now, though, I was used to it.

We'd managed to get more comfortable on the bed quite naturally, and now that I was enjoying chatting to him, my own few nerves had dissolved. We had moved into a semi-lying position, propped up with pillows. We were facing each other and I was able to study his appearance. He looked older than he'd said, but he was slim and had a nice tanned face, although it was only late spring. 'You've been away,' I remarked.

'No – everyone says that. I'm outdoors a lot in my spare time and am pretty sallow anyway.' His tanned complexion suited his eye and hair colour. His time outdoors had left its mark in that he sported a lot of wrinkles, but I've always found that weathered, close-to-nature look very appealing.

I traced a finger around his face as he continued to chat casually. He closed his eyes and savoured the sensation of a stranger touching him with no other agenda than a brief encounter. It was pure escapism – I knew that, he knew that. I thought, I'm going to enjoy this client. It's running nicely already. I'm going with the flow and so is he. I instinctively knew I wouldn't have to put on a performance like I did with some men.

He rambled on a bit about stuff. I wasn't really listening, but we were each looking at the other's mouth and I knew the arousal process was under way. I also knew that I would kiss him. We moved slowly towards each other, both knowing what game we were play-ing, both prolonging the anticipation. We looked into each other's eyes, seeing the escape we desired there. Our lips met in a briefly tender moment, which quickly turned into a frantic mix of tongues and lips. We slowed down, both now in sync, sensing the other's wants, needs, technique. I moved down to his neck and he put his head back to allow me access. I licked his neck from the top of his shirt collar to his lips and gently placed kisses on his neck as he lay back, receptive to it all, eyes closed and moaning softly.

I was under no illusion: I loved the power I exerted over any man I got close to. I knew what to do, I was confident and maybe that was why I could command the rates I did. To be able to get men into a state where they are so stimulated and relaxed that they are at your mercy is very arousing. This had developed in me since I'd started my work. I didn't remember being quite so sexually domi-nant in my private sex life, but it was something I used now because I liked it a lot. My ex-husband was definitely more dominant than me in bed, so I suppose I just followed his lead, never really having a chance to get the sexual upper hand. I believe I'm far more tenta-tive and on an equal par in my own sex life, but the dominant streak seemed to go hand in hand with the confident, in-control work persona I'd created. As a lover, I'm more submissive, but it was interesting for me to play with and discover my dominant side. I found it liberating to express this side of myself and very fulfilling. Admittedly, it was no more fulfilling than what I'd felt when I was successful at other professional employments – I was just paid a hell of a lot more at this gig.

I caressed his neck with my mouth as I started to unbutton his shirt. We were upright now and I knew I was in control, but I sensed that was exactly what he wanted. Control is ours to give away, so if he was allowing me to have the upper hand, it was because that was how he wanted it. If we're to believe what's portrayed in porn movies, it's the ones with power in their day job who want to surrender or be taken over in their private life. In any S&M porn I've seen, it's always successful men wanting to be controlled in some way by a sexually assertive woman. Even a cursory glance at the classifieds will tell you that mainly professional men are looking to be dominated. Likewise, this guy wanted someone else to do the work so he could just lie back and enjoy it. I got this.

As I stroked his bare chest, I knew intuitively that it was time to allow him to feel my skin. I pulled off my sweater and our skin collided gently with the amazing sensation that is skin against skin – does it ever lose its tantalizing quality? He cupped my breasts and looked directly at me. I gazed straight back, deciphering the meaning behind his expression. Had I missed anything? Had I mistaken anything? I thought not. I was straddling him now and felt him hard against my crotch. I got up off the bed, so he could watch as I peeled off my trousers. I didn't remove my bra or panties: I'd leave that to him. I'd let him have that pleasure because it was what he and the majority of men had fantasized about a million times: a woman surrendering to him, allowing him the privilege to expose her nakedness, her breasts and her pussy.

I knelt on the bed again, upright before him, with my hands on my hips. It's a position of power: I knew this and he knew it, but I also knew that I was very horny and liable to do anything. He sat upright too and grasped behind my back to undo my bra. I bent forward, meeting his lips momentarily. He found the clasp, unhooked my bra and tossed it aside. He sucked my dark, hard nipples as deep into his mouth as he could. God, I do love my nipples being sucked. I watched him and admired what he was doing. He gazed up at me while flicking his tongue against a nipple, cupping my breasts with his hands. He wanted to see if I was enjoying it. I was, I didn't have to pretend. I liked to watch. He let go of my breasts and moved his thumb over my nipples. 'Your nipples are so hard, do they like this?' he asked, knowing full well what the answer would be.

'I love my breasts being touched, they're really sensitive,' I murmured. He slid his fingers down slowly, over my hips, towards my panties. He was going to make me wait, looking up at me as he moved closer and closer to the band of pink lace at the top of my knickers. But I had the power – I'd ascertained that that was what he wanted initially – so I ran my nails gently over his back to distract him from what he was doing to me. He moved his head back again to enjoy the change of stimulation and moaned gently.

I moved on to my back. Fuck it, if he likes it real, he's getting it real. I can't be bothered with this waiting any more. 'I want you to take off my knickers,' I stated, sounding in control but really just wanting to give in to it. I love that first touch of my wet pussy. Then the peeling off of my knickers, followed by the groan every man lets out when he feels how aroused you are. It's a testament to how brilliant they are, to their virility, to have you so aroused – not really, but they think so. He obliged and sat up between my legs, slowly wriggling down the panties. I lifted my hips while lying back on the pillows. 'Wow,' he breathed. 'I can see you glistening from here – what a beautiful sight. Can I taste you?' I nodded and he put his face between my legs while gently touching me with his fingers, opening me up before he started a series of long, sweeping licks from the bottom of my vagina to my clit. I held my breath: it felt so wonderful. He stopped for a moment and I exhaled. Jesus, I'd forgotten how good oral sex could be when you're shaved. Good God, the sensation was amazing!

He could see how much I was enjoying it and started again, dipping his tongue inside me as he licked around my whole pussy. He moved his fingers to my clit and circled it with his thumb, giving a different but equally delicious feeling from before. He darted his tongue in and out of me as he continued to circle my clit. He moved back, adjusted his position and gently nibbled my inner thighs, working up to the fleshy part over my pubic bone. He bit down a little harder. I moaned in surprised appreciation: it felt a bit tender, with just the right balance of pleasure. As he was doing this I felt his fingers at my pussy again. He firmly thrust his thumb into me with his hand facing downwards, allowing his fingers the freedom to massage my perineum and butt. He wriggled his thumb inside me, just hitting my G-spot, and moved his mouth down to suck on my clit at the same time.

I'd say some people might be surprised that a paying client would want to go down on an escort, would want to focus on her pleasure like that, but in my experience when men are horny and see a pussy, they just want to get stuck in. I don't want to put every hard cock I see into my mouth, but men just seem to love eating out. I think women generally see blow-jobs as a bit of a chore – probably because there isn't a whole lot of pleasure in it for us, even if we know the man is loving it. Men, on the other hand, seem to find giving oral sex hugely arousing. That's backed up by the fact that almost 100 per cent of the men I've seen have given me oral sex. Strictly speaking, receiving oral sex isn't without sexual health risks, but it's far less risky than unprotected sex and, from what I know, the chance of the woman catching something from the man is far less than the risk a man takes – he's more likely to catch something from her. It's impossible to practise safe sex beyond the shadow of a doubt of succumbing to an STD, but I make it as safe as I possibly can while still providing a service. If I were paying a male sex worker for sex, it wouldn't occur to me to suck him off. I can only conclude that men love doing it not because they're giving pleasure but because it really turns them on. All the little insecurities women have about how we taste, look or smell down there seem totally unfounded. Men love pussy – I think it really is that simple!

Damn. If he kept that up I was going to come, and if I came, I wouldn't have any interest in shagging him. I'd just want to rest for a while in the lovely sleepy aura that happens afterwards. 'Shit, you have to stop,' I said, panting.

'Why? Don't you like it?' he asked.

'I like it too much, that's the problem. I want you inside me. Let me put a condom on you.' I reached out to grab my bag from the floor. He didn't reply, just continued to touch and caress my legs. He sat up as I opened the condom wrapper, ready for me. He was rock hard, but I immediately noticed the curve in his penis. I hadn't actually touched it or looked at it until now: he had been giving me all the pleasure, it's fair to say. 'Oh, you've got Peyronie's disease,' I said matter-of-factly, as I rolled the condom over the glans and down the slightly curved shaft.

'Does it bother you?'

'Not in the least.' I lay down, ready for his cock to get inside me. I glanced at my watch on the locker. It was twelve thirty and I had to be out of there by one fifteen. I was doing okay with timing, but I needed to keep things progressing. Colin looked at me before moving slowly and purposefully into me. I closed my eyes, thinking only of the pleasure, allowing him further into me. He kissed me hard and I could taste myself on his mouth and face. He thrust slowly, then propped himself up on his hands and looked down at his cock moving in and out of me.

'You like watching yourself?' I asked.

'Not usually, but with a bare pussy I want to see what it looks like,' he said, slightly out of breath.

'You like how it looks with your hard cock inside it?' I asked, already knowing the answer.

'Yes, I like it a lot – too much, I'm not far off coming.'

I was glad he said that, even though he hadn't been in me long. I knew I wouldn't come now. I never can when I'm under any sort of time pressure – quickies are not my thing at all. From being almost on the verge of climaxing, my orgasm had retreated to wherever they come from. I wanted him to come now, though if I'd had more time I'd have slowed him down so we could get more enjoyment out of it. I grasped his ass, pushed him further into me. With every thrust, my moaning got ever so slightly louder than was necessary, and I gyrated my hips to get him deeper into me. He started the fast thrusting that signals imminent climax and I was relieved to feel him come. He lay with his full weight on me as he enjoyed a couple of aftershocks, still inside me and unable to speak yet.

I held him close until he had composed himself and was ready to come out. He held the condom as he slipped out of me, careful not to let it move. He lay on the other side of the bed with it still on. I offered to get him some tissues so he could get rid of it, but he said he was grand, he'd get up in a minute. 'How did you know what my curved cock was?' he asked.

'I've seen it a couple of times,' I replied casually.

'My GP says it's rare enough, but it doesn't bother me so he says leave well enough alone. I suppose every man's different anyway,' he remarked, looking at me for confirmation.

'Yep, that's for sure. It takes all sorts to make a world.'

Lying there afterwards, my inquisitive streak wanted to ask Colin why he availed himself of escorts. I tended to ask more questions than was probably right, considering anonymity was as important to them as it was to me, but the men were only too happy to answer. It's an unspoken rule that anything said or done during a meeting is confidential.

'Do you mind me asking? You've been to plenty of girls before – do you do it because you're not happy with your sex life at home or do you just like it?'

'Actually, my sex life at home is good,' he said, looking off into the distance. 'I suppose I just like trying someone new, different personality, different body, kiss, skin, it's all different . . . A change is as good as a rest, so they say.' He grinned. 'Some men like to go away on a golf weekend for a treat or a break. I like to see a girl.'

'Do you tend to visit the same ones?'

'Sometimes, but you find that they've moved on or changed their number, whatever, and, anyway, I like the anticipation of a new woman.'

'Any particular preferences? What do you like?' I asked, as we lay there, gazing up to the ceiling, quite relaxed in ourselves.

'Well, the usual stuff, I suppose – nice face, boobs, curvy figure, not these skinny types. That type of figure might be great for clothes shopping, but it's not the best for sex. Something you can hold on to, that you're not going to break. That's what I like anyway.'

I lay there listening to him and thinking yet again that a lot of us women have it all wrong as regards what men like. Clearly, it's absolutely fine to have a bit of extra padding, and I vowed never to do the celery soup, Atkins or beetroot diets again.

'And personality, of course,' he added, as an afterthought. 'I'd far rather see a girl with a nice chatty personality who can put you at ease any day than a perfect size-eight type with no personality.'

Yes: the need to be a happy hooker prevails over body type. It's common sense, really – nobody wants to pay money to spend time with a girl who is miserable, unfriendly, doesn't talk or makes it obvious she doesn't want to be there. I feel sorry for those girls who work under constant pressure from a pimp. I can't imagine faking friendliness. I can fake orgasms and enjoyment when I need to, for the man's sake as much as my own, but the idea of faking that I want to be shagged by a stranger, perhaps without protection and in dirty conditions, knowing my pimp will get the money – no way.

'Well, I'd better get ready for my brainstorming,' he said, and got up. He walked into the bathroom to dispose of the condom, which was still dangling from his penis, and came back as I grabbed my watch from the locker. It was almost one o'clock and I needed to shower, get on the road, grab something to eat, drop my work things at home, change into a mummy outfit and be at the school by three. I hopped up and said I was just grabbing a shower, if he didn't mind. He told me to help myself. I ran the water for a few seconds – it wasn't hot but it would do. I was showered and out of the bathroom within minutes. As I stepped back into the bedroom with a towel wrapped around me, he headed towards the bathroom to swap places with me in the shower.

'You don't mind seeing yourself out, do you?' he asked.

'No, that's grand. Was that okay for you?' I asked, out of professional courtesy, as I dried myself.

'Lovely, thanks. Are you okay with your money?' He motioned to the cash waiting on the dressing-table.

'I'm sure it's fine, thank you. I'll be out in a mo. Back to reality, eh?'

'Yep, exactly. Back to reality is right, but thanks for the time out. Safe driving now.' He closed the bathroom door and I hurried to get ready to leave.

I pulled on my knickers, dragged my jumper over my head, then put on my jeans and boots. In my rush I left off my bra and socks, but socks aren't essential with boots and no one would notice I wasn't wearing a bra because I'd have my coat on and was driving straight home to change. Putting the cash into my wallet, I checked around the room to make sure I hadn't forgotten anything, then slipped out of the door, pulling it closed behind me.

He was an easy client. He'd probably done more for me than I had for him, but lots of men liked it that way – they found the pleasure in giving and I was only too happy to take, although it was a shame I hadn't come. Ah, well, couldn't have it my way all the time. I knew I could sort it out later by myself with my trusty Rabbit, when I wasn't in a hurry.

I went straight back out the way I'd come in, not bothered about the receptionists this time. It's on the way in that it's important not to attract unwanted attention; it doesn't matter on the way out. I looked like any other busy working woman rushing around about my business. I checked my watch again as I opened the car door: one twenty. Almost perfect timing. I turned the key in the ignition, selected a chat show on the radio to keep me company, switched my work phone back on and headed off.

I checked my messages at the first set of red lights I met on my journey home. Seven missed calls from the same number, which I didn't recognize, and a few texts from new clients, which I'd reply to later. I'd call the new number when I was out of the city, where there was less chance of getting caught by the gardaí using my phone while driving.

Within twenty minutes I was on the dual carriageway, having stopped to wolf down a sandwich and coffee from a garage. I hit Return Call on the new number. The phone rang just once at the other end before a man answered, as if he was waiting for my call.

'Hi there, I missed some calls from you. Is now a good time for you to talk?' I asked chirpily.

'Thanks for calling back,' the man answered, in a quiet tone. I got the impression he was not quite alone and didn't want to be heard. 'I saw your ad last night and was wondering, are you into any fetishes?'

'To be honest, I'm not so I don't usually do them, but what was it you were after?' My inquisitive nature wants to know what goes on in other people's minds.

'Well, it's a bit unusual but . . . I like socks,' he said shyly.

'Socks? What's socks?' I asked, thinking it was an acronym for something.

'Em, the socks that you wear,' he replied.

'And what do you do with them?' I asked, genuinely curious. I'd never heard of a sock fetish before, but this job was one big learning curve, and if I was going to come across it again, I needed to know what it was.

'Well, I'd ask you to wear your own socks on the day that we meet and then I smell them as you wank me off.'

I didn't want to make him feel like a freak, so I didn't laugh or say anything for a moment, but I couldn't believe someone really got off on this. I blurted out, 'You can't be fucking serious!'

'Look, that's why I'm contacting you,' he said, sounding a bit cross and frustrated. 'It's hard to get anyone to do this. I've said it to partners in the past and it didn't go down well at all, so I reckoned if I paid someone, I'd have a better chance of it.'

'And what about anything else – full sex, oral?' I questioned.

'No, not bothered about it – that's all fine with my partner. I just need someone to do this for me.'

I still wasn't convinced he was serious, although he definitely sounded like he was. I could see the toll plaza approaching so I had to finish the call. 'Look, I'll give it some thought. Let me get back to you later, okay?'

'Okay. Please do have a think about it – money isn't a problem for me.'

'I have to go,' I interrupted him. 'I'll text you later.' I snapped the phone shut and slowed down to cross the toll bridge.

I got home just in time to throw on a navy velour tracksuit and trainers, which were in the laundry room downstairs. I ran back up the stairs, taking them two at a time, and hid my hotel bag under my bed. I remembered to take out my bra and socks and left them downstairs in the laundry pile. A quick check in the hall mirror and I saw that my makeup was sufficiently faded so it looked like I hardly had any on. I ran a comb through my hair, spritzed perfume on my wrists and jumped back into the car to collect the kids. I was in and out of the house within minutes, but I'd really pushed it today, leaving no time to spare.

I sat into the car and caught a glance of myself in the rear-view mirror. I looked like any other mother. I paused and took a deep breath to gather myself. It was the end of my working day, time to switch hats and be a mum again. It was not a long working day, only a few hours compared to most jobs, but it felt like a lot more. I was tired.

I drove to the school and pulled up in the set-down area for the second time that day. The home-time bell hadn't rung yet. I looked around at the other parents in their cars, waiting patiently for their children. I wondered if they knew what I did for money. Had they any clue? Maybe it was common knowledge what I was but no one had the balls to say it to me. I told myself to cop on, no one knew, I was just being paranoid. That was part and parcel of the work, I knew that, so I just had to suck it up. The bell rang out and flocks of children started to move *en masse* into the paths and car park. I spotted my three coming out in dribs and drabs with their friends, coats slung over their shoulders. I got out to open the boot and helped them put in their bags. How come children are always so excited to see their parents, even if it's only been a few hours since they left them? They hugged me while chatting busily and all at once about their day and who had done what in class. I was relieved that my working day was over. I wasn't going to take any more calls: I just wanted to focus on my children. That strange sock guy and the other texters could wait until tomorrow. My handbag was on the passenger seat and I slipped my hand in and switched off the phone as I told the kids to buckle up.

When I turned it on the next day, I had several more texts from the sock-fetish guy asking what I thought of his proposition, so I decided to do a bit of research online. Sock fetishism was actually very well documented, and I concluded that he wasn't joking. It sounded harmless to me, but I had no interest in it. I did recall seeing an ad in the classified section of the dating website from an escort in Dublin: 'All fetishes catered for,' it said. I texted the guy, told him it wasn't my thing and included the number of the fetish girl. Ten minutes later my phone beeped and there was a text from him: I have a booking with her. Thank you so much for your help. At least someone was going to benefit from his desire to sniff socks. That was my good deed done for the day.

8. Necessary Qualifications

My criteria for doing the job are: safety, the right price, flexibility and job satisfaction. I operate at the high end of the scale, which I'd say is what most women imagine when they think about what the life of an escort is like and whether they could ever do it themselves. Let's face it, no one relishes the idea of standing on a cold pavement waiting for a total stranger to stop his car and call her over. The women who engage in that sort of prostitution are motivated by other things, and if those factors were removed, you can be sure they wouldn't choose the life willingly. But I'd chosen mine willingly because it ticked the boxes for me. In return, I have to fulfil the clients' criteria: well groomed, good-looking, safe and healthy, experienced and enthusiastic between the sheets.

So how do I measure up? I'm pretty, but not drop-dead gorgeous. I just make the most of what I have. I have a good skincare regime and perfected my makeup application many moons ago: I know exactly what works with my basic canvas. I'm always well groomed. I make sure that my skin is soft and smells good, that I'm clean-shaven where I need to be, that my hair is in good condition and styled, that my dental hygiene is top-notch and that I keep my genitals healthy through practising safe sex exclusively. I possess a wardrobe of reasonably expensive clothes from the pre-recession era and they have stood the test of time in that they still look great and complement my shape. I look expensive – not out-of-reach expensive but middle-class expensive. All of these things show as soon as the client sees me for the first time – he can immediately tell that I've made the effort for him, which is hugely important. He already knows that I'm safe and healthy because I covered all that in the initial phone contact. That leaves him wondering: how good is she?

I think it's a prerequisite of this work that you have to love sex – and I do. I've always loved the sensual thrill of skin on skin – it turns me on. I've also got a very pragmatic streak in my personality, which means I'm matter-of-fact about bodies and not easily shocked or embarrassed. Vaginas, anuses, penises – they're all just other bits of the body to me, so I'm not squeamish about getting intimate with them. Most important of all, perhaps, is that I like and trust men. I know I'm separated, which might make some people assume I think men are dreadful, but that's not the case at all. I really enjoy the company of men: I'm fascinated by the way their minds work; I empathize with their weaknesses and their self-doubt. I have a par-ticularly soft spot for characteristically alpha males who show a hint of vulnerability. I've no idea why, but they make me weak at the knees every time. I love how men make me feel during sex. That may sound a bit obvious, but I know plenty of women who couldn't make a statement like that and really mean it. I like men – all types – and that shone through when I was with a client.

Sometimes I don't realize it until I'm actually with the client, but the whole prelude to the meeting is arousing in itself: wondering what he'll be like, planning my wardrobe, paying attention to my body – even the secrecy, although stressful, is strangely arousing. It must be the adrenalin rush, or perhaps that thinking and planning sex starts off the whole chemical process of arousal in the body, even for sex with strangers. Whatever it is, my body reacts to it, and by the time I get to a meeting, I'm really up for it and hoping it will be a good one.

This seems to be one of the key things that sets me apart from other sex workers: I genuinely get into it and enjoy it with clients, which they love. I think my enthusiasm gives their virility a great boost, so they enjoy the sex a whole lot more. I suppose if a guy feels he can seriously arouse a high-class escort and make her cli-max, then he leaves feeling he's the best shag on earth. After all, he's thinking, escorts shag 24/7 and have been in every conceivable sex-ual position/scenario, so if *I* just gave her a great shuddering orgasm, I really am as good as I've always suspected!

I figured out some time ago that the more real and genuine I was, the more the clients liked it. If I allow myself to relax into it, we both get the best of it – and I have them coming back for more.

I'm not sure if I'm especially fantastic in the sack or if it's just that the whole set-up in having paid sex makes any inhibitions fade into the background, allowing my inner sex goddess to emerge. I was never consciously aware of it before, but I had a slight inkling that I might like being dominant. I'd never had a chance to explore this with any partner, so I was quietly aware that it might be bubbling under the surface, but all the while I'd stayed in the safe zone of straightforward 'vanilla sex', as the pros call it. I hadn't gone into this line of work for what I could get out of it sexually – I was purely financially motivated – but through doing it I realized that I like being dominant and that it's a huge confidence-booster. I'm not sure I could do it without the background of my escort environment and persona, though, and I'm much more likely to try out some new technique in my work life than in my private sex life.

There are another few reasons why it's easier to be a little minx at work. For one thing, it's expected of me. For another, if it goes wrong, I walk away – I don't have to talk about it or smooth things over. I dated a few guys in the past who were either reserved in bed or just inexperienced, and there was no doubt I reacted to that and was equally reserved. I reflected whatever sexual messages I was receiving from my lover. By the same token, when I'm with clients and they know I'm open and enthusiastic, I'm sure it must help them loosen up and do whatever comes naturally. I like letting go and I like seeing men let go because it makes me want to let go more – it's a lustful cycle of sexual liberation!

I don't suppose my dominant escort persona would be acceptable in everyday social interactions. I have learned over the years, or had impressed upon me, that as a woman, it's more socially acceptable to have a slightly more submissive personality. As a result, I smoothed down my embryonic dominant streak from an early age, responding to social cues received in childhood. While men may love me being the boss in the bedroom, I know I'd step on several toes if I were like that in everyday life. I enjoy it, though, and I hope I can explore it further in my private life in future. I've always been an avid fan of sex and I'm a keen reader. I've read so many sex tips over the years, especially when my marriage (and sex life) was on the way out, but I never had the confidence to try them. Strange as it may sound, I felt awkward doing something new with my ex-husband. I tended to stay in my comfort zone. I had read about how to give the best blow-job or hand-job and how to seduce a man, but I'd never put it fully into practice – until I needed to do so for this work. It's been a very pleasant surprise!

I'm absolutely certain that men enjoy sex without the fanfare, by which I mean sex where they don't have to consider my emotions, mood or sense of propriety. That is, of course, very different from the love-making that happens in a committed relationship. I know this because I was that wife in the committed relationship and I don't think my ex-husband was ever as dirty or horny as my clients. I recently read the results of a poll that declared Irish men the best lovers of any nationality. From my experience, I'd say that might be true. They definitely know how to let rip once they're given permission. When I say 'permission', I mean when they're with someone who appreciates them sexually, doesn't judge them and is into it herself. I think that's why I have regulars. From what they've told me, it's great sex, I'm really easy to talk to and a 'lovely' person. Really, I hear that all the time, and it seems to matter greatly to my clients that they have a great time with a woman they consider 'lovely'. I take this to mean that I'm open, relaxed and normal.

I think I'd go so far as to say that if sex work wasn't so frowned upon in society, not to mention illegal, it could possibly have been my occupation of choice. I don't suppose there is any woman alive who hasn't thought at least once, Could I be an escort? I'd certainly thought about it over the years. I was always in gainful employment elsewhere, so it never needed to go any further. Seriously, though, in terms of the myriad needs of the average working mother, it ticks an awful lot of the boxes: self-employed, flexible, creative, well paid, varied, working with people, part-time hours for full-time salary, and minimal childcare fees because you can work around school hours. In return, you need a high libido, an interest in exploring your sexual self, pushing the boundaries of your sexuality, and thinking outside the box in terms of societal norms.

The reality is that even if I hadn't had to make money, I would have enjoyed having so much sex, maybe even more of it. In the real world we have to make money and pay bills, and some of us don't get as much time to devote to our sex life as we would like. In many ways, I'm perfectly cut out for the work. Recession or no recession, there are women who would never do escort work and women who would. I chose it because I needed the money, but I also think I had a natural inclination to work in the sex industry. Indeed, I feel a tinge of regret that I didn't discover this side of myself until so recently. I could have made a small fortune in my twenties when I had the freedom to travel, which would have made secrecy and ano- nymity easy. The sad part is that in my twenties I would never have had the balls to do it, even if I'd wanted to. Isn't life a bitch? We get wise and confident when the flush of youth, with its freedom and opportunities, is long past.

Looking back, I'm not sure how I got to be so sexually uninhib- ited. It wasn't from my upbringing. If we're to believe what we read, our 'love map' – the developmental representation of what we find physically and mentally arousing – is established in childhood, around the age of eight. This was a theory developed by an eminent psychologist, John William Money, in 1921 and his notion of 'love topography' goes some way to explain why women 'marry their fathers' – in other words, they're attracted to similar characteristics, in personality and appearance, to their opposite-scx parent. I'm not so sure about this concept. If anything, I am attracted to men who display polar-opposite characteristics to my father's. As for looks, my father was a bald, bearded, weatherbeaten farmer and I go for men who are well groomed, toned, healthy and with a good head of hair – that's my type. I disliked my father's appearance and there- fore sought out his opposite, but I tend to be attracted to personalities similar to his. Perhaps this is coincidental, but there is a definite pattern. From an early age I felt uncomfortable with my parents' relationship because they fought a lot and never seemed content with one another. It's quite possible that in my efforts to seek out a man of opposite appearance to my father I forgot the personality side of things. This would explain how I ended up with my ex-husband, who is totally different in looks from my father but scarily similar to him in personality.

I was brought up in the typical repressive style of a strongly Catholic rural family. I never saw either of my parents naked, and my father discouraged any show of flesh by his daughters from when we were children. I had no idea my parents had sex until my early teens. If they were ever sexually active during my childhood, I was never made aware of it, and neither were my siblings. Maybe a few of the older siblings knew, but they didn't tell the younger ones. I remember the absolute disgust I felt when I realized where babies came from – it took me weeks to get over the idea of my parents 'at it'. This is probably an accurate reflection of the punitive attitude to sex I had adopted during my childhood. The fact that I felt almost traumatized when I found out what my parents did in bed reflects largely on the subliminal messages I had received about sex from them. To this day, I have never seen them kiss.

We didn't have sex education at school, so if you didn't learn the facts of life from your parents, you relied on your better-informed peers. One thing I was told by my mother was that sex was for married couples only and that pregnancy outside wedlock was unacceptable – plain and simple. That message was crystal clear and my sisters and I believed that a secret abortion was absolutely mandatory should any of us be caught out. Although termination of a pregnancy goes against Catholic teaching, we got the message that it was more acceptable than coming home pregnant. I was a little sketchy on how exactly I would achieve that state, since our parents never gave us any information about our bodies. I was inquisitive by nature so all the secrecy around genitals and sex only made me more curious to find out about them.

I was fifteen before I managed to get an idea of the big mystery.

We weren't given much freedom, so the opportunities to get out and meet someone were few and far between. The summer before I had found a women's self-help sex manual in my auntie's chest of drawers and had acquired from it a fair idea of my anatomical structure. As for any guidance from an adult, there was none, except the messages I picked up from the tut-tutting that greeted a kissing scene on *Glenroe*, or the necessary mid-kiss channel change; I've still never seen an episode of *Dallas* from start to finish. For all their secrecy about it, my parents' attitude told me there was a whole different world that was only experienced by adults, and I wanted to know more about it.

The summer after my Inter Cert exam, I was allowed to stay over at a friend's for the night. Her parents were a lot more open and regularly showed affection in public; they were the first couple I'd ever seen greet each other with a kiss. On the night I was there, they got a last-minute invitation to go out for drinks and trusted me and my mate to stay home alone – we were fifteen, after all. As soon as her folks were out of the door, my friend phoned some of her other friends in the area and invited them over for coffee – honestly, just coffee: underage drinking was definitely out of bounds. Within an hour there were half a dozen people milling around in the kitchen, and it was obvious within minutes who fancied whom. My cocooned upbringing made me want to grasp any bit of freedom with both hands, so I slipped off to the living room with a guy a couple of years older than I was. Because he was older, I saw him as worldly-wise. Whether he was or not, I don't know, but he certainly stands out in my memory for giving me a night to remember.

For starters, he taught me to kiss properly. I wasn't embarrassed by my lack of experience and I was clearly a keen learner, which made up for lack of expertise. We were the happiest teenagers in the country when my friend's mum rang to say they would be staying out for the night and wouldn't be back until after ten the following morning. As the evening drew to an end and the others made their way home, my guy hung back and my friend said she'd turn a blind eye if he stayed over, so long as he was gone by early morning. Without any discussion, I took him up to one of the spare rooms. I had gone from never being kissed to hopping into bed with a young man. I felt very womanly and enjoyed every minute of my adventure. We agreed before getting undressed that we'd keep our undies on – to take them off seemed too far a leap and, anyway, sex was for when you were married. There was nothing to stop everything else happening, though.

I can still vividly remember the first moment when our almost-naked skin touched. My spine tingled and I couldn't imagine that there was anything better to experience with a man. I could have stayed there for ever as we allowed our bodies to do what came instinctively and drink up the thrill of another's touch. We stayed lying down, kissing, with our underwear on, until the sun started to come up. That was when he slowly let his hand move between my legs, chancing his luck to see if I'd tell him to stop. I didn't. I let him put his hand into my panties and feel whatever was going on. I don't recall before then ever being sexually aroused and I'd no idea why I was so wet. I was sure it wasn't pee, but when he touched my wetness, groaned and kissed me harder, I was silently relieved that I was all right down there. He seemed to know what he was doing, and knew what to expect of my pussy – even if I didn't. Sure, I had seen the pictures in the book, but that book didn't mention anything of the delight my clitoris held in store. Wow! How hadn't I known this? Why hadn't I discovered it myself? As for when he pushed his fingers inside me, my God, I had no idea another person could make me experience those sensations. He started to move his fingers faster over my clitoris and I sensed I was supposed to be building up to something, something I didn't know anything about. It didn't seem to be happening for me. He moved my hand down to his cock. I was amazed by its size and very interested, though I still didn't know what I was at. He took his hand off my pussy and guided my hand around his cock. He kept his hand overlapping mine as he started to increase the pace, pumping up and down the length of him until he came. I had no idea what was happening to him except that it felt perfectly natural and we were both enjoying it.

I was far too caught up in the pleasure of it all to worry about what he thought of me, whether he liked my body or if we were going to see each other again. I didn't ask questions. I was too intent on reading his body language, his heart rate and the depth of his breathing to give me my leads. By now, the room was filled with early-morning light and I knew he'd have to scarper soon. He asked if he could take down my knickers, but I still felt uneasy about that. Besides, if I could have so much fun with my knickers on, there was no rush to take them off.

'You haven't done any of this before, have you?' he said, as he cleaned himself off.

'Nope, first time,' I replied, very chuffed with myself.

'You know you can do that to yourself just by touching,' he said, looking down between my legs. I didn't answer, but I made a mental note to try it at the first available opportunity. I assumed that if he knew this, surely all women must do it to themselves.

That night, while reliving every juicy detail, I decided to try and do what he had been doing with my clitoris. I still didn't know what to expect, but there was obviously some crescendo to this for both the man and the woman. I had seen him come and I wanted to find out what the female equivalent felt like. It finally happened, after much trial and error, varying pace, touch and position, but, God, was it worth the wait! After that, I was hooked.

9. The Unexpected Sex-bomb

I took a couple of calls from Derek before he finally committed to making an appointment. He described himself as a retired engineer living in the west of Ireland. He was well spoken, polite and educated, but as he was retired, I was a bit sceptical as to how he might look – let's face it, I don't think grey pubes and chest hair do it for anyone, and I'm no exception. We had about ten days to wait before we could meet because he was going away on a golf trip to Europe and then his son and daughter-in-law were staying with him and his wife for a few days. After that, he was free.

It's remarkable the amount of personal information some people will divulge over the phone to a stranger. Initially Derek wanted me to visit him at his home because, like him, his wife had a full and active retirement and was away overnight from time to time. He gave me the address, but it was a bit far for me to travel, so instead we agreed on a location halfway between his home and mine. Of course, he had now given me his name, address and mobile number, and it struck me that if I'd been a stalker or a criminal, I could have gone to his house, noted his car registration, broken in, found something with his wife's name on it – an envelope or medication in the bathroom cabinet – and blackmailed him. I actually mentioned this to him: was he not concerned that if I went to his home, I could cause an awful lot of trouble for him and his family? Of course I never would, but I felt I had to point out that it could be a dangerous thing to do if he happened to get in touch with a hooker who had a few crazy chips on her shoulder. He agreed it was a very fair point, but that I sounded very genuine and he felt he could trust me to respect any personal information he divulged in our correspondence and subsequent meeting.

During the ten days when Derek was in Europe and then with his family, we exchanged some really saucy texts. He was out at dinner one night when he texted to say he was getting so frustratingly horny thinking about our upcoming meeting that he couldn't concentrate on the conversation. His wife and son had commented that he didn't seem himself, and he had had to pass it off as tiredness after the golf trip. Rather, he was in a state of high anticipation about being alone with me. I was starting to feel that way myself. As the meeting date drew closer, I got excited about it. His texts were sexy, sweet, interesting and entertaining. A good brain is a serious turn-on for me. I don't mean braininess in the academic sense, but someone who demonstrates that all aspects of their brain are fully engaged; sharp, witty repartee is always enticing.

As always, I had asked Derek if he had any specific requirements or preferences in relation to how I dressed and my underwear, and he asked me to wear a dress and stockings with suspenders. I went out of my way to get a decent sexy suspender belt. I can tell you they're difficult to source since the invention of hold-ups, but as every woman with more than stick-insect legs knows, all hold-ups do is dig into your thighs and leave you with two mini-muffin tops – not a good look! With a bit of dedicated searching, I found a black suspender belt and old-style stockings with the black seam running up the back from heel to butt. I decided to wear a fabulous dress I'd bought on impulse in the January sales the previous year. I had had no reason at the time to buy it, I just loved it, but so long as you love what you buy, you'll always find a reason to wear it.

As the day approached for our meeting, I was feeling oddly nervous. I figured Derek was quite experienced, well travelled and refined, and I sensed he could be quite sharp and critical if he didn't get what he wanted. I didn't want to disappoint – I didn't want to disappoint any client, but I particularly wanted to make a good impression on Derek because I was hoping he'd become a regular. I wanted refined, sexy men as my regulars, and so far he seemed to fit the bill.

We had arranged to meet at seven o'clock in the hotel. I arrived there thirty minutes early and got the room set up. I drew the curtains, turned up the heating and put my music-system speaker in place. I arranged the condoms, lube, antiseptic spray, baby wipes and tissues on the bedside locker. I lit some scented candles, checked myself in the mirror and tidied my hotel bag into the wardrobe. I had made a special effort with my makeup as I didn't have any other clients that day and, yes, I was aroused from all our pre-meeting texts and needed a decent shag. I donned the suspender belt and stockings combo, which made me feel sexy, then the dress, and appraised myself in the mirror. Bring it on!

My phone buzzed and Derek informed me that he was just pulling into the car park. I gave him directions to the room and told him to knock confidently on the door, as if he had every right to be there. There's nothing more suspicious than some guy sloping along a hotel corridor looking like he's afraid he'll be rumbled. Faking an air of confidence is as good as the real thing and draws minimal attention from hotel staff or other guests. I arranged two glasses of sparkling water and sat on the bed.

A confident rap on the door announced his arrival. I spritzed my neck and wrists with Chanel and eagerly pulled open the door.

My heart sank. Derek looked much older than he'd sounded on the phone, and I suddenly felt foolish for fantasizing that this meeting was going to be great. His hair was white, his face very wrinkled – probably from years of being involved in outdoor sports – and he was wearing very old-fashioned spectacles. Hoping he hadn't noticed my disappointment, I welcomed him in. I made small-talk about his journey to the hotel and we chatted briefly about his golf trip and how busy he had been since he retired. After a natural lull, I suggested we get started and offered him a shower. I always insist a client has bathed within the previous hour and check with them beforehand. Most men take up the offer of a shower anyway – the soothing hot water has the added advantage of relaxing them if they're a little nervous. I always make sure there are fresh soap, towels, toothbrushes and toothpaste on hand. These are essential for smokers as I can't abide smoking or smelly smoker's breath. I'm generally not going to kiss a client on the mouth but, even so, if they smoke it's hard for me to be close to them with the stale smell of tobacco lingering.

Derek accepted the suggestion of a shower. He stripped off, showing no inhibitions, and threw his clothes on the back of the chair. While he was in the shower I laid out a negligee, to have ready if I took off my dress and needed something more comfortable to slip on. Derek hopped out of the bathroom and strutted around naked as he dried off his rather hairy body. He was skinny, but in an athletic way, with nicely defined muscle tone and surprisingly great legs. I asked him if he'd like to lie down on the bed, but he said he wanted to see me undress as he sat on it. I looked straight at him seductively, unzipped my dress and let it fall to the floor. I kicked it aside, so now I was standing there in a black lace bra and matching G-string-style panties, suspender belt, black stockings and red-patent high heels.

His reaction was a massive turn-on: he grabbed me to him, so that I was standing while he was sitting on the bed, and put his head to my chest, holding me there with his arms tightly around me, as if to absorb my scent, the touch of my flesh, the warmth of my skin. I held his head to me and was surprised to find myself getting rather horny quite quickly. His arms were strong and I was now sensing an intensity in him that I had overlooked when he first walked in. He started to make low groaning noises and told me how amazing I looked. He pulled his head away from my chest and looked up at my face, tenderly touching it, outlining the shape of my eyes, cheeks and mouth. I licked his thumb as it moved over my lips, and he closed his eyes, gasping. I took his thumb deep into my mouth and bit on the fleshy part. He started to move it around my mouth, which was soft and relaxed now. It was clear that we could both feel this incredible sexual energy building between us. I licked and bit his fingers and palms. Jesus, I thought, if this is what kissing his hand is like for both of us, then I'd sized him up wrongly.

I was getting so incredibly aroused, and I really hadn't seen it coming. I touched his mouth so that I was looking into his face as he kissed and licked my hands and he was watching me doing the same to his hands. We prolonged this because it was strangely erotic and felt fantastic. We moved our mouths closer, and when our lips touched, it was like fire. The desire was so intense, it blew my mind. I wrapped my legs around him to get closer. I wanted more of him – I wanted to feel him everywhere. The guy who, minutes before, I had classed as 'unremarkable older man fuck' had the most intense sexual energy I had ever experienced. It was unbelievably exciting to be on the receiving end of it.

He flipped me over and laid me on my back, then whipped off my bra and sat between my legs, holding them in the air, with my suspenders, panties, stockings and high heels still in place. I knew he was admiring me through the sheer G-string and getting an eyeful, so I lay back and let him enjoy what he was seeing. I stared directly at him. I felt incredibly confident about how I looked, especially as it was obvious he was loving what he was seeing. He held up my right leg and started kissing it from my foot to my thigh, to where the suspenders ended. He paused before moving on to my thighs, then tightly buried his head to the right of my groin. He knew what he was doing: if he had gone straight for my pussy, it would have been too much, too soon. I was wet by now, but there was a lot more pleasure to be had and he knew exactly how to tease me into it. With his head in my groin, he used his other arm to lift my left leg and let it rest over his shoulder. He wriggled his shoulder further under my upper thigh and butt, until his skinny athletic arm was under my back. He had such strength, and I can still say to this day that he was the most sexually charged man I've ever been with.

He paused and took a breath, as if to slow things down slightly. I ran my hands through his hair and pulled gently on it. His head was still in my groin and he started to nibble it as he slowly moved his hand down my back and towards my butt. My legs were spread wide open for him. I was really aroused now and so ready for him, wanting him deep inside me. His hand moved down my butt and he pulled my lace G-string to the side and slipped a finger under the fabric. He could feel my wetness on my panties and paused tantalizingly before running his thumb over my pussy to feel the full extent of my arousal. He was sweating at this stage because he was using every muscle in his body to get us both into this position. He moved his head from my groin and buried his face in my pussy, inhaling me deeply. I arched my back in sheer pleasure and he moved his hands over my breasts. With his face still in my pussy, he grabbed my nipples and, although it was a bit rough, it was a very good rough and I received it only as pure pleasure.

'Fuck it,' he moaned. 'I can't wait any more. I have to be inside you.'

He pulled off my shoes, grabbed my panties at the sides and ripped them off. I still had the stockings and suspender belt on. I snatched a condom and pushed it over his very ample firm cock. I lay back; his cock didn't need any guidance. He lay over me and looked into my eyes, our mutual desire for penetration clear on our faces. He rested on his elbows as his cock found the entrance to my pussy. I have to say, that's my favourite part of sex – well, with guys who are good in the sack at any rate. The moment when his cock is just resting at the entrance to my pussy and we both pause momentarily, knowing the first few thrusts are the best by far. It's my all-time favourite part of shagging. Your body soaks up the sensations as you go deeper and deeper into a world of pure bliss. It's better than coming, in fact.

Derek stared into my eyes before forcing himself deeply inside me. We both shouted with sheer pleasure, and I covered his mouth as a reminder to him that we were in a hotel and didn't want to be overheard. He pushed himself deeper inside me and I wrapped my legs around him to pull him closer into me. He pulled me up so that I was on top, in a seated position. He was very flexible and agile. I arched my back so that I was lying with my back on the bed, but still sitting over his thighs and with his cock never losing position inside me. He sat upright and uttered a few expletives, indicating that he was really loving it. Although I don't usually like swear words during sex, being told I was one hell of a sexy bitch somehow seemed fine, arousing, even. I was amazed by how in tune with me this guy was. Christ, it was lovely as a woman not to have to give any direction at all. He seemed to know instinctively when a change of position would be perfect to keep the momentum going.

He lifted my legs up and over so my top half followed and I was lying face down. He pushed my legs as far apart as possible, lay on my back and moved further into me. We were slowing things down now, but only to enjoy a different sensation. I lifted myself on to my elbows as he slowly glided in and out of me. He kissed the back of my neck and I moved off my elbows to lie flat. I arched my pelvis up towards him to get as much of him into me as possible. He grabbed me by my waist and now I was sitting backwards on him. He lay back so he could watch me take his cock into me and see me from behind as well.

'Shit, I have to come,' he gasped.

'It's okay.'

I tried to sit further back on him to get some leverage against his cock. I pushed myself as hard as I could to thrust on to him, using the strength of my calf muscles to push myself up and down. Jesus, I was getting tired, but the very least I could do was give him a great climax, seeing as I'd just had the best sex ever with a stranger. It worked. He literally roared as he came and I was hoping to God that nobody heard, although I suppose couples do have daytime sex in hotels!

We collapsed in a sweaty heap and lay there for what seemed like ages. There was no need to talk: we both knew what we thought of it. After a while, once our breathing had returned to a normal rate, Derek turned to me and said, 'I suppose I'd better get cleaned up.' He kissed me on my forehead, then gently on the lips. What had started as a tender kiss seemed to awaken all the passion we had experienced moments earlier. We kissed for what seemed like five minutes or so, until he pulled back, saying he would love to go again but he had to get home.

As he went into the shower, I put on the negligee and handed him in some fresh towels. I pottered around the room as he dressed. When it came to saying goodbye, he thanked me for a fantastic time and asked would I be happy to see him again.

'Any time, my pleasure,' I said, with feeling.

He handed me the agreed amount of money and said he would

give me a call when he was next free to make a booking. With that, he left. I lay back on the bed, thinking about what had just taken place. I was exhausted in a sexually satisfied way and enjoyed the inner calm I was feeling. Men could still surprise me – he hadn't looked like great sex on legs, but there you have it: he was all that.

I haven't heard from or seen Derek since that day. For all I know, he could be dead and buried. That's just the nature of working in the sex industry: you have no real knowledge of who you're seeing and there is absolutely no follow-up as such. As the saying goes, you pay to walk away, but I do wonder occasionally about some of the clients who made an impression on me, whether they are still in the same relationships, if they ever sorted out the problem we chatted about or if they plucked up the courage to ask their wives for what they would really like in bed.

The thing about Derek was that I could never have imagined he had such amazing energy and was so exciting in bed. I guess a person's sexual personality is unique and private and, really, you've no way of guessing what they'll be like in the sack until you're actually there. It made me think about how the odds were stacked against me finding a partner with whom I was compatible in all the pertinent areas of my life. When I was on official dating sites, looking for a partner, the approach was so superficial: I could only judge someone by what they chose to write about themselves, which they might have fabricated. Then would come the point when we agreed to exchange photos, but I'm not sure if this ever had any benefit: photographs are devoid of all the little subtleties that make someone attractive to us. A two-dimensional picture tells you nothing about a person's smile, self-confidence, how they carry themselves or the effort they put into their appearance – all vital clues. If I had got chatting to Derek on a dating site and he was single, and if he had then sent me a photograph of himself, I would have been put off by his older appearance and wouldn't have considered meeting him for a drink. I would never have been able to tell that, in the flesh, we would have such astonishing sexual chemistry.

When you consider all of the variables that we want satisfied in our choice of partner, it isn't any wonder that there are so many dissatisfied men and women. Just think about the number of areas that are important to you in choosing a partner. My areas of importance are intelligence, manners, kindness, emotional maturity, the ability to empathize, a good listener, financial solvency (or at least reasonably good with money), over five foot eight tall, excellent personal and dental hygiene, and good dress sense. That's what I want before I even snog someone! What if you meet some guy and he ticks all the boxes but there is absolutely no sexual chemistry between you? Or, alternatively, if there are areas in which you are very compatible and others where you don't overlap at all? What is the statistical likelihood of meeting someone who is available and ticks all the boxes on your list, including wild sexual chemistry, and whose boxes you tick? My God, we've no chance, have we?

10. A Confrontation

After almost four months on the job, I had a good idea of what the bog-standard client was looking for and what sex with him would be like. Sometimes I would fervently hope that today I'd get a 'surprise' and have a client who turned out to be fantastic in bed, but mainly what I got was basic, straightforward sex in the missionary position, or with me on top, or doggie style, some chit-chat before and after, and a bit of kissing, if it took my fancy. I was aware that I could get a lot more 'surprises' if I changed my admission criteria and agreed to meet more randomers, but I had made the decision to vet clients based on a solid rationale and I wasn't going to modify that for a more exciting workday. My research had stood me in good stead thus far and I hadn't yet had a bad experience. Yes, I'd had clients I wasn't interested in seeing again, but that was because they were particularly unattractive or just too boring. I had no problem getting clients, so I could afford to be picky now and again. I knew, though, that the longer I worked at this, the more likely it would be that I'd come across a client who was less than a gentleman.

I was just popping out to do the weekly shopping one afternoon when my work mobile rang. I put down my handbag and keys and took the call. Eddie asked if he had the right number – he'd like to enquire about the massage service. I told him he had, and probed as to anything else he might require.

'Well, can I take it that it's a full service?'

'Yes, it is. What is it you're looking for?'

He started by explaining that his wife had given birth to their first child four months earlier. She was breastfeeding and had elected to sleep in the spare room with the baby, so her husband could get a proper night's sleep. He made it very clear that he loved his wife and was delighted with his new baby, but was so sexually frustrated that he had to see someone. He didn't want to start an affair, so an escort seemed the best solution. He told me he was feeling neglected and ignored by his wife. She had had several miscarriages before this child was born and was 100 per cent devoted to her baby. As a result of the miscarriages, she had refused to make love during the pregnancy and had had no libido since the baby's arrival, so he had gone without sex for many months and simply couldn't handle it any longer.

I could empathize with what he was going through. I asked him if he thought he would feel guilty after our meeting. He told me that he used to visit massage parlours when he worked in town, before he was married, but hadn't done so since he'd moved to a rural area to live in an environment more suited to family life. All the while he had been looking for a discreet escort, but hadn't any luck – until now. I took from this that guilt wasn't on the agenda. He had done it before, he knew what he was getting into, and he believed it wasn't the same kind of betrayal an affair would be. I pushed the thoughts of his wife out of my mind: it wasn't my decision, it was his.

He asked me lots of questions, all the usual stuff: what did I look like? (Five foot six, average curvy figure, short bobbed dark hair, blue eyes.) What age? (Thirty-six – a lie, of course.) Size? (Fourteen – men don't know the difference between twelve, fourteen and sixteen, but they may know that fourteen is average, so that was my standard answer.) Was I shaved or waxed down below? (Shaved – neat.) Did I do anal sex? (Yes.) This was very standard questioning for me and I knew what clients wanted to hear in reply. He was very happy with my answers.

I asked him what he would most like to happen on my visit to him. He said he would love a relaxing, erotic, sensual massage followed by a decent hard fuck. He was afraid he'd come too quickly, given the length of time since he'd had sex, so I suggested I make him come first, before I started the massage. That way, he could enjoy the massage and slowly build up to the sex that would follow. He was delighted with that proposal and equally delighted that I'd answered the phone because he was free that evening. I was too, as it happened. He was staying in a hotel for business purposes, so it would be easy for me to visit him there. I told him to text me his hotel name and room number once he was settled in, and we arranged that I would come by at eight p.m.

I'd already seen two bog-standard clients in the morning at a hotel about an hour from my house. I needed to take off my makeup and reapply it from scratch for the evening meeting. I was tired after the two earlier clients and the drive home, but the kids were with their dad and I needed to get the work in when I could. I'd be silly to refuse another client, especially when he was already staying at the hotel.

By seven I was freshened up and on my way. I decided to throw on a pair of denims and a crisp blue shirt. I was wearing a sheer baby-doll one-piece underneath. The outfit was more casual than I usually wore for work, but it was still smart and I felt comfortable – on the third client of the day, style's on the way out of the window and comfort becomes the priority. Eddie had sent me the hotel details and it was easy to get to on the new motorway. I listened to Lyric FM as I drove – apparently classical music reduces the incidence of road rage. I find it chills me out before I meet a new client. I've never been as nervous as the first time, but I still get butterflies when I'm about to meet a man I don't know – there's always that little voice in my head telling me to be extra careful.

I arrived at the hotel in good time, parked and checked myself in the mirror – not bad for a touching-forty-year-old masquerading as a thirty-six-year-old! A quick spritz of perfume, a mint popped into my mouth and I was ready.

I stepped out of the car with my trusty bag of tricks. I strode confidently through Reception, my head held high, looking like I belonged there. The chirpy receptionist bade me good evening and I responded nonchalantly, as if I was fed up with having to greet receptionists in hotels. I spotted the gilt 'Bedrooms this way' sign and proceeded up the corridor. I got into the lift and pressed "2". Another quick check in the lift mirrors before the doors opened and

I spotted the sign for room 202. I did an exaggerated smile and licked my lips before knocking lightly on the door. I always performed this little ritual because apparently the wide smile relaxes the facial muscles, adding softness to the facial lines; the lick makes the lips glisten, appealing to a man's primal instincts.

The door opened and I had my first sight of Eddie. He was attractive and I was secretly hoping he might be one of those little 'surprises'. I went inside and he shut the door behind me.

He wasn't as confident in person as he had been on the phone. He greeted me somewhat sheepishly and immediately said he was nervous as this was his first time since he'd been married. I decided to take the lead and beckoned him to sit on the bed while I arranged my bag of goodies. I made small-talk about work, the weather and the general state of the country. He asked if I'd like payment now or later. I replied that if he'd like to pay me now, that was fine with me. He left an envelope on the dresser and I put it into my bag without opening it. I asked to use the bathroom and told him to take his clothes off while I got into something more comfortable. I undressed to reveal my baby-doll one-piece – always a winner because it's semi-transparent and shows plenty but still leaves something to the imagination.

I asked him to lie face-down on the bed, then straddled his butt so I could massage his back. I poured some of the massage oil into my hands and he remarked on how wonderful it smelt. I told him it was an organic aromatherapy oil that I made up myself. He seemed impressed as I ran my hands rhythmically over his shoulders, but suddenly he asked if we could stop what we were doing – he really wanted to touch and kiss me and was finding the massage frustrating because he was so horny. I got off his back and lay facing him on the bed. He was very attractive in an older-man type of way. He looked mid-to-late forties to me, and when he started kissing me on the mouth, I found myself warming to his touch and responding. I remembered we had agreed on the phone that I would make him come quickly at first, but that plan seemed to have fallen by the wayside. I'd had this before – men say they're worried they'll come too quickly and won't get to enjoy it properly and I always suggest I'll make them come as soon as I arrive, then build up to a second climax. What generally happens is that the nerves involved in waiting for me mean they need a little bit of work to get them going in the first place.

Within a few minutes of starting to explore each other's bodies, we were kissing frantically. I felt myself getting wet and he let out a groan of pleasure when he slid his fingers tentatively inside me. To hell with it, I thought, it's not all that often I get to enjoy my work. He knew I was really into it and this seemed to make him hornier. He said he couldn't last any longer and wanted his cock in my pussy. I reached over and grabbed a condom off the locker, where I had laid out my stuff earlier.

I had it on him in a flash. He quickly positioned his cock at the entrance to my wet pussy and looked into my eyes momentarily before ramming himself deep inside me. God, what bliss! He felt damn good. If only all my clients were that good, I swear I'd never have given up the job. He got into his stride and thrust quickly into me. I adjusted my position slightly to get the full effects of his very hard cock. He started to thrust faster and his breathing showed he was working up to a climax. I wanted to change position – my favourite position is doggie-style because I can enjoy the full feeling of a cock in me, but I don't have to look at the client. Let's face it, they're not all my cup of tea, so I'd rather not have to look at them if I don't have to. I told him I wanted to move before he came and flipped over on to my knees with my head down, revealing the fullness of my ass and pussy with my legs widely spread. I told him to fuck me hard as I knew this would give him a great orgasm. He put his cock back into me and his hands on my ass. As he was thrusting, I could feel that he was interested in my ass and he ran his fingers from my pussy up to it, spreading my juice around my anus. I loved it, and it showed. He was loving that I was so aroused and gently inserted a finger up my ass and rotated it inside me. He tried two fingers next, while still thrusting slowly into my pussy. This was about my pleasure now, but his excitement was in seeing what he could do to me. I also suspected that he hadn't had anything more exciting than missionary with his wife for a very long time.

Surprisingly, he stayed hard for ages and though I couldn't deny that I was enjoying what he was doing, by now the earlier activities of the day had caught up with me. I was starting to get a bit bored and tired and wanted him to finish. I could have done with a quick orgasm initially, but he had stayed hard a lot longer than suited me. He was possibly quite chuffed with himself for managing to contain his climax so long, but I figured we'd been at it for quite long enough. I was always aware with clients, even the good ones, that I was basically in an acting role and only did the job to pay the bills. Time was money and he'd had his time, so now I had to fake a climax and bring the session to its conclusion. I told him what he was doing felt incredible and that I was about to come. 'I want to feel you harder,' I breathed, in my best sexy voice. He fucked me so hard I could feel his cock hitting my cervix. I moaned deeply, contracting my vaginal muscles in quick succession to grip him in me, and gasped. Then I held my breath for a few seconds and sighed deeply, just like I did in my parallel real world where I never had to fake an orgasm.

It worked. When he asked if it was okay for him to come, I urged him on. He rammed himself into me for a few seconds more before crying out. His whole body shuddered, there were a couple of twitching aftershocks, and he slumped into post-coital exhaustion. He moved out of me and lay down to catch his breath. I got up to use the bathroom and returned with some tissue paper to dispose of the condom. I handed him the tissue and he did the necessary, then placed it in the small plastic bag I had brought. I tied the bag at the top, went back to the bathroom, put the little package into the bin and washed my hands again.

I switched on the shower to run the water to a good hot temperature and shouted to him that I was just having a quick wash. I jumped in and washed him off me, imagining his bodily fluids going down the plughole with the soapy water. I ran the soap over every part of my body, rinsed off, then repeated the process until I felt clean again. It wasn't that I disliked the guy, but after the two clients from earlier, with brief showers between them, I wanted to wash all of them off me and have no trace of their scent left on my skin. Being clean is like starting off new again.

I hopped out, briskly towel-dried my body and dressed quickly. I gathered up my bag of goodies, and by the time Eddie stepped out of the shower, I was ready to leave. He told me he had really enjoyed it and hoped to book me again soon. He kissed me on the cheek and I let myself out. I was hoping he might become a regular, especially as he'd been looking for an escort for some time.

Back in my car, I checked my mobile phone for messages and, thankfully, there was none – I was too tired to talk to a client, never mind see another that evening. I opened the envelope he had given me and was just pushing the cash into my wallet when I realized it was just five twenties – he'd left me three hundred euro short. The bollocks! I sat there, trying to calm my breathing. *What the hell do I do?* I had to think straight. Was it an error? Did he accidentally leave me short or had he done it on purpose, hoping I'd be well on my way home before I noticed it? Shit, shit, shit! I had to take a gamble and hope he wouldn't call my bluff. I'd prepared for this type of scenario, but it had never happened for real. It was time to see if the mental preparation would work. All the second-guessing, mind-games stuff I'd imagined and role-played on my own – would it work with a flesh-and-blood man who might not appreciate my take on the situation? I remembered that he'd said he had visited escorts regularly before he got married, so this was either a genuine mistake or he had deliberately meant to con me. I decided to go back to his room and ask for my money. I'd held up my part of the arrangement very well, so it was only fair that I got my agreed fee.

I marched back into the hotel, never giving Reception a glance – I was too angry to care what they thought. I made my way back to his room and knocked firmly on the door. Just as he answered, I made sure to push through the door quickly and get into the room. One look at his face told me he knew I was there about the money. I realized instantly that the shortfall was no error. I was incensed. When I had rehearsed this scenario I'd always been scared, but in reality I was seething with anger. I faked a very confident air to convince him I was in control. I appeared calm yet firm. My heart was pumping in my chest, but I spoke slowly and clearly. 'I'm appealing to your sense of decency. I want you to pay me the agreed fee,' I said.

He murmured that he had no cash on him and was terribly sorry about the 'mistake'. I figured he wouldn't have taken the chance of not having the money in the room, in case I had counted it first and demanded the rest before agreeing to sex. There was no way a man that desperate was going to go without his shag. So I stood my ground. 'Look, I've got the gardaí on speed dial. I can call them now and you'll have to deal with the consequences of the hotel knowing what you were at, and the possibility of your wife and work finding out. Everyone will think you're a total wanker, seeing an escort when your wife's just had your baby – and don't think I won't do it.'

He panicked and started flapping. 'Shit, there's no need for all that. I might have it here in my wallet. Let me just look.'

I stood there, one hand on my hip and the other holding up my phone with my finger over number 1. That was actually my home phone number speed dial, which I'd put in for emergencies, but I knew no one was at home so if I did have to press it, it would go straight to voicemail. 'Come on, hurry up. I need to be out of here – and don't think you can fuck me about like this. You've got ten seconds to hand me three hundred euro or I'm pressing this number.' Jesus, even I didn't know I had this Mafia persona inside me!

'Wait, wait, I'm getting it. Fuck me, you're some piece of work. Here, I have it, please don't dial.' He counted out the rest of the money in front of me. 'There, are you happy now?' he said roughly. I took the money without responding and walked straight out of the room, not even stopping to close the door behind me.

I might have seemed in control throughout that horrible scene, but my heart was in my mouth. I couldn't get out of there fast enough. I looked behind me as I speed-walked out of the hotel, making sure he wasn't following me. The last thing I needed was for him to see me getting into my car: then he would know my registration and have the potential to find out my real identity. As it was, all he knew was my fake name and a non-registered mobile phone number.

I jumped into the car and locked the doors before speeding out of the car park. I was panicked, there was no doubt about that. I drove for about ten minutes until I was sure I was well away before pulling over on the motorway to compose myself. Christ, that had been scary, but I was delighted with myself for standing up to him. What an asshole that he thought he could get away with taking me for a fool.

When I got home, I locked the doors and windows. It was a bit irrational, I know, but I was still freaked by the experience. I made a mental note always to get and check the cash before the deed was done with new clients; my regulars had never tried to do me out of my fee, so it was only the new clients I needed to be especially careful with. I amended my on-line ad, deleting the line about a satisfaction/money-back guarantee: I'd be asking for payment upfront from now on. I took the cash out of my handbag and counted it – it was my consolation. It reminded me why I did this and it was comforting to see the money. I had made 960 euro profit today, after expenses – a record amount, enough to allow me to take a break from work for a few days. After the goings-on with the client this evening, I needed my own space. I switched off my work phone and threw it into the back of a kitchen cupboard. I didn't want to think about men or work. I took a long, hot bath and thanked God I was home safe.

I fell into bed exhausted, but I tossed and turned, unable to sleep. I was still shaken by the experience. It wasn't a big deal in the grand scheme of things, but it had got me thinking about the risks I was taking every time I met someone. Yes, I stuck to my guidelines regarding who I would see and where I would meet them and, yes, I practised safe sex, but there was no denying I was putting myself in a potentially vulnerable situation. I made good money for the number of hours I worked, especially compared to what was avail-able on social welfare, but it wasn't that much. I was making enough to pay the mortgage, bills, the children's after-school activities and the occasional treat, but I was beginning to wonder if it was worth the risks when the payout was just keeping my head above water. The number of clients I saw each week varied – sometimes I didn't get the right type to fit around my schedule – plus there were all the school obligations and holidays when I couldn't work without shelling out for childcare, which would have defeated the purpose. I was losing out on any bit of social life I'd had – even the odd morning coffee was fast becoming a distant memory. I was constantly worried in case I inadvertently let anything slip to my family or friends, to the extent that I was starting to avoid them. I wasn't returning their calls and was being very vague about how I was spending my time.

On the one hand, I loved great sex and the work was good on that front from time to time, but on the other, Jesus, it was totally socially unacceptable. I couldn't imagine that anyone of my acquaintance would understand why I did it if I was ever found out. What if anything terrible happened to me in the course of work and my children had to live with that awful legacy? I had been desperate for cash when I'd started this and hadn't thought further than paying the next bill. I had regarded it as a short-term measure, but now I had to start asking myself how long I could keep it up. The fact remained that I had huge outgoings each month and therefore had no choice but to keep earning. I was seeing on average twelve to sixteen clients a month, but in fits and starts. I could have a great week and then something would crop up, like one of the kids was sick or a client cancelled at short notice, and suddenly my whole budget was out of whack. That put me under pressure to get the work in when I could because I could never tell what was around the corner. There was always something extra to fork out for – a birthday, a car service or something that needed fixing in the house. I suspected that no matter how much I earned, it would all be accounted for in any given month.

There were times when I wondered if I was completely bonkers to have started this. Had I changed something inside me that could never be reversed? Had I placed an unmanageable burden on myself in trying to conceal my secret life from my family and friends? Could I handle the strain of my secret long-term? I knew that the longer I did this, the more likely it was that something bad would happen to me. Lady Luck could only ride with me for so long. What form would an incident take? Would I let my secret slip? Would I be attacked, threatened, rumbled by hotel staff? Or would I end up meeting a client I knew from my real life – worse, one of my brothers-in-law or a relative? How the fuck would I get out of that one? I knew for sure that if my ex-husband found out what I was doing, he would apply for custody of the children and declare me an unfit mother. I was beginning to sense that my luck was running out and that I should cut my losses and quit while I was ahead – but who would pay the bills if I did that?

The events of the evening had given me a kick up the ass, reminding me that I could never become complacent. Perhaps Eddie was genuinely short of money and desperate for a shag and thought he'd chance trying to short-change me. Whatever his motive, it didn't alter the fact that I had had to face down a client and had been scared by it. It had nudged open a door into a bad room, a place where I could be frightened, threatened or worse. But the bills had to be paid and I had few choices. I tried to believe that what I needed the 'universe will provide', and repeated this mantra as I drifted into sleep.

11. Marriage, Children and Loss

All of the experiences you have in life teach you something, and sex work is no different. By now, four months into it, I'd met such a range of men, with such an array of reasons for indulging in an escort service. Some had been boringly predictable – men wanting the bold thrill of anal sex – but other stuff had been eye-opening and forced me to look at my own past life anew, the decisions I'd made and where I'd ended up. I couldn't help but be struck by one of the common threads weaving through the men's lives: that marriages are hard to sustain – sometimes too hard – and that babies throw a major spanner in the works for couples. It had made me reassess my own marriage and where it had gone wrong.

On the eve of my middle child's tenth birthday I was in the kitchen finishing the birthday cake, caught in the memory of what I'd been doing that night a decade ago. I could vividly recall the first pains and then the show. I was so happy to see it because I was five days overdue. After twenty-four hours in labour I had a vacuum extraction, then heard my baby's first cries. What an indescribably beautiful moment! The cake was nearly done, so I popped on the kettle for a final cup of tea. As I waited for it to start whistling, I found myself back in the maternity hospital, watching the clock impatiently for visiting time. I waited in the corridor for my husband, anxious to hold him as we basked in mutual adoration of our perfect little person. We were in our own bubble of bliss, totally and completely in love with each other, with our baby and with life.

I don't know what it is about becoming parents that changes the dynamic of a relationship so fundamentally, but by my child's first birthday we were attending marriage guidance counselling. I suspect that by the time you get to counselling, the relationship is all but officially over. My husband was an attentive and hands-on dad, but he still prioritized himself, his social life, his golf. Meanwhile, as happens to many new mothers, my life had changed beyond all recognition. I rose well to the challenge of parenting, but still had a very busy and demanding career. There was no me-time: I was either an employee or a parent. I've no doubt, in hindsight, that I pushed my husband away, recoiled from his touch and didn't focus any attention on him during those early years of parenting, but I just couldn't. I was frantically juggling my roles and there was no energy left for anything else. Perhaps, had he treated me more like a friend and less like a partner during that crazy time, things wouldn't have got so bad. If he had made fewer demands on me to give of myself as a partner, when I hadn't anything to give, maybe we could have come through it okay. It wasn't just sex, it was his need for me to manage on my own when he was doing his own thing, spending his free time as he pleased. If he had given me more support and space, I would have emerged from our children's babyhood with some vigour for our relationship. I can see, though, that in some ways we were both responsible for what happened to our marriage: he behaved like a selfish git and I behaved like a very pissed-off wife – exactly what I was.

My decision to ask my ex-husband to leave boiled down to one very simple question: was I prepared to share my mind, body and soul with someone who didn't value or respect me any more? The answer was a resounding no. It was that simple. But, of course, it wasn't that simple. Finally admitting to myself that I had to end it was, it turned out, just the start. The years of struggling to prop up a failing marriage had severely eroded my self-esteem, and my confidence was at an all-time low when we separated. I thought at the time that it was probably the hardest thing I'd ever have to do. Boy, was I wrong! We both knew the marriage was over, but he didn't put up any fight to win back his wife and children. That was, I think, the hardest blow. The man I had chosen as my life partner and the father of my children didn't consider us worth fighting for. If he had put up a protest, it would have confirmed that I had made a good choice in him, that he did love us and was a man of integrity and decency. I guess his reaction just confirmed what I was already pain-fully aware of: he didn't value me or our children at all.

Our separation threw me on to the path that led to escorting. When you have children, your priority stops being yourself and becomes them. I had to put a roof over their heads and food in front of them. I had to help them fulfil their potential. I needed money to do that and, for a single mother, money is hard to come by. It was a strange loop that encircled me: I worked for love of my children; I'd ended up in that situation because I had children, which had started the downward spiral that resulted in the end of my marriage.

I can understand both sides: I can appreciate that men want their wife back after the child is born – and that naturally means sex. I can also understand that, as they haven't gone through the deeply alter-ing states of pregnancy and childbirth, men find it more difficult to adapt to life post-baby and can fail to get their priorities in order as quickly as the woman. But there are ways of being a good husband and ways of being a bad husband. When I hear from a client that his wife is recently post-natal or has young children, the real me wants to call him every shade of bastard under the sun – how could he do this, has he no self-respect, no respect for his wife or children? Surely he didn't get to adult life without realizing that paying a hooker is about the most offensive thing you can do to your partner. Why isn't he stepping up to the plate as head of the family and his wife's man? Why does he think having sex with me will solve any of the problems he is facing?

In my working life, I don't afford myself an opinion. I'm not there in that capacity and I am not responsible for my clients' moral integrity.

From what I see in and hear from my friends, many men expect the same amount of attention after a baby arrives that they received before. They feel neglected and left out – as some clients described it – and want their wife's undivided attention for part of every day. If she can't deliver that, they may react petulantly, which only makes the situation worse. If a man is demanding and needy, a woman feels she has two babies on her hands rather than one. It's a complete passion-killer at a time when her libido is naturally decreased, putting even more pressure on the couple. I've heard the male joke about being on a ration card now that there's a baby in the house and only 'getting lucky' on special occasions. There's nothing quite so off-putting as your man asking for sex. It's a bit pathetic and a real turn-off.

I was probably behaving like the wives my clients now complain about – no libido, avoiding sex and complaining about exhaustion. I avoided going to bed at the same time as my husband, faked headaches and recoiled from his touch, knowing that he wanted to have sex, not just to hold me tenderly. It got to the stage that I avoided even a kiss on the cheek in case he saw it as a sign to go all out to get laid. Yes, I felt like shit knowing I was rejecting him, but he would have had a far better chance of getting laid if he had done me any simple act of kindness. If he had spontaneously got up to the baby at night and not pretended to be asleep, I'd have been far more inclined to early-morning sex. It's not that I'd have rewarded him with sex, it's that I'd have wanted to make love to him.

There is another side to this, too, that I'm sure many women are familiar with, and that's the problem of 'wifey sex': a man's belief that when he's in bed with his wife he has to make love to her – not a quick shag, not an experimental adventure, no, it must be lovemaking and nothing more. I've heard this time and again from clients, who say they just can't do the things they want to, sexually, with their wives. Speaking from my own experience and that of my friends, if a man initiated an honest and open conversation with his wife, I think he'd be pleasantly surprised to find that she wholeheartedly agrees and would love to shake things up a bit.

My ex-husband was very experienced sexually before we met and had been quite adventurous. When our sex life started to dwindle after the babies arrived, I suggested we spice things up to get the spark back. I took the initiative – got the sex toys, thigh-high boots, a couple of books and the type of underwear clearly designed for use in the bedroom. I figured I could get him so aroused that he'd have to abandon himself to wanton lust and just ravish me as I craved. His reply? 'I can't do that with my wife.' I told him women didn't always want to be treated with kid gloves and sometimes it was great to get laid with no frills. He told me he just couldn't see me as a very sexual being, especially having watched our children being born. I would have thought that any man seeing a woman giving birth would notice the power and strength of the feminine form and find it compellingly attractive. While powerful women evoke a varied response from men, I believe that a man who is secure in himself can appreciate the beauty of a powerful woman, in childbirth, in business and in the bedroom.

I made suggestions to clients about how they could approach their wives differently but invariably I heard the same sort of response. They declared that they had tried everything possible and that seeing an escort was a last resort, one that seemed preferable to starting an affair with the possibility of one partner getting emotionally involved. I believe that if a couple can hold firm for the first twelve months of their baby's life, it will get easier and they can enjoy a proper relationship again. I know men think this is a hugely long time to go without sex on tap, but I suppose, without sounding too soppy, it comes down to love. How much do you love her?

12. The Young Buck

It was a warm Friday afternoon in May and I had just woken up from a refreshing power nap. I checked my work phone, which had been on silent all afternoon: fourteen missed calls. That was typical for a Friday. It seemed men suddenly realized on a Friday afternoon that they'd had a busy or boring week, had no plans for the evening and that a shag would be a nice way to end the day. The calls always increased at weekends, Fridays and Saturdays. Weekdays were busy because men could phone when they were at work. During periods when the kids were off school, like Easter, it picked up. It was probably down to the stress of intense family time, plus the added hassle of dealing with in-laws and the usual family bickering that happens over holidays. I don't think it's that the men were having a hard time handling the ups and downs of home, it's more that it was their holidays too, and they wanted to treat themselves to something 'special'.

I scrolled through the list of missed calls and rang the first. A guy answered. I said I was replying to his missed call and asked was it a good time to talk. 'Just a moment please,' he said. There was silence for a minute. 'Sorry about that, I just needed to pop outside. I can talk now.' He asked if I offered a full service. I told him I did and gave him my usual sales patter. I asked about his circumstances and what he was hoping for from our meeting. Frank was living with his fiancée and their young child. He said he hadn't been unfaithful to her previously, but things were a bit stale in the bedroom and life in general and he wanted some excitement – nothing too saucy, just straightforward good sex. I pointed out to him that it would be easier to have a fling or a one-night stand, but he said he didn't want to take any risk that his fiancée would find out. He loved her and their child, but he missed the sexual chemistry that had existed between them when they'd first met. His fiancée was fighting hard to keep her job and he had already lost his in the construction industry. He was optimistic that he would be able to manage financially by doing various nixers, but at the moment it was a source of tension at home and he needed a source of release.

He sounded a genuinely nice guy, enthusiastic and down-to-earth, although at twenty-five he was a bit younger than my usual clients. He asked if I could reduce my rates, given his financial circumstances, but I explained that that would be pointless for me. He said he appreciated this, but didn't have the readies to make an appointment. He tried to barter, arguing that he was really good in bed – maybe I should give him a reduction because I would have a great time. I smiled to myself as I told him I regularly enjoyed sex with clients. He sounded surprised by this, and possibly a bit turned on. I added that many men had said they felt used in some way by other escorts, that the experience was clinical and 'conveyor-belt'. He might well be good in bed, I said, but that was no reason for me to reduce my rates: I charged more than other sex workers because I was open and receptive with clients and engaged fully with them, physically and emotionally.

That grabbed his attention! There was no way I was going to start lowering my rates, so I played the great-shag card and waited. If he was really interested, he would come up with the money somehow. Sure enough, he rang me a few days later, asking about my availability. A window of opportunity had opened for him: he would be staying overnight in a city hotel while he was on a training course. The date happened to coincide with the night my children were with their father, so it suited me too.

The hotel was to the north of the city, and it was a straight run for me. His course was due to finish at five and we agreed to meet at seven. Frank sent me a text with his room number, and admitted to being a little apprehensive. I didn't have any worries: in my experience, younger men loved the confidence of an older woman. I was sure his fiancée, about fifteen years younger than me, had a far perkier body and fewer age spots than I boast, but I was way more sexually competent in my forties than I had been in my twenties or early thirties. And it works both ways. I love a younger man's body, especially if he's sporty or works out – that perfect muscle tone, all that testosterone and the beauty of their youthful energy could arouse me no matter what my mood. Frank had mentioned that he worked out at the gym five days a week because it kept him sane. Well, I was certainly looking forward to seeing this toned, fit twenty-five-year-old – and I was getting paid for it!

I arrived at the hotel at seven and made my way up to his room. When he opened the door I was a bit taken aback: he had a shaved head and some body piercings – something I'm not into at all. If I saw him walking down the street, I would have described him as a bit of rough, but he was attractive. He wasn't what I'd go for in my private life, but we can always veer off our 'type' to appreciate another's attributes. I eyed his firm body beneath his clothes and thanked God for young men.

His enthusiasm was sweet, but a bit unnerving. He barely had the door closed behind me when he started touching me, running his hands over my waist and hips and gushing about how hot I was. 'Steady on,' I said sternly. 'Let's get through the basic pleasantries first.' He apologized, saying he didn't want to waste a minute, but he took his hands off me and I asked politely for my fee upfront. He opened the bureau drawer and handed me the cash. I quickly checked that there were eight fifty-euro notes and put them into my bag, thanking him. We sat side by side on the bed and got used to being in each other's company and space. He also had lots of tattoos. I couldn't recall being with someone with a tattoo before. As I had always associated them with low-life types, it made this encounter feel quite naughty. Now I was getting turned on by the thought of having sex with someone I would usually put in the no-go pile. With his shaved head, body piercings and tattoos, I felt like *I* was doing something out of the ordinary, even though I was the escort, which made it quite exciting.

I teased him about his rough-and-ready appearance. It didn't faze him and he offered to show me more. I lay back on the bed and let him strip off to the waist in front of me. He talked me through the stories behind his tattoos, but I wasn't paying him much attention. My eyes were glued to his clearly defined six-pack abdominal muscles. As he moved his arms and shoulders to show off other tats, his muscles rippled in perfect response to his posture. What a treat to look at – he was a great example of the benefits of working out, beautifully proportioned, not too bulky, and toned to within an inch of his life. In spite of his rather tough exterior, he seemed a sweet guy and unaware of what a fantastic body he had. 'I'd like to work on my thighs a bit more,' he said when I commented on how great he looked. 'Anyway, enough about me, what about you?' He climbed back on to the bed beside me. 'God, your skin is so soft,' he said, as his hand roved over my body and under my clothes. 'I think it's only fair you show me yours now.'

He moved in to kiss me and he was a great kisser – boy, am I a sucker for a great kisser – plus he had lovely full lips and a perfect set of sparkly white teeth. We kissed for what seemed like ages before he removed my clothes. He was deceptively gentle; I might have expected fast, almost rough sex with that guy, but he was tender and sweet. His enthusiasm was infectious and he complimented me non-stop about how sexy I was and what a great body I had.

I love hearing those compliments. Given my full-on life, my body's had sod-all attention over the past ten years. Of course, some clients don't comment or compliment me on anything and that's fine too, but when I get a client as complimentary as Frank and find him attractive to boot, it feels great and I lap it up.

Things heated up a notch and I got a condom ready. He said he'd like to do it standing up – never a favourite position of mine as it's almost impossible to enjoy but, hey, he was paying so I agreed to give it a go. I was thinking we'd have to manoeuvre into position against the wall, but to my amazement he lifted me up as if I weighed nothing and held me with my legs wrapped around him. He carried me over to the wall and leaned his back against it. I'm not the size of lady who's used to being lifted up by a man, but it was lovely and made me feel feminine and petite. Far from my usual work persona of being in control, I felt girly and as if I was being taken care of. His size and strength emphasized my womanly characteristics, soft and yielding. He easily managed to hold me in that position until he climaxed, though he lost his balance slightly as he did so. He carried me back to the bed, where we lay in silence for a few minutes.

He went to the bathroom and I was thinking our meeting had concluded, but when he returned and lay down, we started kissing. 'I'm ready again,' he said. I looked down to see his perfectly erect cock ready for round two. That was the fastest turnaround time I'd ever witnessed – I'd say it was ten minutes, max, since he'd climaxed.

'Christ, that's impressive,' I said.

'Yep,' he smiled, 'but I'd like you to come. I know you haven't already. What would you like me to do?'

'Whatever you like.' I meant every word of it.

He moved down to taste me. He quickly got the hang of what I liked and stayed there for what seemed like for ever. I had no choice but to surrender to him until I had an eye-popping orgasm. I've no idea how he didn't get lockjaw and even though I knew our time was way up, I was enjoying it too much to be conscious of the clock. When I came to after the orgasm, I noticed his still-hard cock – God, the poor guy had had that erection for ages. 'Hey, do you mind if I use a little toy on you? Trust me, you'll like it,' I said, thinking he deserved a treat.

'I'm game,' he said.

I reached over to my bag and took out a set of anal beads. They're for individual use only and he saw me rip off the outer packaging. 'Eh, do they go where I think they go?' Frank asked, a bit unnerved.

'Yep, they sure do, and you're going to love it – so let me do the necessary,' I coaxed. I took out some lube and applied it to my hands and the beads. Sitting up between his legs, I massaged his cock and balls, paying attention to the delicate perineum area as well. When I felt he was ready, I gently popped in the beads, one by one, checking all the while that he was comfortable, until the last one was in place.

'What are these going to do for me?' he wanted to know.

'Tell me when you're going to come and you'll know all about what they're for,' I told him. I built up quickly, using one hand on his penis and the other to massage and gently tug at his testicles. I gently rotated the beads, and as he climaxed I pulled them out quickly in succession and watched his face contort with intense pleasure as his cum landed on his chest and arms.

After a few moments he leaned over and kissed me on the cheek, 'Thank you,' he said. 'That was fantastic. Can I get you anything – tissues? Glass of water?'

'Thanks, yes, I could do with some water,' I said, and he went to the bathroom to get it. When he came back with the glass, he said, 'You're right about your fees. You shouldn't lower them – I'm glad I managed to put a bit of cash by when I was last working, otherwise there's no way I could have seen you.'

I smiled. I was glad too.

13. The Needy Man

I had arranged to see Gerry the day after my tattoo man. Gerry was the most unlikely user I had ever encountered: he was a farmer, a grandfather, a businessman and a husband, very much a rural man, not at all an urban sophisticate. It took several calls and many hours of chat before we finally agreed on a meeting, not because he had any reservations but because he was utterly paranoid about getting caught. No matter where or when I suggested, it didn't suit him. He considered himself so well known within a sixty-mile radius that he found fault with every meeting place I suggested.

As the weeks passed, it got to the point that he was phoning daily to hear my latest proposal, while never proffering any ideas himself. Even I began to get a bit paranoid because, with all of the calls and the amount of information we exchanged, I realized he was garnering a fair idea of my daily movements. He rang me once when I was about to pop into the pharmacy to get some paracetamol for my daughter. I took his call, but only to say I wasn't able to talk as my child was sick. By then I knew about his work, his kids and his grandchildren. Many of our conversations never contained any clues as to why we were in contact: they became mundane, nonsexual, and I had no interest in telling him about my children or in hearing any details of his life and family. On the other hand, he had no problem with my fee, was discreet to the point of obsession, was married and understood the type of service I provided. With that in mind, I had to put up with his ramblings.

After three weeks, he finally agreed a meeting place and time in an area he wasn't familiar with. They say women are bad at reading maps and following directions, but this man was pathetic! I practically had to stay on the phone with him for his entire journey from his home to the location and talk him through every traffic light and turn. Even when he had arrived – I saw him drive in as, yes, he had told me what car he drove – I had to tell him where to park, which entrance to use and exactly how to get to the room. I stayed on the phone to him until he knocked on the bedroom door. I was tired of him before I had opened it.

When I did open it, I was pleasantly surprised by his appearance because he was dressed quite stylishly, which wasn't the picture I had formulated in my mind. I don't know if it was nerves or his personality, but from the moment he walked in he talked incessantly about stuff I had no interest in discussing with him – politics, the recession, my personal and family life and his family life. In order to move things along, I took control and instructed him as to what would happen. I ordered him to undress and, as he slipped off his trousers, he said, 'I suppose you're used to having great lovers and very experienced men.'

'Ah, not really,' I said, not reacting to his irrelevant rhetorical question.

'Well, I'm sure I'll be a disappointment for you,' he said resignedly, as he folded his vest and shirt over the back of the bedroom chair.

I had to ignore the irritation that was rising in me. 'Look, it's not about me,' I said cheerfully, 'and I'm not comparing anyone, so please just relax and enjoy it.'

I told him I'd prefer him not to talk so that he could concentrate on what was happening and the sensations it produced in his body. Really, I just wanted him to shut up. I'd give him a massage and he'd erupt into chat again, but I told him to be silent and relax. As he was getting more aroused, I asked him if he was ready to put on a condom. 'Well, really I don't want to have sex because I've been married for thirty-two years and have never been unfaithful to my wife, so I wouldn't want to start at this stage in my life.'

'Oh, right, that's fine,' I said, thinking, if I'm being honest, that he was an idiotic hypocrite. By his logic, penetration equalled unfaithful but paying a sex worker and being in bed naked with my hand around his cock wasn't a problem. You've got to love some men's notions of fidelity! He asked if I could do a bit of oral and finish with a hand-job. Thankfully, it didn't take him long to come and I cleaned up and got out of bed. He declined a shower, but accepted a cup of tea. Christ, did I regret offering that cuppa. He stayed for another *hour*, wanting to be critiqued on his performance. What performance? Plus isn't the idea of paying for it that you're not being critiqued, compared or scrutinized? Not this guy: he wanted to know how his penis compared with my other clients'. 'I suppose I'm small, am I?' he asked doggedly.

'Not at all, you're perfectly average,' I replied.

'Ah, you're only saying that, come on, tell me the truth, I can handle it. How do I compare?'

He was so lacking in any sort of sexual or self-confidence that I ended up feeling a bit sorry for him. I tried to think of some nice things to say, so I told him he was well groomed and had a good body for his age and that anything that happened sexually was all perfectly normal. In fact, it was ultra-boring, but that wasn't what I was paid to say. Then the questions got more bizarre. He wanted to know if his cum was the normal amount, whether he was noisy or quiet when he climaxed and did he take long to come compared to my other clients? I tried to pass off his questions in a casual and light-hearted manner, but I was pretty stunned. I'd been asked a lot of surprising things in the course of my work, but nothing like this. By the end of the meeting, aside from being heartily sick of him and feeling very sorry for his wife, I had decided he was the neediest man I'd ever met. We've all heard complaints about needy women, the kind who need constant reassurance and are insecure about everything in their life, but no one had ever warned me that a man could be just the same. Boy, was it off-putting.

A full hour after we'd finished the deed, he was still sitting there, talking shite, and I was getting seriously pissed off. Eventually, I had to tell him that I had another client arriving and, much as I had enjoyed our meeting, his time was up and he had to leave. He went to wash his cup in the bathroom, but I took it from him and told him I'd look after it – could he please just pay me and go? I really was under time pressure. I had forgotten to get the cash upfront because we'd been arranging the booking for so long that I'd begun to think of him as a regular. He fumbled awkwardly in his trouser pockets for the cash, then in his jacket, before finally locating his wallet in his shirt. He was so slow in everything he did. He counted out the twenty-euro notes one by one, then looked at me and said, 'Now, are ye happy with that? Are we settled up fair and square?'

'Yep, that's lovely. Thanks very much – but now I really have to rush.'

He dithered a bit longer, then cleared his throat and said, 'Will you see me again, even though I know I'm not good in bed and you probably didn't enjoy it compared to other fellas? Will you see me next week because I'd like to see you once a week?'

Every fibre of my being was silently screaming, *Piss off!*

I agreed to see him again, just to get him out of the room. When he'd waved his final goodbye and I'd shut the door after him, I rested my head against the wood and breathed deeply. A man like that didn't need an escort, he needed a life coach or a morale-boosting seminar, some sort of service that I certainly couldn't provide. For the next two months, his number flicked up on screen once a day without fail, and each time I guiltily ignored it. I know he could have been a reliable regular but, honestly, that level of neediness wasn't worth any amount of money.

14. The Rough and the Smooth

It was late June and I'd booked a holiday apartment about an hour away from home to use as a base for work over the next month. It would be easier working from one location, plus I'd noted what other escorts were advertising online: they'd visit various towns on rotation, saying to clients that they were around for just a few weeks. My children would be doing a few summer camps and going away for a week with their dad towards the end of July, so I wanted to book as many clients in that time as I could: I'd have little or no opportunity to work for the rest of the summer until the children were back at school.

I was dubious about booking the apartment, fearing that the owner would ask too many questions, either directly or informally through casual chat. I needn't have worried. I don't think she could have cared less what I wanted the place for so long as she was getting the rent. I paid her cash up front and didn't see her again until I handed back the keys four weeks later. The apartment had two bedrooms, a small galley kitchen, a bathroom and a living room, which meant I could greet clients casually, offer them tea or coffee, then proceed to the bedroom when we were both ready.

When I arrived for the first time, I made up one of the bedrooms and left a stash of necessities in the bedside locker, such as condoms, tissues and lube. There were several sets of spare bed linen in the airing cupboard and a washing-machine, so I could rotate the laundry myself. All in all, it was perfect for my needs: self-contained, with secure parking.

I contacted my regulars to let them know I was in residence and the phone started to ring – summer meant lots of clients and I was kept busy answering queries and making new contacts. One morning in early July, I took a call from a guy named Hugh. His situation was a bit different, to say the least. During our initial phone conversation, he explained that he had an unusual arrangement with his wife: she stayed at her parents' house during the week with their child while he worked on their farm, then his wife and child joined him for the weekend. He was in his forties and, from what I could gather, his wife wasn't too interested in him; their only bond was their child. He was shy and reserved on the phone but he sounded genuine about making an appointment so we agreed a booking.

He arrived at the apartment on a washed-out summer's day at one o'clock. When I opened the door to him, my heart sank. He seemed self-conscious and awkward, looked a bit unkempt, in that farmer sort of way, and had difficulty making and keeping eye contact with me. He was polite enough, but an alarm bell started to ring in my head. I greeted him in a friendly, relaxed manner, but I was thinking, I hope to God he comes quickly so I can get him out of here soon. I can't say why I took such an instant dislike to him, but instinctively I didn't want to be alone with him for long. His inability to make eye contact, even as we shook hands, spooked me. It's not the action of a confident, sane man, and wasn't how clients usually behaved.

I went through my usual patter, making small-talk about his journey, the weather, blah blah, but there are some clients you just know you're not going to want another phone call from, and he was one of them. I usually find something to like about a client regardless of his looks, but this man unnerved me, for some inexplicable reason. My managerial head took over. I clock-watched and spent ages massaging his back so I wouldn't have to look at his face or converse with him, then moved on to the back of his legs, his arms, hands and his horribly cracked feet. Luckily, the music and scented oils I was using on him seemed to be working their magic and he appeared oblivious to my discomfort. He tried to make chit-chat a couple of times, but I encouraged him to just kick back and enjoy what was happening, hoping he would drift off for a while and make my job a lot easier.

When I had dragged it out as long as possible, I asked him to turn over. I didn't want him to touch me, so I needed to give him such a good hand-job that he wouldn't want anything more, that he would be so focused on the intense arousal he was feeling that he wouldn't even be able to speak in case it distracted him from what was happening with his cock. I knew I couldn't bear it if he asked for penetrative sex. Thankfully, I had a sachet of lubricant that heated up on contact with skin, adding to the sensation and, hopefully, hurrying things along. I used the whole sachet on him, I knew from client feedback that it felt much better than without, and I caressed his balls at the same time with my other hand, pulling gently on them. Luckily, he had what he called a 'mind-blowing' climax and I breathed a sigh of relief when I saw him come.

I went to wash my hands and offered to run a shower for him, which he declined. 'Okay, so I'll let you get dressed, then,' I said, as I threw on a dressing-gown and went into the living room. He came out shortly afterwards and thanked me, saying he would like to see me again. He counted out the money and handed it to me. I took it – I'd been so unnerved by him when he'd arrived that I'd forgotten to ask for it upfront – but didn't answer his remark about seeing me again. I apologized to him if it seemed like I was rushing him, saying I had to get ready for another client – I had taken a second booking the previous evening. In truth, I was glad I had an excuse to hurry him out. I didn't want him near me any longer than necessary. I thanked him and let him out of the door, vowing not to see him again.

Hugh made my skin crawl. I sensed that he could turn aggressive or violent. I've no particular reason for saying that, it was purely a matter of gut instinct. I don't recall any other client ever making me feel so repulsed. It wasn't his looks – I've enjoyed sex with attractive and not-so-attractive men, and I've seen clients of all ages, sizes and shapes. In every instance I have found something likeable about them, but there was none of that with Hugh. He was creepy and I couldn't see past it. Something told me he was not similar to the other men I'd seen and that I couldn't let my guard down with him. Over the previous months I had developed a good sense about men and was able to size them up quickly. Of all the experiences I've had in my work, that one made me feel the most uncomfortable, even though it sounds innocuous. In another way, though, it made me glad: I was glad to know that I was now savvy enough to have reliable instincts about a client and experienced enough to deal with them effectively.

Hugh phoned and texted me for weeks after our meeting, but I never replied. He had no way of finding out who I really was, where I lived or how to contact me, apart from the number of an unregistered mobile phone. It reminded me yet again that the longer I was at this, the more likely it was that I'd meet someone nasty or have a bad experience. While I could bring down the shutters on Hugh and never worry about him again, I was a bit annoyed with myself for rushing the booking and seeing him in the first place, but summer was an expensive time: I had allowed my money worries to lead me to be less selective than usual. If I had spent longer sussing him out on the phone before agreeing to meet, perhaps I would have realized he made me uneasy and avoided the whole thing.

After Hugh had left, I had a shower and got ready for my next client – I'd arranged to meet him at his place. I'd seen Ian about four times in the past four months, always at his apartment, so I knew the route well and that I'd easily be there within the hour. His home was bright, clean and spacious. He was a lovely gentleman, the kind of man I'd probably date in my 'real' life. He worked away from home regularly in the same town and had an apartment there, where he stayed several nights per week. He really missed sex while he was away from home, or that was what he told me – perhaps he just had more time to think about it when he was on his own. He'd had a few one-night stands in that small town, but found the going out, chatting up, drinking and drunken-sex scenario unappealing. He was a busy professional, did a lot of international travel and was a committed father. His time was precious and limited, so when he found my ad online, he knew it might be the answer to his predicament, providing him with a discreet, guaranteed and regular service.

When I say that Ian was a gentleman, I mean that he liked ladies to be ladies. He was quite traditional in that sense, but he behaved like a gentleman in return, paying great attention to me in the way that older men do – opening doors, topping up my drink, complimenting me, making a big effort with his appearance and ensuring that I was enjoying whatever we were doing as much as he was, even though he was paying.

The first time I had visited him I had been intrigued by his past and upbringing. He had several unusual pictures and ornaments displayed in his apartment and I couldn't help but ask how he had come across them and what stories lay behind them. I'm always interested in the story behind the person and in how he came to be where he was in his life's journey. I noticed that he didn't have any pictures of his wife and family on display, and when I asked him about this, he quickly dismissed it, saying he didn't want them looking at him while he was with me. I sensed he felt shame or guilt or maybe both, but I didn't press it. I was glad he didn't have family photos looking down at us: it makes me uncomfortable, too, even though I tell myself it doesn't. I always try to erase the imprint of a wife's face from my memory, but it can be a hard thing to do.

Most of the men I visit at home bring me to the spare room and not to the one they share with their wife. However, there was one occasion when the guy didn't seem in the least perturbed by taking me to the marital bed. I just couldn't do it and asked him if there was anywhere else we could go. I pointed out that any woman would know if another had been in her bed and, anyway, it was hardly hygienic. He apologized for not having had the foresight and led me into the spare room. He was one of the bog-standard clients, and while I was on my back waiting for him to hurry up, I was looking at a wall covered with his children's official school photographs. I wasn't the only parent who'd been guilt-tripped into buying them, I thought – but it's just not right to imagine a picture of your child in the shredder of some photographer's office. I noticed a smaller photo of what must have been his wife at a child's confirmation and looked away immediately. I didn't want to recognize her in town. It was his business what he did behind her back, not mine. My business was to provide for and raise my children. Of course, from the uniforms his children were wearing, I could tell which nearby school they attended. It struck me for the umpteenth time that men never gave a thought to protecting their privacy in these situations, which seemed very strange.

Ian was a great storyteller and very funny in a couldn't-give-a-shit-what-people-think sort of way. He was an easy and enjoyable companion to pass time with. He told me he was fifty, but had looked after himself from a young age. It showed – he was in great shape, with a far better body than some thirty-year-olds I'd seen. I liked going to his place. It was tastefully decorated and stylish, unlike some of the other homes I'd visited. He always had M&S food in the fridge, plenty of good wine and a great music system that was piped to his bedroom. It was spotlessly clean, as was he. He always smelt gorgeous and was well turned-out. In truth, it was becoming a bit of a treat for me to see him.

On my first visit to him, in March, we had ended up sitting on his sofa, sipping wine and chatting for a long time. I didn't need or want to clock-watch: he was my only appointment for the evening and I found myself enjoying our conversation so much that it started to feel like a first drinks date where we were getting to know each other. Although Ian had expected that I would be well presented and well spoken, once he had met me and found out a little about me, he was intrigued by my decision to work as an escort and wanted to know more. I gave away no specific personal details, but I explained to him how it had come about. He asked about the types of men who contacted me, the difficult situations I had got into and how much money I had made. I told him that the vast majority were just ordinary guys who wanted what I considered to be normal sex – not a huge feat, really, for any emotionally and sexually mature woman.

The conversation moved on to the recession and the economy. We discussed the various measures people were taking to make cutbacks in their daily lives. I taught him a few ways to save on his various insurances and household expenditure, and joked that I might have earned him back the money he was going to pay me. Every time I visited Ian I got to like him more.

I tidied the apartment, pushed Hugh firmly out of my mind and headed for Ian's place, arriving there just over an hour later. I rang the doorbell and he welcomed me in warmly. He poured me a small glass of red wine, knowing that was what I preferred, and settled me on the sofa. He went over to change the CD, putting on some classical music, and we relaxed, quite happy in each other's company. I was glad to be there, in the cosy ambience he'd created. We sat in silence for a bit, listening to the music, then he asked me about my day. I told him about the creepy guy and he lectured me about the dangers of my work. He was going on a bit, so to justify taking his money later, I switched the conversation and got more comfy with him, knowing it would lead to sex. He moved his hand over my cheek, allowing his thumb to brush against my lips. 'I want to kiss you,' he said softly. I put down my glass and kissed him gently, barely letting our lips touch, until I felt myself start to tingle. I looked into his eyes and knew that he was enjoying the anticipation.

'Let's go to the bedroom,' he said, taking my hand and leading the way. We spent the next hour enjoying what can only be described as tender but passionate sex. He was really lovely to be with in bed and so concerned with my pleasure, always checking if his touch was okay, not too hard or too soft. It still amazes me that the majority of my clients care so much that I enjoy myself – it's a million miles away from what I would have expected. Isn't it a shame, though, that the occasional oddball can ruin a rewarding career? Afterwards we showered, had a cup of tea and I organized myself to head off. I kissed him goodbye before he opened the door to let me out. Just as I got home, he texted to tell me he had really enjoyed the evening and would be in touch soon.

There was one tiny glitch. Ian had fallen for me and asked if he could date me – the real me. In fact, he asked me out during my very first visit to him. He proposed taking me out for dinner once or twice a month, but I would be there as his date and therefore not paid for my time. I was flattered, and perhaps in a different situation

I would have accepted, but as I explained to him, all my time was allocated either to being a parent or to making money. If I was out for an evening as his date, it would be a lost opportunity to make money and, for the time being, that was my only focus. He could see where I was coming from, but I did say that if things changed for me financially, I'd like to go for dinner.

That evening, he had broached the subject again, asking if my finances were any more secure yet. I smiled ruefully – if only! I was making up to twelve hundred euro per week, but with the mortgage, household bills, school demands and extra-curricular activities, I was only just breaking even. I was feeling a bit bolder now that I knew him better, so I asked him, out of interest, would he have any concerns about dating someone in my line of work? Apart from the fact that he was married and shouldn't be dating anyone, I wanted some insight into his opinion of sex workers. Wouldn't it bother him if I were dating him and still working as an escort? His answer was surprising: he thought that, from what I'd told him, it had been a brave decision to make and he admired my strength of character. That wasn't what I'd expected to hear. It occurred to me that perhaps men's attitudes to sex workers were changing. I felt it was a good omen: if I ever had to tell a prospective partner about what would then be 'my past', it was good to know that some men could see it for what it was – a way to make a living.

15. The Three Most Important Lessons

In order to be successful in every area of my work, I have to prioritize three things above all else: safety, health and discretion. I'm in it for the money, and I really need that money, but I can never let my guard down in relation to those three things. I need to keep myself safe so that I always return home after a meeting; I need to ensure that neither my health nor the health of my clients is ever compromised; and I need to protect my identity and my clients' identities.

When I started thinking about doing this work, the question of safety was probably the first thing I considered. Could a woman do this work safely? From my initial research, I learned that the rape of an escort is quite rare. It's far more common with street workers. It's usually a big enough thrill for the escort's client to be paying for sex. Obviously you can never know for sure how a man will behave, but it was reassuring to know that attacks on independent escorts don't happen very often. There is a huge amount of information, from the UK, USA and worldwide, on the statistics and variables of sex workers and the industry as a whole. The incidence of violence, drug use, abuse by pimps and sexual-health issues are well documented, but there is also a distinct line drawn between street workers and escorts.

The latter is considered safer in her work. This is backed up by statistics, with far more independence and less risk of violent attack; also, escorts are far less likely to resort to use/abuse of drugs/alcohol. A 1986 study by Diane Prince found that call girls (escorts) and brothel workers (similar to escorts and, again, very different from street workers) had higher self-esteem after working in the industry. In fact, 97 per cent of call girls who responded to Prince's study liked themselves 'more than before' (that is, before they had worked in the sex industry). I don't know if the findings of the Prince study about self-esteem are correct (I don't know the parameters of the study or have access to the full report), but there are considerable differences in the work conditions of street prostitutes versus independent escorts, who choose the work of their own volition, without being coerced, threatened, violated, abused, subdued or pimped.

Next to being found out, my greatest fear was of rape or other violent abuse. I handled that aspect of my safety in two ways: the screening process I set up; and the persona I used with clients. Screening the men ensures that I mostly keep the oddballs at bay, while establishing a good stable of reliable regulars.

The persona I created for my escort *alter ego* is a confident, dominant and in-control woman. She is ballsy and doesn't take shit from anyone. She knows exactly how the meeting will go and she directs it that way at every turn. If I sustain this role, the men respond to it as I want them to. I am very aware that my meetings with clients are a subtle – and sometimes not so subtle – power play. I also know that how I behave physically, how I carry myself and how I interact with the client from the moment I open the door are vital in establishing the ground rules and maintaining control to avoid compromising myself physically or otherwise.

In my previous sales training I was taught a lot about the simple movements and body language that show power and gain the attention and respect of a client. I basically modified these techniques for my work as an escort, to let the client know that I was the one in charge and calling the shots. We've all been told that confident behaviour leads other people to comply, and I've found that this really is the case. If you give an instruction confidently, people respond as you expect them to. Humans are quite predictable like that. It's equally true that practice makes perfect – the longer I work as an escort, the more confident and assertive I become. Really, that's a lesson for any walk of life. Now whenever I have a potentially stressful interaction to deal with, I'll rehearse what I'm going to say and how I will deliver it. I look at myself in the mirror in the clothes I plan to wear and decide on the best posture and facial expression. It's been a revelation to me that I'm much more capable and ballsy than I ever thought.

As well as giving me a safe zone within which to work, I find that my confident, no-bullshit sexual persona really appeals to men. They seem only too happy to let a woman do all the thinking in the bedroom. I guess for some men the thrill is that this is very different from the norm they've come to expect. Talking to clients, they often say that sex at home is predictable and boring, with the traditional roles of man and woman being brought wholesale into the bedroom. Of course, sexual interaction can be fraught with mind-games and the residue of earlier fights, grievances and disappointments, which can be very wearing if all you want is to switch off and get laid. I'm not saying this is women's fault, far from it, it's simply the battlelines of sex that can be laid down in any long-term relationship. Of course, all of that goes out the window when you're paying a woman to have sex with you and, from what I've seen, men find that truly liberating. My super-confident sexual persona adds a huge frisson for my clients, which is why I think so many choose to become regulars.

When I'm with clients, I carry off this assertiveness by telling them where to sit once they arrive at my hotel or, if we're at their hotel, by telling them to sit on the bed while I get ready. I direct them to the shower and tell them where to leave their clothes and in what position to lie on the bed. Of course I do it all gently and politely, but the message they receive is the same: I'm the one in charge. Interestingly, in my private life I wouldn't behave like this as I would find it too taxing always to be in control. I'm much more laidback in reality, but this is work: we all have a different face for work than for our private life.

I use confidence tricks like this to stay safe when I'm the 'host', but naturally I'm more nervous when I'm going to the client's turf, be it home or hotel. I have less control in those situations. I don't know how the room will be laid out, and I can't do all the things I do to make a meeting run smoothly if I'm in a client's hotel room. I invariably have to work much harder in those situations to stay with my work persona, remaining confident and in control as much as possible while still respecting that I'm in the client's space. I find those meetings particularly tiring.

I mentioned before that the type of men I meet and how our exchanges work out has been one of the most incredible revelations of my job, and that's very true. When I was growing up I believed that only very desperate women sold their bodies – and usually for their next drug fix. The only type of prostitution I had ever heard described involved victimized women putting themselves in very dangerous situations with unsavoury characters. If you went by what the media portrays, that's the only story you'd ever hear. You'd be aware of the horrors – rape, murder – and nothing else. I've never seen a report or news story about the positive experiences of women in the sex industry. Judging by my own, there must be lots of other independent working girls who are meeting nice clients like mine. I don't know if I've been unusually lucky – life doesn't work like that, does it? – but I haven't had a single really nasty experience while I've been working as an escort. I've never faced a threatening situation. My clients have been upfront, respectable men who wanted to enjoy my company, not raving loonies hell-bent on humiliating me. The problem is that sex work is illegal.

The second most important consideration is health. I have to be able to guarantee that I'm 100 per cent healthy because that's what my clients are paying for. They know I'm not charging four hundred euro because I'm the greatest fuck on earth, but rather because they can have a good time with me and walk away with nothing but lovely memories. There is no shag so good that it's worth risking contracting HIV or hepatitis. The men I see all have other lives and lovers, so it's imperative that we are all very conscious of the health risks and take every precaution. I'm a stickler about condoms and my clients appreciate this. That goes against the image of desperate men seeking out desperate women and having no-holds-barred sex, which is how it's often portrayed. Instead it's two adults agreeing to have sex together responsibly and safely, so everyone goes home happy.

Finally, discretion is the foundation of my entire business. I can't let anyone find out my identity because it would ruin my life – it's as simple as that. My children can never know what I do to earn my living because it might drive them away from me. It would be a very difficult thing to hear about your mother, and I'm well aware of that, so I put a huge amount of effort into concealing and protecting my identity. This suits my clients perfectly because they're in the same position: no girlfriend, fiancée or wife is going to stay with a man who's revealed to have had the odd – or regular – tryst with an escort. It's a sacking offence, and every man knows it, so they take precautions, too, and trust in my need and ability to keep us both safe from detection.

My first line of defence is myself. As I said earlier, a client has to provide a contact number and speak over the phone initially. If a man is serious about making an appointment, he'll want to know what I sound like and confirm that I am Irish (very important for some men, to be able to enjoy the banter) and that the service I provide is suitable for his needs. For the first year, when I was working full time, I'd keep a caller talking for anything from twenty to sixty minutes, getting as much information as I could to ascertain what he was like.

Once we'd arranged to meet, there was greater potential for things to go wrong. I got chatting to a close friend who works in the hospitality sector one evening and brought up the subject of sex workers using hotels as their base, saying I'd read something about it in the papers that week. I wanted to sound her out and see if there were any tips, from a hotel employee's point of view, I could take on board. She told me that hotel staff are trained to spot women using the hotel as a base for sex work. They look for the obvious signs, such as more than one man visiting a room, sex noises in the daytime and a woman who is dressed in 'hooker style'. She told me a story of a sex worker who was openly seeing several clients a day from a hotel where she was working. It quickly became obvious that the escort intended to stay for several weeks – her room was booked for a month in advance. The hotel management didn't want to call in the gardaí because they didn't want other hotel guests witnessing any sort of a scene and risk the reputation of their hotel. The escort seemed very obvious in her appointment scheduling, and CCTV footage clearly showed a client leaving her room with another waiting in the corridor. However, the hotel didn't have absolute proof that she was selling sex.

They came up with a plan designed to get rid of her with minimal fuss. The manager asked one of the barmen if he would pose as a punter. The barman agreed, but how was he to book the appointment? He would have needed to get the girl's work mobile number. They decided that the best option was for him to knock on her door and pose as her next appointment. If she welcomed him in and asked for the cash upfront, that would confirm she was indeed selling sex and they would have enough proof to get her out of the hotel quickly.

The plan went perfectly. The escort answered the barman's knock on her door by inviting him in and asking for her payment upfront. The barman made his excuses and left, saying he had changed his mind. The hotel manager was waiting outside the door. Once the barman gave him the nod, the manager knocked on the door and introduced himself, indicating that the 'punter' was in fact his barman. He told the girl that if she packed her bags and left immediately, nothing more would be said. If she didn't leave or attempted to use the hotel in this manner again, they would promptly notify the police of her activities. She left twenty minutes later.

My friend and I laughed over her story, but I was filing away the information carefully. It was helpful to me in planning how to approach hotel bookings and arrangements for my clients. I had always gone to extreme lengths to cover my tracks. I carried business files and folders with me and laid them out on the dressing-table, along with my laptop and diary, to give the impression that I was a businesswoman. I brought my own disposable bags to get rid of the condoms and any other sex paraphernalia after the client had left. I lit scented candles so the place didn't smell of latex or sex. I kept my bag of sex toys and lingerie under lock and key at all times. When I was staying overnight and seeing more than one client, I brought my own sets of clean sheets. I'd whip off the hotel set, dress the bed with my own linen, then remake it before I left with the hotel sheets so that it looked like only one person had been in it. I washed any cups or glasses that had been used. I tidied the bathroom, folded the towels, opened the windows and pulled back the curtains. Most importantly, I only ever saw a small number of clients and never more than two on the same day at the same hotel. If I had to see a third, I would book another hotel close by. I wouldn't dare see three clients on the same day in the same hotel – that would be asking for trouble and I don't think my nerves could have taken it!

I also booked hotels and self-catering apartments in my local town. This seemed cheeky, but I decided that if I wanted to cover my tracks, I needed to be brazen about it and book a place where I was known and where nobody would suspect anything untoward going on. I had to work around school hours, so a local base cut out the time and expense of commuting.

In terms of people's perception of me, I've been careful not to overspend. I was never raking it in, but nowadays it looks odd to be seen laden with bags of shopping. Nobody would have paid a blind bit of notice a few years back, but in a small town like mine, where curtain twitching is fairly constant, I don't like to be seen bringing in shopping bags from the car and avoid splashing out on any luxury items. I pack my 'work bag' at night and leave it in the car boot because it's less likely that anyone will see and start to speculate about what I'm up to. If I look 'made up' from a daytime appointment and am popping down the town or meeting a friend for coffee, I take off my makeup and dress down so I blend in with the stay-at-home mums out buying the groceries. I don't want to hear, 'Oh, you look nice – where are you off to?' I also don't want any of my clients to recognize me outside work, so I ensure that I look very ordinary – no man would do a double-take, let alone recognize me as the sex goddess who rocked his world!

I had a couple of slip-ups, though. Once when I was chatting to a client, I inadvertently used my real surname. I immediately started to backtrack and tried to cover it, but the client didn't seem to notice, or if he did, he wasn't bothered and didn't mention it. I had to be extremely careful with my work mobile phone because my kids are well able to have a nosey if they want to, so I made sure it was password protected and kept it out of sight as much as possible.

Recently, I was putting a new insurance disc into my car and noticed that my full name and address featured on the old one. I panicked momentarily – it had never occurred to me that I was parading my identity around like that. After skipping a few heartbeats, I reminded myself that I had always been very careful to park at the furthest reaches of hotel car parks because I didn't want clients to see my car and registration. It seemed unlikely anyone could have checked out my disc and discovered who I was. A double life is very exhausting because you have to be hyper-aware all the time. I dislike having to watch what I say and frequently resort to white lies with my family and friends, but the truth would hurt far, far more than the little falsehoods I use to protect everyone – me and those I love – from the reality of what I do.

16. Czech Mate

I'd been working as an escort for just six months, but already I felt changed by my experiences. I'd confronted my body-image issues, realized I could enjoy being dominant in the bedroom and I'd had sex with men I wouldn't have looked at before, only to find out that we were very compatible. It had been a strange sort of learning curve – all the things I'd thought I might be thinking weren't in my mind at all. And those hidden experiences were starting to impact positively on my private life, which I definitely hadn't considered a possibility. But it was true – my eyes had been opened and I could appreciate things and people I wouldn't have noticed before.

It was July and the weather had been unusually glorious for the past week. I'd even managed to get a tan doing a bit of sunbathing on the days I didn't have clients. That weekend I couldn't work as much as usual, though, because I had to go to a family party. My youngest sister was having her birthday bash in town on Saturday night, and as it was my weekend to have the kids, I had to book a babysitter and drive home afterwards. Parties and sobriety aren't my idea of fun, but I couldn't decline the invitation because my sister would hold it against me for months. I planned to stay a respectable length of time, then slip off home at the first opportunity. My sister's friends were single or cohabiting but none of them was married or divorced. They'd be doing shots, snogging anyone fanciable and generally behaving like mad-for-it young things. I was used to attending get-togethers on my own by then, but I'd no interest in watching my sister and her friends get drunk and leery.

On Saturday evening, between feeding the children and getting them ready for bed, I had to get myself into something decent for the party. I reckoned it was a night for my LBD – I'd throw it on with my black suede wedges *et voilà*! I'd more than got my money's worth out of that dress, but there was still plenty of wear in it. Its deep, plunging neckline, cap sleeves and knee-length A-line skirt were perfect for my shape – well, according to Trinny and Susannah they were.

By eight thirty I'd parked and was making my way to the restaurant. I spotted my sister's group through the open door – they looked well oiled already. Damn. I hated being the sober one and having to listen to drunk talk. I stretched my mouth into a wide smile as I walked through the door and went straight over to give my little sister a big hug. She did the introductions. 'There's a couple of people from work joining us for drinks after dinner,' she added.

'Lovely,' I said enthusiastically. 'It looks like it'll be a great night.' I was glancing at her mates and thinking they'd all be dying of hangovers in the morning and it was probably just as well that I was driving. A few more of my family arrived in dribs and drabs until we were all gathered, whereupon we were ushered to the dining area. The tables were set in long rows, bench-style, and occupied by two raucous hen parties and a mixed group that were equally boisterous. It looked like getting drunk was the objective of everyone in the place, except the restaurant staff and me.

The night dragged on, the chat getting crazier and louder with each course. My sister had sat me beside the rest of my family, but with the way the table was set up, it was hard to chat to anyone except the person directly opposite and on my immediate left and right. The ever-rising noise level gave me a headache before dessert had even arrived. I sneaked off to the bar to get another sparkling water and surreptitiously popped a couple of paracetamol. It was quieter there, so I took a seat for a moment's time out.

As I was sitting there on my own, another small group arrived in the door and made their way over to my sister's table. I didn't know any of them, so I assumed they were the work crowd she'd mentioned. One came over to the bar where I was sipping my sparkling water and stood beside me to order a drink. Then he turned to me. 'So, are you a friend of Barbara?' he asked, in a foreign accent I couldn't place.

'She's my sister,' I replied. 'I presume you're a work colleague of hers?'

'Well, I've just started work there. I think she asked me because I'm the newest immigrant – Irish hospitality.'

His English was perfect and he was very polite. I took a proper look at him while he was paying for his drink. He was about six foot two, had very short dark hair, greenish eyes, obscured by his glasses, and a young face. He was wearing slacks and an open-necked blue shirt, like he just came from the office, except it was Saturday. He was a bit nerdy, and it wouldn't have surprised me if he'd worked in IT. 'So what are you doing in Ireland?' I asked, as he sipped his drink.

'I've taken a year off college to do some travelling. I'm doing some office work to pay my way.' His drink had fizzed up tiny droplets on to his glasses, and he took them off to clean them. 'And you, what do you do?'

I could see his eyes properly now and they were green with the most amazingly thick dark lashes. He was actually quite beautiful. Everything about his face was in perfect proportion, from his high cheekbones to his gorgeous strong jawline, clear complexion and slightly pouting lips. He was good-looking enough to be a model – shame about the dress sense. I suddenly realized I was staring at him and awkwardly pretended I'd been distracted. 'Sorry, I currently don't work outside the home,' I said, sounding very politically correct. 'Anyway, you sound much more interesting. Where are you from, what are you doing at college, are you in Ireland on your own?'

He laughed at my quick-fire questions, but told me that he was from the Czech Republic, was studying history and taking a year out to visit Irish heritage sites. He had a particular interest in Irish folklore, was here on his own but hoped his girlfriend would join him in a few months' time. I was fascinated by this charming young man and, while chatting to him, I forgot about my headache. After half an hour or so, I felt it was time to get on the road – it was past midnight and I had a long drive ahead of me. I began to gather my things. 'Well, it was really lovely meeting you, I hope you enjoy your time in Ireland,' I said, smiling as I put out my hand to shake his.

'Oh, you're going home already? Where do you live?' he asked, looking a bit unsettled. I suspected he would feel like a spare part when I was gone because he didn't know the crowd well. I told him where home was and was a bit taken aback when he said he planned to visit some castles in my area. He suggested I give him my email address so he could look me up when he was down my way. Out of politeness I gave him my contact details – why not? He'd been lovely company and a welcome respite from the drunk talk. No doubt he was getting contact details from as many locals as he could, so he always had options when he was touring on his own. I said good-night to him, then went over to my sister to thank her before leaving. I caught a look at the Czech guy from a distance as I left – he really was a beauty, and there's nothing more charming than a man with old-fashioned manners. Lucky girlfriend.

By Monday, I'd forgotten about the Czech beauty. The week went on as normal, with a few clients here and there, all pretty typical and a tad boring. I'd made a fair bit of money, though, and was going to treat myself to some new work undies, although that hardly rated as a treat, I suppose, more of an investment. On Wednesday I popped into M&S on my way back from seeing a client in his home. It was totally unremarkable, straightforward sex. Some sex is just like a typical day at the office where nothing worth talking about happens. I cheered myself up with a new underwired plunge bra and matching knickers in a deep aubergine. The rich colour looked great with the sheen of the satin fabric and thick lacy detail on the edging. Pleased with my investment, I stored it in my work-undies drawer when I got home before changing into Mummy attire, ready to collect the kids from school. I had about ten minutes before I needed to leave the house, so I switched on the computer to check my emails.

There was one from the Czech beauty. I clicked on it quickly, wondering why he was contacting me. His message said he would be visiting my area that weekend and would I be free to meet for a coffee? My first thought was, Oh, no. He's looking for free B&B or a tour guide. I emailed back, asking if he needed some advice about places to say, bus routes or opening times of the places he was coming to visit. I omitted to mention whether or not I was free for coffee. He must have been checking his email from his work desk because within minutes I received a reply, telling me he had all his arrangements in place and just wanted to meet up. He had enjoyed my company the other night. Okay, that sounded innocent enough – no cadging for freebies there. I agreed, and we arranged to meet on Saturday afternoon.

On Saturday morning I pottered around the house, catching up on the laundry and planning next week's dinners. The Czech beauty texted to say his bus was on time and he had just left town. We arranged to meet in the pub opposite the bus stop in my local town. Not thinking much about it, I threw on jeans and a T-shirt over some undies that had definitely seen better days. After putting on a bit of mascara and some perfume, I headed down to the pub to wait for him. It was empty, so I chose a comfy corner seat and ordered a coffee. Out of the window, I watched the bus pull up across the road and the Czech beauty get off. I was more than pleasantly surprised to see him: he must have been wearing his work clothes last week because he looked very different now, dressed casually in a pair of chinos and a tight T-shirt. His rucksack was slung over his shoulder and I could see the outline of his chest muscles as he walked across to the pub.

He smiled as he greeted me with a kiss on the cheek. We stumbled through the first few minutes of conversation, but once he'd ordered a coffee, we settled into it and got talking about his plans for the weekend. I couldn't help but notice the soft line of hair going from the top of his chinos up his T-shirt as he stretched. After a while, there was a lull in the conversation and he leaned his arms across the table and looked directly at me. 'So, what now?' he asked.

'What do you mean, what now?' I asked, thinking he was referring to directions to one of his historical sites.

'I like you,' he said softly, running his fingertips across my forearm.

'For God's sake,' I said crossly, 'stop touching me – we're in public, you idiot.' He pulled his hand away with the look of a scolded child. I took a deep breath and glanced quickly around the pub. 'This is small-town Ireland and people are very nosey. And, anyway, have I missed something here?' I asked, genuinely confused. I hadn't seen any of this coming. 'Haven't you a girlfriend?' I said. 'And even aside from that, I'm way older than you.'

'It's true I have a girlfriend,' he said. 'I'm not going to lie about that, but I do really like you. I thought you were interesting.'

I sat there, totally stumped by what I was hearing.

'And,' he continued, 'when I find someone interesting, I also find them very attractive.' He took a sip of his coffee, never taking his eyes off me.

'Listen, that's all lovely and I'm flattered, but you're still in college. I don't even want to ask what age you are,' I said, folding my arms in what must have seemed a matronly stance.

'Don't ask,' he said, with a shrug.

'What are you on about – don't ask what?' I said, getting frustrated with not knowing what was going on.

'You said you didn't want to ask my age, so don't ask,' he said, with a saucy grin.

The penny dropped and I sat back to consider it. 'But why do you like older women?' I asked. I certainly wasn't a wealthy cougar, so if he was thinking I'd fund his tour of Ireland, he had the wrong end of the stick.

'I'm not interested in hearing about the latest must-have nail colour. With girls my age it's all drama, and down-to-earth conversation doesn't happen. Older women have something more between their ears and that's far more appealing for me,' he said, with his gorgeous foreign lilt.

This was all too much for me. 'I don't know about you,' I said, 'but I'm going to have a drink.' I rooted my wallet out from my bag.

'I'll join you. What will you have?' he asked, standing up and accidentally giving me another little glimpse of his abdomen.

A couple of white wines later and I knew there'd be no driving to heritage sites now. Almost without thinking I blurted out, 'Do you fancy getting something to eat at my place?' He fancied it all right, and bought a bottle of wine from the bar to bring with him.

Within minutes, we were at my home, looking through the menu for the local Chinese takeaway. I excused myself for a moment and ran upstairs to change out of my old undies. The new ones I'd bought for work were relocating to the personal-use drawer. When I went back downstairs, the Czech beauty had found his way around the kitchen and poured two glasses of wine. He was quietly confident and made himself at home. I liked that. We weren't ready to order food yet, so we took our drinks out into the garden.

We sat on the bench, enjoying the warmth of the afternoon sun. 'Do you mind if I ask you something?' he said.

'Go ahead,' I said, sipping my wine. I was feeling a little tipsy now and quite relaxed.

'How do you feel about F-mates arrangements?'

'God, your turn of phrase is very up to speed,' I said, surprised.

'Why? What do you call it?' he asked.

'"Friends with benefits" is a little less blunt than fuck mate or buddy,' I informed him. 'Anyway, I've never tried it.' I knew where he was going with this. 'It's not something I'd agree to without sampling the goods first,' I said, giving him a naughty glance. He leaned into me and sucked softly on my bottom lip, running his tongue gently over my mouth before pulling away. 'That's a mini taste for you. There's plenty more where that came from, if you're interested.'

'I'm interested,' I said, took him by the hand and led him to my bedroom. I couldn't remember the last time I had had a man in my own bed. It felt so damn good. Everything I wanted was at my fingertips. I flicked on a CD with the remote control and we spent the next couple of hours kissing, exploring, fucking and chatting. His youthful body was delightful. It was the nicest afternoon I'd had in ages and all the better because I knew he'd be gone shortly. Lovely and all as he was, I'd no interest in having a man in my space. I was beginning to see the benefits of a Czech fuck mate arrangement, though!

By now we were both ravenous and I phoned to order a takeaway delivery. It was all amazingly relaxed and comfortable. We had dinner, then he dressed and phoned a taxi to take him to the B&B he had booked for the night. I was glad he didn't hint at staying over with me because I didn't want to blur the boundaries. If this was just sex, then it needed to be simple, straightforward and hassle-free – so far, so good! 'Maybe we can meet again tomorrow before I get the bus back to town?' he asked, as his taxi pulled up.

'Give me a shout and I'll see if I'm free,' I said. He kissed me goodbye and let himself out.

Over the following months we got to know each other really well, both inside and outside the bedroom. We had fascinating conversations about our different backgrounds, upbringing, societal norms, and how all of this had influenced the people we became and our choice of partners. We found we shared a nerdy interest in the origin of words and spent ages arguing on the specific meaning of words in different contexts.

One day, about two months after we'd started seeing each other, I mentioned that I was taking the kids to the National Gallery in Dublin that weekend; he said he'd love to join us, if I had no objection. I didn't object at all – the more healthy male role models my children spent time with the better, as far as I was concerned. They hit it off with him and thought he was great. He was funny, thoughtful and sweet with them. It felt perfectly normal and natural for us to spend the day together and he was very careful not to do anything that suggested to the kids we were anything more than friends. As we got more and more comfortable with one another, he once brought up the subject of what I did for a living. I looked at him and said, 'Don't ask, you really don't want to know.' In spite of his maturity and open-mindedness, I was sure no guy would accept what I did for money and I certainly wasn't going to tell him just to see if I was wrong on that score.

Over the next six months, he really grew on me. Maybe in a different environment, at a different time, we could have had more than a fuck mate relationship. But after his year was up, he returned to the Czech Republic and his girlfriend. She had tried to find work in Ireland during his year there, but wasn't successful. I was secretly delighted because it had kept everything separate and simple. It was his birthday recently, and when we talked on the phone, I teased him that I had never actually found out his age. It wasn't important any more, so I was now ready to ask. He told me that he was twenty-four when we met, which meant I was sixteen years older than him. Wow!

The thing is, thanks to my work, age really doesn't matter to me. I know I have a friend for life in him and vice versa. I confided things in him that men twice his age couldn't handle. We thoroughly enjoyed our time in the bedroom and he taught me more about my own body than I had ever learned myself. I experienced sexual firsts with him that I haven't managed to repeat with anyone else. I'm very grateful that my escort work allowed me to have the guts and open-mindedness to say yes to him. The pre-escort me would have nipped things in the bud in that bar. I would have laughed at his forwardness, felt a little thrill of delight that he found me attractive, then told him he didn't stand a chance with me. I would have kissed that whole opportunity goodbye. Instead, I went with the flow and allowed it to unfold in its own way, enjoying his body, his mind and his attentions to the full. It's funny what life can teach you!

17. A Bad Patch

The summer months should be about light, energy and positivity, but somehow I fell foul of a bout of depression in the middle of them. My body ached and I had zero energy for anything. I found myself staring resentfully at the joggers and walkers and smiling people going by my door – they all looked so healthy and happy and there I was, a shadow of myself. When I'm feeling like this, my existence is miserable.

I went to see my GP, who prescribed anti-depressant medication. She talked to me a lot about stress, how it's a major cause of all kinds of conditions, from sleep deprivation to chronic mental illness. I joked that in recession Ireland there must be a lot of stress about, and she told me she had been inundated with patients seeking help because they couldn't cope. As I was walking along the street to the pharmacy to fill my prescription, I couldn't help looking at all the people rushing by, their faces tense and their minds focused on everything they had to get done that day. We were all in this together, weren't we? And yet everyone felt so totally isolated and alone. I know I did – struggling to make ends meet, every week an unpredictable race to the finish line of paid bills and maybe even a good night's sleep. I looked at the people around me and saw the exact same thoughts and stresses reflected back at me. Sometimes it seemed like no one was happy.

I handed over my hard-earned cash for the anti-depressants. I hated having to spend money on myself in this way, but I was desperate to get to the other side of it – I couldn't afford to be ill, mentally or otherwise. That was a stress in itself – none of us could take a breather or let any of the plates stop spinning, because the whole thing was so finely balanced and fragile. It was enough to drive a person mad, and no wonder that the newspapers were full of reports of suicides. I've never felt that bad, thankfully, probably because my children rely on me, but I can understand how a person could feel that the world had closed in on them and there was no way out. If you have a bank manager on your tail, maybe a credit-card company, maybe the electricity and gas bills are overdue, it can seem like a problem to which there is no solution. During the Celtic Tiger years, Irish people were given to believe that they could have it all and enjoy it. But there are only twenty-four hours in the day and something's got to give. I learned this the hard way.

I know my decision to work in the sex industry was unorthodox, but I can't help thinking there's a lot of people out there who would understand it. As a parent, you don't have the choice not to provide – you have to do whatever you can. Ireland was lifted to dizzying heights during the boom years, but now we've been dashed hard on the rocks. I think people feel it socially and personally – like we're all little wrecks, washed up and with no prospect of being repaired. It's just so damn tiring to keep on fighting that we all end up depending on caffeine, nicotine, sugar, prescription meds, alcohol or cocaine just to get through the day.

When the depression hits, the world looks dark and dangerous, and I take on too much personally. I get terrible headaches at night and can't sleep. Sleep deprivation is a form of torture. I guess, though, that I'm lucky in some ways: I suffer long episodes of feeling depressed, but they're countered by long episodes of feeling well – I remind myself of this on the bad days. When I'm stuck in an episode, it feels like my life isn't worth living – nothing seems worth any effort, not my family, my friends or even my children. That's how low I feel. Thankfully, I know that this is the depression talking and that the real me is stuck inside a cage of misery. I know that if I take my medication and give it time to work, the real me will emerge again.

That bout had lasted for three weeks and I was still feeling drained and defeated. When I looked at the calendar on the kitchen wall, my heart sank when I saw how close it was to the red-ringed day for the mortgage payment. I didn't have the money in my account. I took out my work phone and there were umpteen missed calls. They were all from potential clients and I was unable to muster the energy to call them back, let alone meet them and have sex. I stared at the phone and switched it off – I simply couldn't do it that day. I filled the bath, took my medication and a pick-and-mix of nutritional supplements, then lowered myself into the water for a long soak. Afterwards, I climbed wearily into bed and swallowed a strong sleeping tablet. Please, God, let this pass soon so I can get back out there.

18. A Good Day

It was nearing the end of August and I was a lot better. I actually felt enthusiastic and wanted to work, a very good sign. I had to be productive while I could. The children were delighted to find me more like my usual self, and the morning chaos went smoothly – I got them up and out of the door to summer camp on time. Back in the quiet of the house, I flicked on the kettle for a strong coffee and switched on my work phone to see what awaited me.

I'd been lying low for four weeks so there were many missed calls. I started going through them one by one, sending apologetic texts and letting the caller know I was available again, if he would like to call about a booking or chat about his requirements. Most of those callers would either have a different Sim card or a mobile phone that their partner didn't know about that they used for their extracurricular activities. As it was mid-morning, some would be able to find a quiet moment to ring, if they wanted to. Sure enough, the phone was buzzing before I'd even finished my return texts.

I answered the first call, sounding chirpy and friendly. The guy at the other end was called John and I hadn't dealt with him before, so I asked him his age and marital status: forty-eight, married and travelled with work. As it happened, he was staying overnight at a hotel that very evening and would love a visit to his room. The location was an hour away from where I live, so it suited me perfectly. It was Friday and the children would be with their dad for the weekend. I arranged to be with him at seven. I recognized one of the numbers in the list as Kevin's, a regular. I called him back and, as luck would have it, he also wanted to see me that day. We arranged to meet at one o'clock at his home.

I hung up, and saw that a text had come through from Liam, another guy I'd seen a few times. He had a window of opportunity that morning. Fantastic! He was a perfect client: paid upfront, never asked for any unsafe sex acts, and what he loved most of all was a great hand-job. He never lasted longer than an hour in total, but I still got three hundred euro. He was about sixty years old, and his wife was very religious, more concerned with the goings-on in the parochial house than in her bedroom; they had sex a couple of times a year, at best. I responded quickly and enthusiastically, agreeing to an eleven o'clock meeting at our usual hotel, which was ten minutes away. I had thirty minutes to get ready and on the road.

Damn! I hadn't carried out my basic maintenance in the past four weeks and, needless to say, the superfluous hair was a tad too obvious, as were my grey roots and milk-bottle white skin. I made up a portion of hair dye, some eyebrow dye and some depilatory cream. I took my watch off to time everything exactly and got my accessories ready. First, I applied my hair dye and took a note of the time: it would take exactly ten minutes. Next was the depilatory cream, which I spread on my upper lip and chin. Last, a quick eyebrow shape and an application of dye for a few minutes. I jumped into the shower once the ten minutes were up and washed off all the lotions and dyes. I stayed under the shower for another ten minutes, until the water was running clear, and shaved the essentials while I was there. I jumped out to dry myself off, then stood back in the shower tray to spray on an instant-dry fake tan. Okay, so the smell was pretty toxic at this stage and I was coughing with the fumes, but for time management it can't be beaten. As the tan was taking, I applied a one-second coat of polish in vamp red to my finger- and toenails. That was it – I was good enough to go.

I'd a reliable working wardrobe at the ready. It was exactly what men wanted and what flattered me: a crisp white shirt revealing a moderate amount of cleavage, well-tailored jeans, chunky jewellery and high-heeled boots. A quick blast of the hairdryer, some eyeliner, mascara and lippy and I was almost ready. I kept my hotel bag in a locked case under my bed. It contained the following working girl essentials:

- red satin full-length negligee
- pink polka-dot baby-doll negligee
- pale blue see-through uplift bra and knickers
- red lace bra and diamanté G-string
- black pure silk lace short negligee and kimono wrap
- red-patent high heels (Penney's finest!)
- mini music system
- small selection of toys
- washbag containing torch (to examine penis in dark lighting to ensure it looks healthy), condoms (lubricated and flavoured in various sizes and colours – giving a blow-job with a condom *in situ* is horrible, but it really helps if it's flavoured and pre-lubed – *marguiretta* is the best, I think), individual sachets of lubricant, antiseptic spray, waterproof plasters, latex gloves, aromatherapy massage oil and rocket balm, which is a stimulant that helps to speed up a guy if he needs a little help

I checked that everything was in my bag, grabbed my car keys and was out of the door by ten thirty. It was a twenty-minute drive to the hotel and I phoned en route to make the room booking. I knew there would be no problem with the reservation as one hotel a week was closing down, so there were bargains a-plenty. I told the receptionist I was on my way from the airport, with a long car journey ahead of me, so would need a room for a few hours to have a nap and freshen up after a transatlantic flight. This was a standard request when I was making short-term bookings and was never queried by any hotel. I figured they didn't really care why you wanted a day booking so long as you were a good customer and paid the bill.

At the hotel, I parked the car, grabbed my bag and Filofax and strode confidently through the doors and up to the desk. I used my own credit card to check in, then texted Liam to tell him the room number. While he was on his way up, I closed the curtains, dimmed the lights, pulled back the duvet, put my washbag on the bedside locker, poured a glass of water and switched on my music system. Last thing was a little bit of lube on my bits, so that when Liam touched me, he'd think I was wet from arousal, something all clients love, of course. It's an occupational hazard to need a little extra moisture at times. A knock at the door let me know he'd arrived.

We greeted each other like old friends, with a hug and a kiss. We sat down and I asked what he would like. A massage, a blow-job and him using my vibrator on me before full sex, he replied. It wasn't his usual request, but it was fine by me. I was still on a high at being out and about, fit for work and having three clients booked for the day. He handed me an envelope containing three hundred euro and, as a courtesy to him, I didn't check it, just thanked him and put it straight into my handbag. I helped him undress, kissing his neck tenderly, murmuring that he deserved to relax, switch off and enjoy himself. He told me work wasn't going great and he was getting nothing sex-wise at home. He needed to release the pressure in order to give himself a bit more energy.

Liam was very dapper, a real old-fashioned gentleman who always wore a suit and bow-tie. His body was quite good, considering his age, and sexually he was in full working order. He was also sweet, reliable and well-spoken. I had often wondered why he didn't have an affair if he was finding his sex life so frustrating. I knew he would easily find a lady companion who would enjoy his company and body. I had said it to him once, but he told me that an affair was out of the question: he'd be terrified of getting caught and disowned by his family. Anyway, he said, 'I don't believe in infidelity.'

I couldn't help it – I laughed out loud at the irony. 'Do you not regard what we do as infidelity?' I asked.

He looked a bit sheepish. 'Well, I suppose it probably is, but the fact that I pay you makes it feel less personal. An affair would be personal, feelings would get involved.'

His illogical response reminded me of Gerry, the client who declined penetrative sex with me because 'I've never been unfaithful to my wife and I'm not going to start now.' I guess we can make ourselves believe and justify anything.

I told Liam to lie face down on the bed, naked, and straddled him. He could feel my shaved soft pussy on his butt and groaned. I started to massage him slowly with patchouli and lavender oil, a combination that is both relaxing and arousing. I am an accomplished masseuse, even though I've never had any formal training. I'm sure it's because I love a good massage myself and have had loads over the years, plus all the practice on my ex and my clients had paid off. I massaged Liam all over, keeping an eye on my watch to ensure I didn't skimp on time – he was a good client and I wanted to give him his money's worth. I asked him to turn over and opened a sachet of lube. I sat between his legs, with his knees bent up to give me full access to his balls and cock, which was by now rock hard. I looked directly at him and started to massage his cock with the cool lube. He loved it, so I decided to take my time and not rush his climax. I placed a condom in the side of my mouth and put my mouth over his cock while flicking out the condom over the tip of his penis and rolling it on to him gently with my lips – I try to give clients the best blow-job I can, considering that all men hate condoms and that they reduce the sensation. I continued to move my mouth over his cock while massaging his balls and perineum with my already lubed hand. I gently inserted a finger into his ass to check if he liked it, but he asked me to stop because he felt like he was going to come and he wanted to use my toy on me first.

I grabbed my vibrator from the bedside locker, applied a little lube and handed it to him. 'I'm not sure how to use this so give me a few hints, will you?' he said.

'Of course I will,' I said encouragingly.

He got the hang of it after a few attempts and as I lay there with my legs wide open, he could see that the buzzing rabbit ears were hitting the spot exactly. Liam was still hard throughout all this and though I was enjoying what he was doing to me, I knew he needed to come and I wasn't far off either. 'It's time to fuck,' I murmured. He didn't comment, He let me apply a fresh condom as I told him I wanted it hard, from behind.

I love the feeling of penetration from behind and, to be honest, it makes me really horny to turn men on. By now, having had Liam use my vibrator on me, I was ready for it. I knelt on the bed, exposing my pussy and ass for his full admiration, knowing it would speed him up. He pushed his cock into me and gasped, saying I felt fabulous. I told him I wanted to be fucked as hard as possible and that I wanted to come. I stroked my clit and closed my eyes as he fucked me. I concentrated on the sensations I was experiencing and tightened my pelvic muscles so he could feel me grasping his cock. His breathing got deeper and his thrust was steady and rapid. I hadn't had sex in four weeks so I was really up for it. I guess I've a very high libido anyway, so I'd genuinely missed it. My clit started to throb and I quickened the pace with my fingers. I was going to come, and told him not to stop, to keep fucking me. He continued to fuck me as hard as possible until I felt the release in my pussy that I'd needed so badly. I had a fabulous orgasm, which seemed to go on for ages, while he continued to fuck me. He knew I'd come and that pushed him over the edge. With one final deep thrust he moaned loudly, his body jerked a few times, then went limp with exhaustion. He lay down on my back and we bathed in the afterglow. Climaxing simultaneously mid-morning with no strings attached felt damn good!

I got up, ran the shower for him and switched on the kettle. He sighed contentedly and said it gave him the best feeling to know he could still please a woman at his age. He'd missed having a sex life for so many years, and we chatted briefly about what a fundamental part of us sexuality is. I passed him a fresh towel as he hopped into the shower, then tidied the room. When he emerged, I had a cup of tea ready for him and I was wearing a negligee. He took a couple of mouthfuls – I really only make the tea out of manners, because generally clients are eager to get going once they've showered, but it's a nice touch, I think. We checked he hadn't left anything in the room, then kissed goodbye. He asked if I'd be available again in two weeks' time. Of course I'm available any time for such an easy client!

I closed the bedroom door behind him, making sure to stay behind it so I couldn't be seen by any housekeeping staff in the vicinity.

I jumped into the shower, careful not to wet my hair or makeup; it would last a while longer with just a touch-up. I opened the curtains and windows, tidied the bathroom, pulled up the duvet and made sure there were no condom wrappers lying around. I ordered a scone and tea to my room and repacked my bag for the next client. I changed into my blue see-through underwear, threw on my jeans and shirt and was off to the next appointment.

One hour later I pulled up near the home of my next client, Kevin. I'd seen him three times before, so I knew the drill. I parked one street away and carried my tote bag and laptop case. The laptop case was empty, but who was going to check? With it, I looked like I was making a legit business call to his house. Kevin worked from home and clients visited him there regularly. I licked my lips as I knocked on the door to give them a sheen. He opened it and shook my hand for the benefit of anyone who might be watching us.

Once inside, he asked me to remove my clothes and join him for a drink. He undressed very quickly, as did I. Our clothes lay in a pile in the hallway, but this wasn't a prelude to frenzied sex: Kevin was a naturist and had no one to practise it with. His wife had always been appalled by the idea, so he paid me to have a chat and a drink in the normal environment of his home, with both of us stark naked.

Having looked into naturism, I can see the appeal. We're judged by our outward appearance, so without clothing, the impression we give is based on conversation and personality. In addition, exposing one's skin to the sun is considered by many to have several health benefits. I think his wife was overreacting to it, but Kevin told me she had never been comfortable with her nakedness, and always insisted the lights were off when they made love. She said he was an exhibitionist, but from the little I know of it, showing oneself off has nothing to do with naturism, which has nothing to do with sex. It's about feeling a sense of freedom with the removal of the socially imposed (and climate-essential) outerwear, so that one may feel more in touch with one's whole self. While I'm not pushed one way or the other about it, I can at least appreciate it and see no harm in it. It was unfortunate that Kevin had to pay someone to share his interest. He really didn't need a sex worker – he just needed to meet some like-minded people. If he had been a little more forthright, he would have discovered that there were a few groups in Ireland who met regularly and several societies abroad that arranged naturist get-togethers and holidays.

I sat naked at the kitchen table while he put together coffee and scones for us. We chatted about what was in the news, the state of the economy and the weather. I tried to behave as if I was totally comfortable with this but, like most women, I'm a lot more comfortable being scantily clad and in dim light. The ordinariness of the kitchen seemed in total contrast to what was happening: I was being paid to be naked, and a stranger was making me coffee with his todger dangling in front of me. I must be a good actress, though, because he seemed to accept that I was totally relaxed. I understand that naturism isn't about looking good but about being comfortable in your own skin, feeling free and more at one with nature. He suggested we move to the conservatory, where the sun was shining in. I couldn't help but glance at his dick as he set the beautifully prepared tray on the table. He noticed my eyes on it and asked if I was comfortable with 'this'. I said I was, of course, that I was just admiring how he'd prepared everything.

When we were seated in the sunlight, sipping coffee, we got into a conversation about religion, of all things. It was topical because it was in or around the first anniversary of the publication of the Ryan Report, the investigation into the widespread abuse of children in Church-run institutions. There had been a huge amount in the media about it, concerning priests who abused their positions of authority to interfere with and rape children in their care. I don't know anyone who suffered at the hands of the Church, but Kevin did. He told me a terribly sad story about a family member who was receiving 'spiritual guidance' from a local priest in the wake of a sibling's death, only for that priest to compound the grief and confusion by abusing the child. I asked him if the priest was arrested for this dreadful crime, but he replied sadly that people didn't talk about such things in those days. Kevin was in his late fifties and, thankfully, things have changed a lot, but back then people didn't dare mention anything negative about the clergy because such comments or accusations simply wouldn't be believed.

It really was quite surreal to be having that intimate and distressing conversation with no clothes on. But after a while our nakedness seemed unimportant – we were just two people, listening to each other. Thinking about Kevin's story now, I'm incredibly moved by the power of the human spirit to live and survive beyond the most unimaginable grief. When he'd finished talking, he composed himself, then thanked me for letting him talk about it for so long. He said his wife was so used to the story that he rarely brought it up any more, but he had found it very therapeutic to talk openly about it again. I guess some things run so deep you never really get over them.

After another while, he asked if I would like to get dressed. As I was putting on my clothes, I was thinking I'd feel shit taking money from him because he had shared that painful story with me. I didn't have to face an awkward moment, though, because he had left the payment by my bag, without a word. He thanked me once more for letting him be himself and said he'd call me again.

I left feeling very emotional and sat into my car. I needed to hear my own children's voices after all that heartache. How anyone could harm a child I really do not know.

I was home by three and threw off my work clothes, changing into my comfy tracksuit. I wiped off my makeup and put on a hydrating mask before sitting down to watch trashy daytime TV with a cup of tea. I needed to be ready again by seven for my third client of the day. Three in a day is a lot for me, but I was so grateful to be making a bit of money again that I didn't mind at all. I felt pleased that I had the energy for three. My money situation had deteriorated rapidly in the weeks I wasn't working. The landline had been disconnected for non-payment of bill, which meant I was also without the Internet. As the Internet was my only method of advertising, it was a top priority to get it reconnected: if I couldn't advertise, I couldn't get work. Now, though, I'd six hundred euro in my wallet from my two clients this morning. Subtracting the cost of the hotel, I was left with a profit of 560. Tonight's client was a new guy, so he'd be paying the first-time rate of four hundred euro. By the end of the day I'd have enough to pay the phone bill and get my Internet access reconnected. It would also cover half the mortgage that had gone unpaid last month. Happy days!

By the time I was leaving home to visit the last client, I was feeling the effects of a busy day. I was tired and not as enthusiastic as I'd been earlier in the day when I'd taken the booking. John would get a raw deal in that I'd have to feign interest and I wasn't up to much chat.

He was a quiet older man, so he probably didn't have much of a sex life. Anything would be a bonus, right? I went through the motions. He responded. I hastened things. He reacted accordingly. He came. He went. End of meeting. If he'd had any complaints he could have withheld my fee, but as he didn't, he obviously felt it was worth the money. I figured as he didn't know I was usually way better, he didn't realize he'd been short-changed. I must make it up to him if he books me again, I thought.

I headed home, tired but delighted to have my mojo back and money in my pocket. I'd pulled through the abyss and the future looked more promising.

19. *Sex Toys*

When you work in the sex industry, one thing you learn a lot about is sex toys. I'd say most women under forty have a vibrator stuffed into the back of a drawer in the bedroom, but the huge plethora of toys on offer mightn't be so familiar to them. Before I became an escort, my knowledge of sex toys was confined to dildos and vibrators. I wasn't sure what men would want in terms of toys when I first started out, but after a few months I had built up a stock of the most in-demand items, namely double-probed vibes, anal beads, clit stimulators, cock rings and butt plugs. I find that men want to push their own sexual boundaries, and where better to try this than in the non-judgemental company of a paid escort who has the expertise (allegedly) and know-how but is minus any tendency to judge or criticize? Obviously a sex worker needs to have a good working knowledge of what's available and how to use it, but I'm pleased to have acquired this knowledge for my private sex life, too. Based on what I've surmised from giggly conversations I've listened to among my friends, I think it's information worth sharing.

Unfortunately for women, there isn't a try-before-you-buy option with sex toys – they can be quite expensive and you don't want to shell out for something that isn't right for you. The most regular purchase women make is the vibrator – a sex toy made commonplace by TV shows like *Sex and the City*. By now I know what I like and pretty much stick to the same texture, size and control settings. There's nothing worse than some fiddly vibrator with sensitive controls that you can accidentally hit off, changing the speed just when you were beginning to enjoy it. And as for the ones where the controls are almost the size of a TV remote but still connected by wires to the shaft, you'd need an engineer beside you to operate it, plus a few more pairs of hands for all the buttons – way too complicated.

It's like everything else, I guess: you get what you pay for. A really good, compact, robust vibrator that is well designed, hypoallergenic, waterproof and almost silent will set you back at least eighty to a hundred euro. To that you have to add the cost of sterilizing spray and lube. If you pay less, you can expect less from your toy.

There's also a plethora of new 'luxury toys', which look more like beautiful ornamental pieces rather than something that needs to be stashed out of sight. These are ergonomically designed, and made with the highest-grade materials – titanium, ceramic, glass and silicone. Some have fantastic features, like memory systems – yes, unlike your average man, your toy will recall just how you like it so you don't have to alter the settings. Don't you just love advances in technology? I like the custom-made engraved gold vibrator I spotted recently on the Internet. Just in case you ever get into such a frenzy that you forget your own name mid-play session, all you have to do is glance at the engraving!

As a woman, I consider a really good vibrator to be a basic staple of life, but there are plenty of other options and ideas, depending on likes and areas of sensitivity. Thankfully, the days are gone when it was very difficult to get your hands on good-quality sex toys. Once upon a time a woman had to brave the pervy sex shop, the kind where you rang the doorbell, nobody made eye contact and nobody spoke. That's all changed now, and sex shops are customer-oriented businesses, like any other retail outlet. Most have excellent websites that describe the products in detail, respond to queries or particular requirements, and guarantee highly discreet postal packaging.

When you visit a modern sex shop, you'll find the staff friendly, approachable and helpful, with very good knowledge of all the products. It helps to know beforehand what you like in terms of size and pressure, and areas of particular sensitivity, but I've also taken a gamble on a new toy occasionally, only to find it way better than I would've expected. As a result, I now own a tiny mini vibrator that is absolutely perfect for clitoral stimulation and is powerful, silent, waterproof and literally small enough to conceal in the palm of my hand, which makes it ideal for travelling. It was actually a sales assistant in a sex shop who suggested I try it, which proves that staff can be a great source of help and inspiration. If you're not very familiar with sex toys, I'd recommend starting on a reputable website and getting an idea of what's out there, then treat yourself to something. Try a clit stimulator/mini vibrator and any of the more expensive toys that are designed by engineers to fit the contours of a woman's body and will reach G-spot, clit and perineum simultaneously.

There is a huge range of toys available to titillate and satisfy men, too, including anal probes/beads/plugs and anal vibrators, which are angled to massage the prostate. Other toys, such as cock rings and cock vibrators, are designed to increase or alter the sensation on the penis, to prolong and intensify the experience, and can be used solo or with a partner. If you're lucky enough to have a partner with whom you're sexually compatible, you can easily overcome any misgivings with a suitable toy. Once you get over the initial shyness about your man having some bright pink or purple bit of silicone around his willy and realize that said silicone is very, very nice when he's inside you and it's vibrating against your clit, you'll be happily converted.

I particularly like penis enhancers, which are male toys that add length and width to the penis, while also having some sort of vibration for additional clitoral stimulation on penetration. If you prefer clitoral stimulation prior to climax, then these toys will do the job very well. I find it a great turn-on when men are liberated and comfortable enough to try these often odd-shaped toys. Sometimes the fun and arousal may simply be in trying something new, but other times you can find a real gem that becomes a favourite for you both. My favourite to use with clients was a clit stimulator to enhance my orgasm, but clients loved watching me use my vibrator on myself and then having a go at doing it for me. I found that very few were experienced with using toys on a partner and needed a bit of guidance and feedback on what felt good.

I've heard female friends joking about turning to sex toys because their boyfriend/husband doesn't know how to make them climax. I don't think it's okay for a woman to expect her lover to be able to turn her on when she doesn't know what she likes/dislikes herself. Women owe it to themselves to know their minds and bodies well enough to be able to tell a lover what they want and what will work for them. It's hardly fair for a woman to expect her man to bring her off with his fingers if she doesn't know the pace, pressure and variation she likes. This isn't the sole preserve of sex workers: every woman should have a good working knowledge of her own body so she can maximize her pleasure and her partner's.

If you've never done it, have a one-to-one date with your lady bits as a matter of priority. Allocate some time when you're not rushed or likely to be distracted, have a glass of wine or a bath to relax and read some erotic literature or imagine what you would like your fantasy partner to do to you – I'd say George Clooney and Brad Pitt have been responsible for some serious orgasms over the years that they're not in the least aware of! Let your hands roam over your body, paying attention to how the different areas respond to touch. Focus on the sensations. Vary your position depending on what feels right – the obvious one is to lie on your back with your knees bent up, but try lying on the floor with your feet raised on the wall, get on all fours, or into the X position, which is exactly as it sounds, in the shower or lying on your side curled up but with your upper leg raised. Personal favourite: in the bath. I move myself around so that my legs are raised upright against the wall in a V position – I'm not sure why, but it works.

Once you know where your hot spots are, you'll have a better idea of what you may like in a toy. Buy yourself a new one in the same way you would a new outfit or hair-do, by treating it as an investment in your sex life. Toys can be a great way to break the monotony of sex with a long-term partner. When it gets to a stage where you know your man's sexual repertoire and can predict his every move in the bedroom, then it's time to stir it up a bit to avoid things going stale. While some women may feel a little uncomfortable talking about spicing up their sex life, it's worth being honest and upfront as that will quickly get you both over the hump of any embarrassment. If anything, suggesting new things for the bedroom shows that you care for your partner and want to continue enjoying your sex lives together, which can only bring you closer as a couple. When you next need to drop hints about what you want as a gift for a birthday, Christmas or anniversary, send your man an email with a link to the toy you have your eye on, hand him the catalogue or tell him outright. I can't imagine that any man would react with anything other than delight.

When you're choosing a sex toy, especially a vibrator, consider your man's ego: most men would feel a little threatened if they saw you enjoying a huge eight-inch vibrator. If your partner is one of the many who worries about penis size, don't choose the biggest vibrator on the market: use a little sensitivity with regard to how he may react. If he enjoys anal sex, would he like to use a toy with an anal probe on you, or would he prefer you to try some anal beads on him? Think about what will enhance the experience for both of you. Here's a tip from experience: it's remarkable how many men love to watch their partner using her toys to bring herself to climax – I got asked for this all the time. Don't worry what you look like while you're doing it or what he might be thinking – trust me, he'll love it! As for hand-jobs, men often tell me that no one does a hand-job as well as they can do it themselves, so ask him to masturbate while you watch and get a lesson in exactly what he likes.

From listening to my clients, I know that the biggest threat to a satisfying sex life is 'long-termism'. If you've been making love to the same person for years, it can be difficult to keep it interesting. When children come along, it's all too easy to relegate sex to the bottom of your to-do list, forgetting that you're actually a couple as well as parents. Without wishing to sound dramatic, I can say from experience that this can be a way to lose your man to other women, or to escorts. So many of my clients are happily married, apart from the sex bit. It's lovely that they desire their wives, but not so lovely that their desire is continually frustrated, which leaves them feeling isolated, neglected – and justified in seeking out other companions.

I'm speaking now as an ex-wife as well as an escort: don't neglect your sexual relationship. Make your lover your refuge in good times and bad and you'll stand a much better chance of weathering the storms of a long-term relationship.

The best sex I've had, whether in my professional or personal life, is when I've let go of everything and allowed myself to become a physical being – not a thinking being, not a stressed-out being, just a bundle of nerve endings and sensitive skin, with my entire focus narrowed down to my body and its sensations. I remember reading somewhere that the brain is the biggest sex organ in the body, and I really think that's true. If you can tune your mind into your body and your lover's, tuning out everything else, you'll be able to relax, take your time and just enjoy it. Whether it's sex toys, positions, technique or fantasies, it comes down to one final piece of advice: remember, it's just sex.

20. The Blow-in

I'd fallen out with my mother. Again. My dad says we argue because we're so alike: too feisty to wait for the other's point of view; too stubborn to admit the other has a valid opinion. We can get on great at times, when we see eye to eye on things, but when we don't, it's awful. The latest row was about a family party my mother wanted to hold in September. She rang me to discuss it, but she wanted it to be a surprise party and I knew how much the person it was aimed at – my dad – hates surprises, so I told her. From there, we managed to insult each other about a number of things, with her ending on a high note: 'You don't understand the dynamics of a long-term marriage because yours only lasted a few years.' After that, I hung up, which was childish.

Of course, I couldn't concentrate on anything for the next hour and it bugged me to leave it like that. I knew she was too stubborn to call back and clear the air, so for her sake and mine I eventually picked up the phone, ready to make amends.

'Hi, Mum, it's me again.' Her reply was brief and frosty. 'Look, I'm sorry we argued, and if you want to have a party, you should just go ahead and arrange it. But I think you shouldn't mention the birthday – just make it a family get-together and everyone will enjoy that. No need to make it about a specific date in the calendar.'

There was a pause and then she softened a bit. 'I suppose I could just go ahead and do that, and you're right, everyone would enjoy it regardless of the reason for having it.' She was warming up now and I could almost hear her mind ticking over, the entertainment plans taking priority over staying cross with me. 'That's actually a really good idea, darling. You know what? I'm going to get started on it straight away.'

Phew! She sounded upbeat and I knew the argument was over

and we were friends again. We'd be okay until the next silly argument – that's the way it always pans out; I know the drill. We chatted briefly about me, then said our goodbyes because she needed to phone the caterers immediately to see when they'd be free.

It bothers me no end that it's always me who gives in when we argue. I know I can be really stubborn at times, but shouldn't it at least be that we take turns at being the one to hold out the olive branch? On the other hand, she's a fantastic grandmother, still works hard in my father's business and was a dedicated and loving mother when we were growing up. The problem is, she doesn't seem to realize we're not children any more. She still speaks to me as if I was a child and can't seem to relate to any of her children as independent adults. Some things from my childhood I try to replicate in my own parenting style, such as insisting on good manners and a healthy respect for authority. Others, I hope I don't fall into – I'd hate to think I couldn't treat my children as adults when the time comes.

I was just walking away from the phone, towards the kitchen, when it rang again. I picked it up. It was my mother. 'And while we're at it, you never call me these days, your phone always goes to voicemail and I haven't a clue what's going on in your life.'

It was true. We used to talk almost every day, but lately I'd been avoiding her calls. I was on the road so often during the daytime to appointments that I'd press 'silent' when I saw her name come up. It was easier than trying to explain where I was going and what I was doing; there are only so many excuses I can come up with. I always intended to call her back, but somehow the days flew by and I'd forget.

'You're right, Mum,' I said, in a conciliatory tone. 'I've been impossible to get hold of lately. I'm just so busy with the kids and this long-drawn-out divorce is doing my head in. I suppose I just haven't been in the humour to chat.'

'Well, it would do you good to talk more – it's not right keeping things to yourself.'

'Okay, Mum – I'll do my best.' I made a mental note to return her calls in future and text her every day. I didn't want her getting suspicious of how I was spending my time or asking me any tricky questions.

Two weeks later I dropped the children over to their father's, then drove the eighty miles to my parents' town and my old home. I had to stay over – at my mother's insistence – but I wasn't looking forward to doing that without my children to provide a welcome distraction. In fact, I was dreading the whole thing. I could already tell what would happen. Among my siblings and my parents' circle there was no recession – it wasn't PC even to mention the R-word. They seemed entirely unaffected by it and continued to parade around in their new model SUVs, chatting about their forthcoming foreign holidays and modelling the latest styles from the most expensive boutiques in town. I had no idea how they did it, but my theory was that some were living off credit now to keep up the life-style they'd once managed easily. I'd have to listen to my siblings and relations telling me how wonderfully my cousins were doing in Singapore/New York/London, or how lucky their eldest was that they'd got their 4,000-square-foot house on three acres built just in time before they fell delightfully pregnant. I'd listen smilingly and nod and say, 'God, that was good timing – it would be so hard to be building a dream house and pregnant at the same time.' And I'd be thinking, Who the fuck needs 4,000 square feet? For them, though, that was the way life was. They were old money, you see, a different kettle of fish altogether from the brash upstarts who had it all in the boom and lost it all in the crash.

After entertaining the self-congratulatory stream of conscious-ness, I'd have to face the worst part of the proceedings. 'So, are you still working for so-and-so?' The lies would pour out of me because I'd be too embarrassed to tell them I was officially unemployed, that my outfit was borrowed, that my Scrooge of an ex didn't pay main-tenance and that my car was about to be repossessed. I wouldn't be able to tell them I occupied a very different world from the comfort-able little bubble in which they all existed, but all the while I'd feel like a complete fraud as I laughed and pretended that life was good when really it was a complete fucking mess. Nor would I be able to numb the pain with alcohol – I'd be too afraid that it would loosen my tongue and then there might be a bit of *in vino veritas*, as they say.

That was exactly how the night went – except for one unexpected element. My parents had invited some of the new 'blow-ins' out of neighbourly decency. Mum introduced me to a few, saying, 'And this is my daughter, she works in . . .' then proceeded to tell them the name of my last employer, in that way conveying her disapproval of my current employment status. I was right to feel they were embarrassed by me – they didn't even say I was separated. A friend of my father's asked, 'And who did you marry?' thinking he might know the family.

My father butted in before I could answer: 'Oh, she's settled away down the country with her three lovely children.' The friend looked from my father to me and, sensing he shouldn't have asked, excused himself to get a refill. I could feel my cheeks burning and sloped off to the upstairs bathroom to take a break.

On my way back down the stairs, I met one of the blow-ins Mum had introduced me to earlier. We were on the landing, between the first- and second-floor bedrooms, an area sufficiently big enough for it to seem a reasonable place to have a chat. Blow-in smiled at me and said, in a conspiratorial tone, 'I wonder if your folks knew my marital status, would they have invited me?' I wondered what he was on about. 'I overheard your dad when that man asked who you married. I'd say you would have liked the ground to open up and swallow you.' He laughed.

I was caught off-guard and not at all impressed by his comment. I gave him a half-smile and continued down the stairs. 'Oh, I'm very sorry,' he said hurriedly, in a different tone. 'I didn't mean anything personal by that. I'm divorced, and have noticed in these parts that it's still frowned upon. I've had some funny comments myself.'

I realized he hadn't meant any harm by what he'd said, and that if I hadn't been so hurt by my father's insensitivity, I'd probably have laughed. So I lightened up a bit and asked did he not know what an established area he was moving into. We chatted for a bit. Martin was in his mid-forties, an accountant with two grown-up children.

He was getting used to the area, but was amazed by the old-fashioned attitudes of his new neighbours. He'd adopted a policy of not giving away anything about himself because he'd noted the look of suspicion when he told anyone he had moved down from the city and was living on his own. He described 'the look' as a cross between people wondering was he an ex-convict or a paedophile – why would anyone be living on their own in their forties after all?

Just then, the voices downstairs hushed. We presumed someone was saying a few words so we headed down to join the others. My first impression had been replaced with a more favourable one: he'd seemed quite nice, except for his grey hair. Is there anything more ageing? My mum was busy thanking everyone for coming and announcing that dessert would be served shortly. The caterers had done a great job and I'd eaten far too much. While the guests were tucking into desserts, I joined the smoking crowd outside for a change of scene. Blow-in arrived out for a smoke and the rest of them made their way back in. When we were alone, he asked if he could have my number, wondered if maybe I'd like to go out for a drink some time. I didn't think he was my type but what the hell? It was only a drink.

The party trundled on until the wee hours, with the usual die-hards making the most of the *craic* and free-flowing booze. Shortly after one a.m., I made my excuses and went to bed. I was sleeping in my old room. It looked so much smaller than I used to imagine it as a child. Mum had insisted on the bedrooms looking more or less the same as when we all lived at home, which was bizarre. My mind wandered to the hopes I'd had as a young girl, growing up. I got uncomfortable being jerked back into my childish self – what does a child know of life? I switched off that train of thought. I'm good at blocking out things I don't want to be reminded about. I filled my mind with some lighter thoughts to help induce sleep. I just had to get through breakfast with my parents without giving anything away, then I could escape back to my house and my children – and my recession-tastic life.

21. Girlfriends, Gossip and Guilt

In the eight months I'd been doing this work, I'd told two people the truth, two people I would trust with my life. One was Mags, my closest friend in the town where I now live; the other was Liz, an old schoolfriend I've known for thirty years. I told them because I trust them completely.

I am blessed with many good friends, but I wouldn't tell any of the others about my work. It wouldn't go down well and they don't need to know anyway. There's a problem, though, in that I'm desperately self-conscious in front of my friends and family, living in terror that I'll let something slip that causes them to wonder how I have acquired all this sexual knowledge. I have to remain hyper-alert when I'm with people, which can be hard with friends. I have to bite my tongue, pause, rephrase my comments and think carefully before I answer even the most innocent question.

One of the ways I cope with the double-life conundrum is to take alcohol only in very small amounts when I'm out socially. I live in fear that I'll overdo the drink some night and confide my dark secret to someone – friend or stranger. When anyone carries a big secret, there is always a pressure to offload the burden, and I'm no different. I can't afford to get tipsy and start thinking that everyone will understand and be sympathetic. I feel like Batman sometimes – hidden behind a social persona and having to maintain it not just for now but for the rest of my life. My secret would be equally devastating if it emerged in five, ten or fifteen years' time, especially for my family and my children. I hope in time it will get easier, but so far it has been the opposite. The more experiences I have, the more knowledge I gain and the more stories I hear, the more I have to remember to keep secret and the harder it becomes not to let the mask slip. I have had a few minor slip-ups when I mentioned something that happened with a client, but luckily I was able to cover it quickly. I don't think anyone noticed. I rely on my friends never imagining me as an escort and putting my stories and knowledge down to the books I read.

A few weeks into this work, back in late February/early March, myself and a few girls from a previous workplace met up for dinner. They're a good bunch and always up for a laugh. We got on to the topic of the week's social gossip in the media and who was the latest footballer to be caught playing offside. One of the girls said the man in question was a 'total ride and I'd hop on him in a shot'. We were all having a good giggle at this and other comments that were flying around. I'd had a few gins, which had loosened me up. Another of the girls said she wouldn't shag said footballer if she was paid and that she much preferred David Beckham. I blurted out that if she was being paid, she'd shag whoever turned up for his appointment on time. No sooner had I the words out than I realized what I had just said, but the girls took it for granted that I was joking and continued giggling. If this had been a group of sex workers, they would have got the joke precisely, but these were my mates. It was really stupid of me. A few more comments like that and it wouldn't be long before someone started to put two and two together. I put down my drink and poured myself some water. I decided then that letting my hair down with the girls, or anyone else, was too risky. From then on, apart from the odd glass of wine, drinks with the girls became a thing of the past.

Given all this, why did I share my dangerous secret with two people? Well, I guess I just had to confide in someone and though I couldn't have been 100 per cent sure of the reaction, I'd like to think I know my friends well enough to understand their level of tolerance. The first time I said it out loud was to my local friend. It was two days after I'd seen my first client, and we were out walking. She was the friend with whom I had laughed only a few weeks earlier at the very thought of selling our bodies.

'Hey, I've something to tell you,' I said, in a way that warned her it was something serious.

'Okay, go ahead,' she replied.

I knew by her tone that she was prepared to hear whatever I had to say. I had opened with that warning and if she had felt unsure she would have said something like 'If it will put me in an awkward position, I don't want to know.' I started off tentatively: 'Please tell me to stop if this is too much to take on.'

'Right,' she said. 'I'm all ears.'

I started by reminding her of the laugh we'd had in my kitchen about being so desperate for money that we'd go on the game. 'After you left, I got to thinking that maybe it wasn't such a bad idea. I've looked up a lot of stuff, and I'm doing everything as safely as possible and, basically, between the jigs and the reels, I've seen some clients already.'

'I don't fucking believe you!' she said.

I was relieved that there was no hint of disgust in her voice. I figured that for her sake, as much as for mine, she didn't need to know the gory details, so I talked about it in very bland generic terms.

I was pretty sure I could trust her not to be too shocked: she's had a varied and interesting life, and is very open-minded. She's now happily married and totally faithful to her very Catholic husband, yet she's never judged me and her attitude is 'You do what you have to do.' Telling her turned out to be a good idea in more ways than one because, as well as support, she gave me sound advice about safety, such as always to have a contact number for a client and to make sure I'm in charge of who I take on. She knows nothing about this work first-hand, so it was mostly common-sense stuff that she reinforced for me. She also pointed out that it probably wasn't a good idea to deposit substantial sums of cash into my bank account in case my ex-husband found out and started to ask questions before our divorce. She's a solid person whose company I always enjoy, even if we're chatting about something miserable. She's one of the few people to whom I can say absolutely anything. She has a very different life from mine, but what we have in common, I would say, is our resilience, our determination, the fact that we don't tolerate bullshit and aren't afraid to call a spade a spade. My friend has been through very tough times in the past, both emotionally and financially, and she's the living embodiment of the old adage 'What doesn't kill you will make you stronger.' I consider her a very strong person who sees obstacles as challenges and always looks at ways around them rather than being daunted. I'm very lucky to have a friend like her: she is one of the few people in my life I can be honest with.

'What do you think?' I asked. 'Am I mental?' I had outlined for her what my working life was like.

'Fuck it,' she said, and we continued on our walk.

The second friend I told about my entrepreneurial pursuits is also a strong character who seeks solutions to life's problems. Liz had planned to visit me one evening for a catch-up chat. We don't live close to one another, so meeting up has to be planned in advance. That particular evening we agreed to get into our comfy trackie bottoms, order a takeaway and fill each other in on what had been going on since we'd last met. We settled down for a good old natter and, of course, the subject of money and mortgages came up. 'Jesus, how are you managing for money now that you're out of work?' she asked.

'Well,' I said, with a long pause, 'I'm using the assets I was born with.' I looked at her to see if she'd twigged; she looked confused. 'I'm on the game,' I blurted out.

'Oh, my God, are you serious?' she asked, and her face told me she knew I was. She wasn't shocked, but it did take her a while to get her head around how I could manage and arrange the work and how I went from introducing myself to someone to shagging them within minutes. As with Mags, telling Liz was a good idea because she offered support and help. She has a fantastic business head and she gave me superb advice regarding my business plan. Thanks to her, I realized the importance of putting in place a workable time frame, to ensure I didn't just drift on indefinitely with the sex work. For me, it was a great help to put things into perspective with someone who wasn't biased. She didn't judge me for my choices: she said she admired me greatly for being a 'tower of strength' in prioritizing the areas of my life that were of the utmost importance to me. When I confided in Liz, she told me I was an inspiration. I don't believe she was complimenting my choices as such, but she understood them and admired my tenacity and resilience.

Liz agreed to be my 'business mentor' and to review my business plan and advise me on how to attain my end goals. One of the necessary goals we established was to have a Plan B in place for making money and paying my bills: I was to think about where I wanted to be in my life, then work backwards to take steps to achieve it. I know my future is in my hands and, as a person who instinctively thinks outside the box, I believe anything and everything is possible. Having a Plan B helps to take the insecurity out of life. Let's face it, I'm not going to become a madam and run a string of massage parlours or sell sex when I'm fifty and getting ridiculously wrinkly. I devised a Plan B of where I wanted to be in a year's time, in five years' time, and also what I would do if I didn't achieve my original goals. I was much more likely to do so now because I'd taken the time to think about them and write them down. It helps, when times are tough, to know that if I don't achieve my goals, I have an alternative option to work towards.

The short-term goals I identified were things like paying the most pressing household bills, continuing to generate money and starting to put a tiny bit aside. Building up a mini nest egg was the medium-term goal: it would allow me to go back to college or reinvent myself professionally. The long-term plan was to keep the roof over my head, raise the children to independence and get a job that I could be proud to talk about openly. I had a Plan B for each of the goals as well: for instance, I wanted to pay fifty euro a week towards my utilities, but if that wasn't possible I'd pay something just to keep on top of them. I also had a Plan B – maybe it was C or D – that if I ever got found out, my mini nest egg would get me and my children out of Ireland immediately. It wasn't something I ever wanted to have to do, but the funds would be there if it came to it.

Both Mags and Liz are strong and wise, have been through a lot themselves, are slow to judge or criticize others and know the real me. Being with them is easy because I can talk about my life without watching every word I say. When I refer to seeing a client, I tell them I've been 'at work/doing some work' just as I would with a regular job. Interestingly, neither of them has ever asked me any specific details about the sex or the clients. We're adults, we know what sex is about and there's no need for any detail, unless it's a particularly interesting or funny story. When I'm chatting with them they ask, 'How's work, is it going okay for you?' just as they did when I was in previous jobs. I'm lucky to have them as friends and I hope they can say the same about me.

Neither of these friends knows the other. I have a very diverse set of friends because I've had a diverse working life. I don't even know if they'd get on. I have several good friends who have never met one another. Some women have a close bunch of friends who all went to school/college or worked together, but I tend to have one good friend from each of the chapters of my life. I value my close friends highly. The two staunch friends in whom I confided will never be a source of gossip about me. However, I'm also very aware that a small town is a hotbed of gossip, rumour and intrigue. I was very careful not to draw any attention my way and tried to remain below the radar. I rarely went out socially in my local town: apart from the fear of bumping into a client, I would have risked letting something slip. The worst place possible to let the cat out of the bag would have been on my doorstep, so it was best to avoid it. A neighbour of mine is very involved in local community activities and committees and she's a terrible gossip. I used to dread her visits and idle chatter, but now she was an important source of information on what was being said about me around the place. If there were rumours about my work, she would have heard them first. I ensured that we had a pot of tea together fairly regularly, so I could hear what was going on and satisfy myself that no one had guessed my secret.

One day when she called around, she told me breathlessly that I had been the subject of talk in the local pub. My heart skipped a beat, but I kept my face calm. She went on to say that some people were muttering about the maintenance my ex must fork out to me because I seemed able to maintain a good standard of living. My heart rate slowly returned to normal. It was the sort of speculative gossip I hated, but it wouldn't do me any harm. After that, I knew that if she heard anything about my work, she'd be only too delighted to tell me. She unwittingly became another element of my defence net.

The only other way someone could get wind of what I do is if one of my clients said something. I seriously doubt that possibility. My client selection criteria have minimized that risk: I've chosen middle-class, attached men who have something to lose if they're found out. I do sometimes worry that in the future one of my clients may separate or divorce, then have no reason to keep my secret, but the public perception of men who pay sex workers is so poor that none of my clients would want to be associated with it. So, for now, I feel I have the gossip bases covered.

That leaves the guilt factor. It isn't really a problem because I don't need to feel guilty about being a good parent to my children. The men might have cause to feel guilty, but that's their business and I'm not going to get involved in it. I don't have a heart of stone, though, and I will admit that the hardest moments are during home visits, when I catch sight of family photos with smiling wives. My way to deal with that is not to take in too much information. Pictures of family, letters with the wife's name and the client's surname sitting around are surplus to requirements for me, and if I glance at something of that nature, I look away immediately. I have developed the ability to filter out unnecessary information and erase it from my memory. I would hate to recognize a woman from a photograph while I was out shopping or at the school gates. I know I would feel guilty – at least, I think I would. I've protected myself from clients' guilt by insulating myself against their private lives. I think of it as a normal job where you have your professional self and then your weekend self. If I'd been any other responsible and committed professional from Monday to Friday, would you have expected me to feel guilt if on Saturday I wore a mini-dress, drank ten cocktails and had a one-night stand with a stranger?

22. Porn Stars and Headstands

It was a crisp blue day in late September and I had a booking for the afternoon. Noel had rung that morning and sounded young, maybe early thirties. I didn't know him; he was just visiting the area with some of his friends. He fitted in as a suitable client because he was married, and polite on the phone. When I asked what he wanted from our meeting, he said simply a decent shag. Grand. I could handle that, I was sure. I booked a short-stay studio apartment attached to a well-established urban hotel that I'd used a couple of times. It was fine for what I needed: it had the benefit of the hotel's services with the facilities of an apartment, which ticked a lot of boxes for me. It was nice and private, too, with plenty of secure parking – always a bonus.

He arrived in a casual polo shirt and golf shorts. He'd played a round earlier with his friends and hadn't changed in case his mates asked any questions about what he was planning to do for the afternoon. I offered him a shower and he accepted. He handed me my fee without being prompted. He was attractive, tall, with blond wavy hair, and a relaxed disposition. I caught a glimpse of him as he stepped into the shower, and his body was lean and tanned. This one will be easy, I thought, as I lit some scented candles. I realized that the shower had stopped and turned as he stepped into the room with a towel wrapped around his waist. 'That's better,' he said, then smiled. 'I'm all yours.'

I asked if he had any particular requests. He had indeed got something specific in mind: he wanted to re-enact a scene he'd seen in a porn movie.

'I'm no porn star.' I laughed. 'You didn't mention anything about this on the phone.'

'It's just a suggestion,' he said, with a shrug. 'If you're not happy to do it, that's entirely up to you. No pressure, honestly.'

I believed him, but I was curious to know what he wanted and asked him to explain his idea to me. He described a scene in a porn movie in which the couple were having anal sex. That's straight-forward, I thought. The tricky part was the position the stars were in. The man had entered the woman in a face-to-face, lying-down posi-tion, then he lifted up her pelvis and she put her legs straight up in the air, in front of his face. He raised her until she was almost standing on her head, with him supporting her and still with his cock in her ass. It sounds impossible to me. I'm no acrobat and that seemed to demand the flexibility of a contortionist. I told him so. 'That's the whole point,' he said. He didn't think it was possible either, so he wanted to find out whether it had been staged for the movie. I agreed to give it a go because it was a bit different and therefore a bit exciting, but he knew he had to stop if I was uncomfortable. As I undressed, I thought, I should be charging danger money for this.

We did the basics, and when we were both ready, he instructed me to lie down on my back. He slipped on a condom, told me to tilt up my pelvis as far as I could, knelt before me and entered my ass slowly and steadily. He told me to lift my legs up in front of him, which I did, and he managed to stay well inside me. He told me he was going to lift me up more so that I was vertical and upside-down. He was taking his time and being considerate to my comfort, check-ing all the while that I was okay. He put both his arms around my legs and, with some almighty strength, lifted me so that I was upside-down, apart from my head, which stayed on the pillow. He held me there, then started thrusting. The ass stuff was fine, but the position was downright uncomfortable, and as he thrust more and more, he was struggling to keep me vertical and I started to slump. I'd no control whatsoever, and while I wasn't frightened of the cli-ent, I was concerned for my safety. I really didn't fancy a slipped disc or torn muscle, so I asked him to hurry up and come so I could get the hell down.

'I'm almost there,' he said and, with a few not-so-pleasant thrusts, he was. I breathed a sigh of relief. I felt a bit light-headed so I lay there until the dizziness passed.

'Well, how did we do? Are we as good as porn stars?' I asked.

'We sure are,' he said, with a big grin, delighted with himself. 'That's exactly what happened in the movie, but I really didn't think it was humanly possible to shag in that position. Jesus, you're flexible.' He shook his head admiringly. 'How did it feel for you anyway?'

'I felt *exactly* like a porn actress,' I said sarcastically. 'I was acting the whole way and, like with your porn stars, I wouldn't have done it either if I wasn't being paid.'

'Was it not at all nice for you?' He sounded a little surprised that being fucked in the ass while practically standing on my head might not be the most pleasurable of sexual encounters.

'Quite honestly, no, it wasn't good for me but, hey, it wasn't painful either and you wanted to try it, so now you know.'

'Fair enough,' he said, as he hopped up and started to dress. 'Thanks for letting me do it, though. I loved it.'

'You're welcome,' I said.

He organized himself, checked he had everything and left.

I put on the kettle for a sugary cup of tea and vowed that, in future, I wouldn't try to be something I was not. I was an escort, not a porn actress – lesson learned.

23. The Blow-in Again

It was a Wednesday evening in October and the children were milling about the house. I was in the middle of preparing dinner when my non-work phone beeped – a text message from Martin, the guy I'd met at my mother's party. Could he call later for a chat? I replied that I'd see what time the kids got to bed and text him back. I couldn't see anything romantic happening there, but maybe as he was new to the area and didn't know many people, he was just looking to broaden his social circle. We can never have enough friends, I reasoned, so what harm?

He called after ten o'clock and we ended up talking on the phone for three whole hours. This happened every night for the next week and I joked with him that I'd have to put a time limit on our chats because my eyes were dark-shadowed for want of sleep. In all those hours of talking, he didn't mention anything about meeting up. We chatted about his circumstances and mine, and I told him everything – except the obvious, of course. If we were going to be friends, I wasn't going to lie about how tricky things had become financially. Having been through a divorce himself, he could at least relate to that part, even though his children were grown-up when he and his ex-wife had decided to part.

I liked listening to him: it was reassuring to know that there were many others in similar circumstances to me. I didn't talk to my family about my ongoing divorce proceedings to save them from the embarrassment that one of their own had a failed marriage.

This marathon chatting went on for a fortnight and I began to wonder if he had any other friends. I mentioned that my birthday was coming up and hoped he'd take the bait. He did. He offered to take me to dinner somewhere we wouldn't bump into any of my family. What the hell? I agreed.

He picked me up one Saturday afternoon and we drove to a castle hotel in the west. The conversation was easy on the journey: we were used to each other's chatty style by now. Check-in was a bit awkward because I approached the reception desk first, only to realize that I didn't know his surname. He stepped in and made the necessary payments. It was a little odd being shown to our room, but what else were we going to do? We were in our forties, after all, and of course sex was on the menu – it was tacitly understood.

After dropping our bags, we grabbed a bite of lunch in the bar and he insisted on ordering a bottle of champagne to toast my birthday. The bubbles went straight to my head and I started to feel way too giddy. We decided to go for a walk to clear our fuzzy champagne brains. The area was so quiet and peaceful, I could feel the tension lifting from my shoulders as we strolled around. We stopped to admire some foals frolicking about, and there, with a bit of encouragement from me, we had our first kiss. It wasn't great. He was a little bit sloppy, which worried me because I think a man's kiss is indicative of what he's like in the sack. I pushed that thought aside and we made our way back to the hotel to get ready for dinner.

Our room had a beautiful claw-foot, free-standing bath that was definitely made for two – it was huge. He ordered a bottle of wine to the room and I ran a deep bath. I was sure he was hoofing into the booze out of nerves, and I was glad of it for the same reason. He poured two large glasses and we got out of our clothes and hopped into the hot bubbly water. If it hadn't been for the drink, it would have seemed odd being in that plush hotel with a man I had met only once before but, because of our late-night chats, we felt we knew each other well.

We polished off the bottle of wine in the bath and stumbled out to dry off. My head was spinning – I was positively drunk, unused to more than the occasional tipple. I lay down on the bed with a towel wrapped around me and asked him to get me a glass of water. Pissed before dinner is not me and I really wanted to sober up. He passed me the water and lay down beside me with a towel around his waist. With all the drinking, I hadn't taken much notice of his body, but now I couldn't help but look. It was promising: he was in good shape for a forty-something. The grey hair niggled at me, but I told myself he was a genuine, kind and generous man, and that a few grey hairs didn't change that.

Inevitably, lying on the bed quickly turned into kissing, which turned into him being about to enter me. 'Aren't you forgetting something?' I snapped, as I moved my pelvis away from him.

'What?' he said, looking confused.

'Condom!' I said, in a rather harsh tone.

'Oh. I didn't bring any with me,' he said, surprised.

'Jesus, that was a bit stupid,' I said, swinging my legs out from under him and hopping off the bed. 'Luckily, I had the sense to bring my own.' I rummaged through my washbag and grabbed a couple. I quickly jumped back into position and rolled on the condom. He started to enter me but lost his erection, and we lay there feeling like a pair of inexperienced teens.

'I'm really sorry,' he mumbled. 'It must be the alcohol.'

'It's really okay,' I assured him. 'I could probably do with a nap more than anything – drinking in the day always did make me feel exhausted.'

'Yep, I'm pretty sleepy myself. Let's set the alarm for an hour – that'll give us enough time to get ready for dinner.' We snuggled up and dozed off.

Later, we went down for dinner looking like any other elegant couple in the restaurant. Still feeling a bit tipsy from earlier, we refrained from ordering wine with our meal. We had a nightcap in the bar before going up to bed; I was hoping round two wouldn't be as disappointing as round one.

As we lay in bed kissing, I asked him why he hadn't brought condoms.

'I didn't see the need for them,' he replied.

'What do you mean? Did you think we wouldn't end up having sex?'

'No, no, not that, but you told me you hadn't dated anyone since your husband, and I know I've no diseases, so I didn't think we'd need them.'

Bloody hell! Sure I hadn't dated anyone since my ex, but I'd shagged loads. How naïve of him to believe what someone claimed about their past sex life. Everyone knows that people lie regularly about the who, what and where of their past dalliances. It's not until you've had an up-to-date STD test and agree to be in a monogamous relationship with someone that the latex budget can be jettisoned. I explained to him that I was very particular about safe sex and would always use protection, unless the relationship was very serious. He was fine with this, and when we were both ready, we made love.

It was forgettable, sad to say. I was secretly hoping that he would be a dynamo in bed, and that, with his charming, kind personality and single status, we'd go on to have a great time together. He seemed happy enough with his performance, but for me, it was just downright boring. Fuck, fuck, fuck, why couldn't he have been great in bed? Still, I consoled myself that, with all my experience, I could teach him a few things and, with practice, we would be great.

The following morning, he wasn't interested in sex and wanted to get out walking. I beckoned him back to bed, saying we were in no rush and surely hotels meant a lie-in, but he didn't pick me up on it, or if he did, he declined to accept. I found it rather strange for a red-blooded male not to want the Sunday-morning hotel shag. Maybe he was a little embarrassed about yesterday. I decided that was it and put it out of my mind. We spent a lovely day together, stopping off for lunch on the way home. He texted me that night to say what a lovely time he had had with me and that he hoped we'd do it again soon.

He phoned the next night and we chatted away like everything was great. He invited me over to his place mid-week. The kids would be away on Thursday night; he knew their routine by now. I told him I'd go over late because I didn't want anyone to see my car parked at his house. Knowing the neighbours, my parents would hear about it before morning, and I didn't want the inquisition.

On Thursday I waved off the kids, then made a huge effort with my hair and makeup, before packing my nicest black silk negligee into an overnight bag. It was wasted on him: he wasn't in the mood for sex because he had work in the morning. We shared a short kiss in bed, which I thought would lead to love-making, but he turned over and said goodnight! I lay there in disbelief and frustration. *Fuck that!* Why had he bothered to ask me over? If this was the beginning of a relationship, we should have been at it like horny rabbits!

Well, no one could say I didn't try. I continued to see him over the next few months and, to be fair, we had some great nights out. We shared a love of live music and he booked tickets for some really good venues. He always paid and he treated me like a lady, but the sex never improved. He was happy to have it about once every week or ten days, which meant his libido was much lower than mine. Sometimes I'd hold back when I was with a client, saving my arousal if I was seeing him later on, but it didn't make any difference.

My work was easy to cover up: he knew I was officially unemployed, so I didn't have to lie. His job kept him very busy during the day because he travelled around the country. It flashed through my mind that maybe he was seeing escorts and using up his sexual energy with them, but I knew he was just too square to do anything so risqué. I would phone him in the morning and check what part of the country he was in, on the off chance that he might spot my car if we happened to be in the same town.

I hoped against hope that things would improve for us in the bedroom. He had so many qualities that I wanted in a long-term partner, and as it was me who was unhappy with our sex life, it would have to be me who tried to change it. The problem was, I really liked him and felt uncomfortable asking him to do anything a bit more adventurous. I cared what he thought of me. He told me once that he was taking it slowly out of consideration because I hadn't been with a man for a long time. I couldn't say anything to that, could I? I did make a few suggestions outside the bedroom, but they didn't happen once we were in bed together. Every time we had sex, I'd lie in bed after he came, frustrated as hell and dying to get home so I could finish what he'd started. We were just sexually incompatible, and eventually I got irritable and cranky with him. He thought I was a moody bitch. He was so well-mannered and polite, he thought dirty talk was offensive, regarded one-night stands as the actions of those with no self-esteem and he had never intentionally watched porn because it degraded the very essence of a woman. How could I have said to him, 'Well, actually I love dirty talk and I fuck guys for a living'?

After a while, I had to accept that our libidos were polar opposites, and no amount of trying was going to change that. It also takes two people to work at improving communication in the sack, but Blow-in just seemed to be on a different sexual planet from me. I'd probably have tried harder and put in more effort if I had felt very, very strongly about him and thought we had a chance at a future together, but I didn't. There was just too much work to be done with him if he was going to change in bed and, quite frankly, I wasn't interested in the challenge.

I can see now that he was so rigid in his way of thinking that he was never going to open his mind to the possibilities in letting go a bit.

During this time, my Czech mate's phone was hopping. After a night with Blow-in, I'd have to call him and see if he was free. Sometimes my Czech mate would get the train out to the end of the line, I'd drive up to meet him and we'd fuck in the car. I felt guilty about this because I cared about Blow-in, but being with him was like being constantly teased with no chance of fulfilment. It's odd that I could be so open in my work, yet when it came to my personal life, I was tripped up by the usual insecurities: what will he think of me? What if he goes off me when he realizes what I want? I, of all people, should have known that if you can't talk sex to your partner, he needs to become your ex. I knew that from my work, as well as from my marriage.

After four months of hobbling along, hoping we'd find the spark somewhere, I ended the relationship after spending a whole weekend with him *sans* sex. I think he was definitely a candidate for a little blue pill. Much as I liked him, there's far more to relationships than companionship. I might settle for that when I'm eighty, but not now.

24. Three in a Bed

I was in the car, on the way to pick up the kids from a play date, when my work phone rang. I pulled into a lay-by to answer it. The guy at the other end was on a hands-free set and said he was calling from his car on the way to work. We established that my fee was out of the question for him, so that seemed to be the end of that.

Even though there was no business to be done, we ended up chatting for a while. Owen told me he used online sex sites to find extra-marital fuck mates, who do it for free, but that he was easily bored and tended to swap around quite a bit. For some reason, he hadn't clicked with the last two women he'd arranged to have NSA (no strings attached) sex with, so he thought he'd give me a call and see what the deal was.

Of course, I had to stick my nose in and ask him what he was into and which sites he found the best. He'd had a regular fuck buddy for the past few years, in addition to the irregular ones he saw in between; he was married and his sex life with his wife was good. His regular F-mate was married and bisexual. They liked having a guest member to join them when it could be arranged, but what with work commitments, spouses to deceive and the hassle of finding a suitable guest, the *ménages à trois* weren't as frequent as he would have liked. He asked if I'd ever had any girl-on-girl action. No, I hadn't, either personally or professionally. He suggested that it was something I should get some experience in, as good guests were hard to come by and it would be a great selling point for my service.

I agreed to give it some thought; if it was a market niche, I was interested. I had no objection in theory to sex with women, but the difference between theory and practice can be too vast if you don't have the facts.

What did we ever do before online search engines? Later that day

I surfed various sites and discovered that threesomes, with the various combos, were almost normal for younger couples, those between their late teens and early thirties. It seemed the *ménage à trois*, or at least girl/girl action, was in vogue, thanks to its increasing incidence in TV programmes like *Glee* and *Gossip Girl*. This wasn't reflected in what clients had told me, but then my clients are generally within the forty-to-sixty age bracket. They regularly asked if I did threesomes as part of my work, and made it clear that if I arranged it, interest would be high, many wanting to experience a first. In areas where several women are working together, arranging a threesome is no problem. An escort just asks one of her friends in the business to join her with an interested client. For me, though, discretion and confidentiality are key. I don't know any other escorts and I would never approach or source a third woman to join a meeting. Too risky.

From my reading on the subject, it's obvious there is a lot of etiquette involved in it – imagine deciding to try it out only to realize that the other woman would have the starring role. That just wouldn't do, now, would it? Many Irish sexual adventurers travel to Berlin, the swinging capital of the world, to avoid the possibility of bumping into their neighbours, although several groups coordinate events in Ireland. Ironically, you're actually more likely to bump into someone you know in Berlin because they, too, will be avoiding the scene in Ireland, for fear of being recognized. There's a very well-organized club in the city that arranges parties for discerning and discreet ladies and gents. The focus is mainly on the ladies, some of whom may be bisexual or gay or just bi-curious. The event organizers do a nice hand-holding arrangement for newbies and first-timers, where everything is structured to allay first-time fears and make the experience as enjoyable as possible. There's no pressure to join in: if a couple or threesome leaves the bedroom door open, it means they're happy to have an audience. Sounds great if that blows your skirt.

I was considering pushing the boundaries of my sexual repertoire and giving it a go. At worst I could just observe and put it down to professional research. I decided to call the club later that night, when there was no chance of being interrupted.

Once the house was quiet, I rang the number listed on the website. A man answered and I told him I was interested in finding out more about his get-togethers. He wanted to know a little about me: age, physical description, and if I'd like to attend alone or with a partner. Once he'd sounded me out, he explained the usual arrangement, where it took place, the entrance fee – to cover canapés and drinks – and when the next get-together was scheduled. I asked him the policy on safe sex. Yes, condoms were essential: no glove, no love. I then asked what was safe for girl-on-girl sex and what the infection risks were for female oro-genital contact. He couldn't tell me: he'd never been asked that before. I wound up the conversation, saying I'd have a think about it and maybe get back to him. I thought he should have known more about infection risks and how to prevent them. As far as I was concerned, safety wasn't his number-one priority, and I wasn't impressed.

I set about investigating the infection risks for girl-on-girl sex. I was surprised by what I found out. It's absolutely second nature to practise safe sex with men, and the glossy magazines are full of articles on sexual health for straight women, but where is the information on safe sex between girls? It turns out that HIV transmission is quite rare between lesbians, but one British study found that 85 per cent of women who had sex with women also had unprotected sex with men. Lesbian sex is perceived to be relatively safe, but if almost nine out of ten of those women have had unsafe sex with men, that creates a whole other story. The usual array of STDs can be passed on by infected persons, but hepatitis and HIV are my main worries, and I discovered that some forms of hepatitis, such as B and C, can be passed from woman to woman.

Is there anything quite as off-putting as reading about genital health? That sort of research almost makes me want to cross my legs and hang a *Closed for Business* sign around my neck. Almost.

I investigated further and discovered that the female equivalent of a condom is a dental dam. It's basically a square of latex that you put over your mouth to prevent any contact with bodily fluids – in other words, when you stick out your tongue to bestow some oral pleasure on your girl, your tongue is encased in the latex. That sounded like an awfully poor invention to me and I could understand why they weren't used much – they sounded so impractical and awkward. You'd be trying to control your swallowing while deftly showing off your tongue acrobatics and supposedly enjoying the once-in-a-lifetime must-try experience of dining out on the same sex with the equivalent of a piece of clingfilm stuck over your mouth.

Next, I tried to find out how readily available dental dams were. Condoms, as we all know, are everywhere from pubs and restaurants to shopping centres, so why aren't the female equivalent so easily accessible? The clue is in the clingfilm: it's a simple matter of supply and demand. They're not readily available because there's no demand for them, which implies that a lot of ladies out there assume that girl/girl sex is safe without protection. It seemed like very dodgy territory to me – far from the level of control I like to have when it comes to my sexual health.

I called the guy at the club again to let him know I wouldn't be attending. I told him I wasn't ready for it yet because it was easier than saying I was concerned some of the practices were unsafe. That was his business and I didn't want to get into conversation about it. In fact, I didn't want to give him any reason to remember me other than as another enquiry.

I put the whole question of lesbian acrobatics out of my mind, but then, out of the blue, Owen called me again. He'd decided my fee was manageable after all, so would I be interested in joining him and his bisexual married female F-mate as a special guest? I could have charged more for a threesome, but four hundred euro is a hefty amount, so I didn't say anything about it. Okay, my research had pointed up some issues, but his proposal was worth thinking about. The organized events would possibly have the same circle frequenting the scene, so the chances of everyone being STD-free were compromised. But in Owen's case, his F-mate was married, her husband knew nothing of her kinkier side or extra-curricular interests and she always practised safe sex. He told me she was happy to use protection, was aware that it would be my first time and was very discreet. She was a respectable wife and mother living in a small town, so she wasn't going to take a chance on her secret getting out. Sounded worth exploring, I agreed, but I told him I needed to mull it over – first-time nerves, I laughed. He called me back about forty minutes later and suggested a nice hotel about two hours from my home, and a time: the following Wednesday at two p.m.

All right, I thought, let's do this. He'd said to call if I'd any questions.

I didn't do any research into positions in preparation for it because I figured the couple knew what they were at and would direct me if I needed it, but I was confident that I could just go with the flow and use my imagination.

Early the next morning I had a text from Owen, asking me to call him. I rang him, and when he answered, he sounded distinctly forlorn. His F-mate had wanted to know all about me but, of course, he didn't know anything, except what I'd told him over the phone. She'd wanted to know what I did for a living and, rather than making something up, he'd told her I was an escort. She'd blown a gasket, called him an asshole and demanded to know how he dared to degrade her by thinking she'd ever get jiggy with a slag. What was she thinking? Escorts were low-life, filthy trash, and she wouldn't go anywhere near one. She ended with a flourish: she never wanted to see him again and that was the end of their F-mate arrangement.

I was disappointed, I'll be honest. After a night of mulling it over, I had started looking forward to a new experience, but I also thought he must be an awful idiot not to have known how she would react to me being an escort. Of course she would think of me with the usual disdain, not realizing that I was the exception rather than the rule when it came to discretion and safe sex. Owen was absolutely raging that he had cocked up so badly and was trying to contact her to see if there was any way of salvaging their arrangement.

I put the phone down and sat there thinking about the woman I'd never met and nearly shagged. Apparently it was okay for her to live a lie with her husband and shag random men and women she met online, but it was not okay for me to have safe sex in a structured environment and get paid for it. Hypocritical bitch. I had to take a few deep breaths to calm down and try to purge from my mind the things she'd said about me. That was as far as my exploration of the fairer sex went: it ended before it had begun. I wasn't curious enough to pursue it. If I was propositioned by an attractive couple in my personal life, I think I'd give it a go, but it's not something I'd go out of my way to do. I also concluded that it wasn't a market niche after all. Yes, I got requests for it, but it was only provisional enquiry-type interest. For the time being, my clients were happy with one escort.

25. Sexual Healing

When I started having sex with men for money, I presumed that was exactly what it would be: full sex, and then some. If a man was parting with his hard-earned cash for the experience of having sex with me, I would expect him to want bang for his buck, if you know what I mean. What I didn't expect was the number of men for whom it wasn't really about sex, and penetration didn't occur.

As I met more and more clients, I was struck by how many were looking for a little TLC, some relaxing massage and pampering. They were easy enough to spot by their low voice and slumped shoulders, which seemed to be symptoms of long-term stress. When I knew that was what they were there for, I would select music to match, such as Enya. I saved the pumping/shagging club-type music for those who just wanted a good fuck.

About 20 per cent of my clients were happy just to turn over their minds and bodies to me for a couple of hours as a sort of therapy for stress. Of those, I'd say 90 per cent climaxed – whether by penetration, hand- or blow-job. But they all loved the slow build-up, starting with relaxation, music and massage as I gradually revealed my body, increasing the sensory input as the client chilled out. With this type of client, I felt like a pseudo sex therapist, giving a stressed-out man the opportunity to switch off from the outside pressures and tune into himself and his body. I enjoyed those experiences. They made me feel like I had a bond with the man, and it was good to help people who were bowed down by life's demands. I was like that, too, so in helping them I also helped myself.

One such guy, who really made an impression on me, was Peter. He was very much in love with his wife, but there was an obstacle to their sexual relationship. From what I gleaned in our initial phone calls and texts, his wife was beautiful, had a successful career and he respected her as his wife and life partner. However, because he respected her, he felt he could only 'make love' to her, but often he just wanted to fuck her without the kid gloves on. That was where I came into the picture.

I asked him to tell me in detail what he felt about his sex life and how he wanted to change it. That would give me an idea as to the best approach to take with him. He told me that he craved hot, hard fucking, but couldn't do this with his wife. Because he loved her, he had tried to put this need for raw sex to the back of his mind, had buried himself in his career and hoped that maybe his testosterone levels would settle down a bit and he wouldn't be so distracted by his desire to have very different sex from the sex he was currently experiencing. He was only in his early thirties, and it was clear he had reservations about seeing an escort and was worried about the potential risks. He was also burdened by guilt about betraying his wife, but found himself constantly fantasizing about straightforward, selfish sex, where he didn't have to consider her satisfaction and pleasure.

As he talked, I had reservations myself because I had zero interest in clients who felt bad about what they were doing with me. That was their own shit to sort out in their own time. If I had the impression a guy was feeling sheepish during the initial contact by phone, I always probed further to ensure that, if we did meet, I wasn't left with some needy, insecure man who wanted reassurance that what he was doing was okay. No, thank you. But I felt that Peter wasn't the needy sort, so I kept talking to him, with a view to securing a booking.

I told Peter that I understood his situation because I had once been that wife, on the receiving end of 'wifey' sex. Had he ever considered the female perspective? Had it ever occurred to him that his wife might be bored to tears in the sack, too, and want exactly what he wanted – a plain old decent fuck? He explained that while he hadn't ever discussed it with her openly, she seemed reasonably happy with their sex life.

I was flummoxed. 'But how can you know that if you haven't

spoken honestly about it? Let's face it, your wife hasn't a clue what you want in bed or you wouldn't be considering paying for it, so you can't possibly know what she's thinking either.'

He was quiet for a moment. 'Well, I suppose that's a fair point, but it's been like this for so long that I wouldn't even know where to begin the conversation.'

I tried to explore this further. After discussing it for a while, he admitted that he did see his wife as a sexual being and could appreciate that she might be bored with the sex they were having, but he didn't encourage her to talk about it. In the early years of their relationship, there had been no need to discuss how satisfied they were in bed because they were so close emotionally that gentle lovemaking seemed suitable, appropriate even. As their relationship progressed, however, it seemed they had got stuck with this type of sex and with not checking if the other was satisfied. It sounded like they had established a sexual pattern that had worked well for a time, but now needed to be reviewed, revised, revamped and revved up.

Peter had never discussed his sex life so openly and thoroughly before, he told me, but it had made him realize that he needed some pointers on how to start off the conversation with his wife and find out how she felt. He also knew he needed a bit of mentoring in the fine art of sex: he wanted to know more about how to experiment with his wife and to expand his own imagination. We agreed to meet on the basis that we would have straightforward good sex, but that I would critique him and demonstrate techniques he could try out with his wife. I also agreed to demonstrate how I used my sex toys, so that he could observe the way a woman likes to masturbate. Through this, he would get a better understanding of the pace and pressure some women preferred, and I would talk him through the physiology of what was happening. This approach was probably Peter's way of justifying to himself why he was seeing me. It wasn't extramarital sex, it was an investment in his marriage and his wife's happiness.

We arranged to meet at a hotel at two o'clock the following Tuesday. He lived about three hours away from my town, but was

paranoid about security and privacy. He needed an absolute guarantee that our meeting would never be revealed to anyone who might
know him or his wife. I assured him that, as a mother and respectable woman, I was in exactly the same boat and that discretion was
part of my service. He seemed content with this. In view of the
considerable distance he would have to travel to meet me, he opted
to block-book me for an afternoon and an evening. That was great
for me: it meant a fee of seven hundred euro and it was easier to
spend several hours with one client than with a few consecutively.

Finally, I asked if he had any preferences about how I dressed. He
requested a schoolgirl-type uniform, but I wasn't comfortable with
that. Instead, I offered a compromise that I said I would keep secret
until we met. I could tell he enjoyed the anticipation this created. I
knew I could pull out one of my female fantasy books, memorize
one of the fantasies, substitute the character in the story for a
schoolgirl and ad lib as needed. I love dirty talk and when I know a
guy is loving it, too, I find it really arousing. It would get us both in
the mood, I reckoned. It was such a huge turn-on to listen to a man
confiding his secret fantasies and then to play them out for him. If I
wasn't comfortable acting out a particular role, I'd add it into an
erotic story to tell him while I was caressing him or I'd ask him to
talk me through his fantasy. If time was ticking by and I was becoming aware that he needed to get a move on, it was also a very handy
way of getting him to orgasm. Dirty talk is an arousing and reliable
time-management tool, if ever there was one – but you have to love
it!

The day before my meeting with Peter, I reviewed my books and
planned what we would do and how I would share my knowledge
in a way that he could apply at home. I had built up a pretty good
library by this stage, from erotica and fantasies to books on technique and overcoming various problems. These products are a
godsend: they're well written, packaged and presented in such a
way that they don't look out of place on a bedside locker. I checked
that my hotel bag had adequate supplies of everything I would
need, then selected an array of sex toys to bring along to give him

an idea of what was available and show him which toys stimulated which areas best. I also brought a selection of male sex toys to use on him, so that he could experience the different sensations.

On the day of the meeting, I arranged a sitter for the children; I could well afford it with what my take-home pay for the day would be. I drove an hour and a half to the hotel, collected my room key from Reception and went upstairs. I arranged the toys in the bed-side locker – I didn't want him to see them until the appropriate time – put my watch and phone on it, placed the books on the floor next to the bed and put some acoustic music with a strong beat on the music system. I wore my red silk, floor-length negligee and its kimono-style matching robe. By the time I heard his knock on the door, the candles were flickering and the whole scene looked inviting and seductive. A quick flick of the hair and lick of the lips, and I was ready.

I opened the door and was greeted by a friendly young man. It took us a few minutes to acclimatize to how we looked physically – he was very attractive, and complimented me on my appearance. He loved the outfit! We chatted for a little while, then he took out his wallet and started to count out the fee we'd agreed. I was delighted to be getting such a wad of dosh for what promised to be a good old session. Peter then asked for a shower after his long drive. Afterwards he walked out of the bathroom naked, drying himself. He had a good body, about five ten, with dark hair and green eyes. I could tell even from his flaccid penis that it was going to be at least seven inches when erect – yep, he was well endowed, lucky wife! I checked with him that we were still in agreement as to what should take place.

'Yes, sure, I'm still happy with all of that, but there's one thing I don't think I mentioned on the phone.'

Uh-oh. 'And what's that?' I asked.

'Well, you know how it is, I've been thinking about this so much and talking with you and I just don't know how long I'll last before I come.'

'That's no problem,' I said, relieved. 'If you prefer, I'll get you to come quickly the first time and then you'll be more relaxed to enjoy the rest.'

'That sounds perfect,' he said gratefully. 'I'm sorry about this, but I don't tend to last too long anyway and I'm especially horny.'

We moved on to the bed and I asked him to lie on his back so I could give him a quick hand-job. Then we'd get on to our sex lesson. I sat between his legs and got some lube warmed up in my hands; his cock was already fully hard. I started to stroke him gently, allowing him to get used to my touch and the sensation of the lubricant. He mumbled something I couldn't understand, then totally without warning his body clenched and he shot his load. What the fuck? I hadn't even had my hand fully around his shaft; I had barely touched him. He began apologizing profusely and appeared very embarrassed. I was quite taken aback and a bit lost for words, but I composed myself to appear calm and assertive and reassured him that it was okay. Clearly, Peter had a far bigger problem to overcome than what we had talked about on the phone. Far from needing to be able to fuck his wife, experiment with toys, broaden his sexual horizons and have an honest sexual discussion with her, he had to work on a bad case of premature ejaculation. Why had he failed to mention it to me? Had he hoped it wouldn't happen? Or was he incredibly self-conscious and embarrassed about it?

After a few awkward minutes he was cleaned up and lying on the bed beside me. 'Peter, how long do you last inside your wife before you come?'

'It varies, I guess, but not very long.'

'Well, would you like to last longer or do you feel your dick's the one in control?'

'God, yes, I'd like to last a lot longer, but it's been happening like this for a while now. I was kind of hoping it would sort itself out, but it doesn't seem to be.'

'How long is a while? A few months? A year?' I probed.

'I suppose it's about two years now, if I'm honest with myself.'

'Do you think you have premature ejaculation?'

'I was hoping I didn't, but I don't think there's any denying it now, is there?'

'Well, it's very, very common, far more so than you'd imagine, but you blokes don't talk about important stuff, do you, so I guess you think you're the only one in the universe with this problem.' I could tell he was relaxing a bit now that it was out in the open and we were speaking frankly. I explained to him that there was plenty he could do to address the situation and that it was in no way a life sentence.

We started to talk about how the problem might have developed for him: he reckoned it could have been a result of him not wanting to disappoint his wife in bed. This was, of course, the elephant in the bedroom for them. The more he suffered from PE, the more frustrated he felt with himself and the more pressure he felt to be able to make love to her without the stress of shooting off early. He had thought that if only he could fuck his wife, instead of having to go through the ritual of making love, his problem would be solved. He had blamed the pressure of having to make love for the PE. As a result, he felt huge anxiety at the mere idea of making love, and the only notion he could deal with was shagging.

Well, I was glad we were talking about it because he clearly wanted to get the problem solved. I ventured to ask him how much he had discussed all this with his wife.

They had never had a heart-to-heart about it. Each time he ejaculated too quickly, he would apologize and she would say it was okay and then they would lie there, in silence, separate in their own thoughts, without reaching out to one another either physically or emotionally. How lonely for both of them, I thought, but particularly for him.

'Permission to speak frankly?' I asked.

'Yes, please do.'

'You contacted me because you could only see your wife in a certain way and were only able to make love to her when, really, you wanted to be able to just fuck her or have any type of sex that didn't idolize her and that you both enjoyed, yes?'

A nod.

'But the reality is that you can only do the boring wifey sex because anything even marginally more adventurous increases your premature ejaculation.'

Another nod.

'But even with the same old boring sex, you still can't last long and it ends up as a bit of a disaster, with you barely managing to stay inside her for any length of time. It's a huge disappointment for you both and it's getting worse, so you called me.'

'Yep, I'd agree with all that,' he said quietly. 'I think I tried to pro-long the foreplay in an attempt to sustain my erection and delay ejaculation, and I've probably convinced myself that I can't see my wife as a sexual being and that I can only make love to her in a certain way.'

'But, actually, we can now see that the problem is you have pre-mature ejaculation and are in denial about it and haven't spoken to your wife, although clearly she knows you have it and is also avoid-ing talking about it.'

'Yes, yes, you're right. But why the hell can I talk quite openly and bluntly about it to you, a total stranger, and not to my wife, the woman I love and want to be with?'

'Well, I'd say that it's because you don't care what I think. You're not out to impress me or satisfy me in any way, plus you know that I'm really into sex and all its connotations and issues, and that I've probably come across this loads of times before and know of things that can help.'

He smiled at me. 'That's all true, but do you know of ways to help that don't involve going to my GP? I've thought of going to him, but am just too mortified.'

At this stage we were lying back on the bed, relaxed and comfort-able, with my legs resting over his. There was nothing sexual in our position, just comfort from the skin contact. I knew if Peter was ever going to open up, it was now. I asked him a few questions about his attitude to sex, his upbringing, any negative sexual experiences, and his relationship with his wife outside the bedroom. There was nothing untoward in his background or his attitude to sex, but he and his wife were certainly not as close as they used to be. They were so busy working and pursuing active social lives that he felt they were going through the motions and not having real conversations like they used to.

On reflection, he could see that they definitely didn't share those little stolen tender moments they had once enjoyed. Their phone chats were about practicalities and texts were to the point: *Can u get milk on ur way hme, ta*. Somehow, the romance had drifted way off course and he admitted that neither of them was doing anything to stop it drifting further. We chatted about how our activities in the bedroom are only as good as the relationship outside the bedroom, and that if he wanted clear, open and honest talking in bed, he had to have it outside bed as well. If something isn't being talked about, you're both relying on guesswork, and that can create a gaping abyss of misinterpretation and misunderstanding.

I told Peter all I knew about PE: that it affects up to 30 per cent of men at any given time, that it's the most common sexual dysfunction in males but also the most untreated, and that only one per cent of men seek treatment, for a variety of reasons that include shame, embarrassment, and the mistaken view that it's untreatable. In fact, it's very treatable and by various approaches, including occasional medication, topical medication (applied to the penis), psychotherapy, specific exercises and, interestingly, varying where, when and how sex takes place. It seems repeated sexual scenarios are more likely to increase PE, so Peter continually making love to his wife in the same way wasn't helping matters. Solving the PE problem would be relatively simple, so long as he spoke to his wife honestly and had her co-operation. There were also some things he could do that would make a big difference, particularly Kegel exercises.

It's a common misconception that Kegels, or pelvic-floor exercises, are only for post-natal women to prevent incontinence down the line. In fact, they are just as important for men: the more you practise and strengthen the pelvic floor, the more control you have in that area, which is where it all happens during sex. Kegels can assist with all sexual health problems in both men and women, can increase sensitivity and can help to produce more intense orgasms. The old test that a man should be able to hang a towel off his erect cock isn't too far off: if he has a strong pelvic floor, any man will easily be able to do this. Kegels also engage the core muscle group, which most people are familiar with from Pilates, callisthenics and yoga. It wraps around your lower back and abdomen, protecting the lower back from injury, giving a flatter stomach and adding stability to every movement of the body. The benefits of Kegels cannot be underestimated and if you commit to doing the simple exercises daily, your bits will thank you for it – as will your partner.

I explained all this to Peter and showed him how to locate his pubococcygeus muscle, so he knew he was exercising the right area. Once he had grasped the importance of pelvic-floor exercising and had the technique right, I demonstrated the start/stop squeeze technique that is commonly used to prevent early ejaculation. This involved Peter being more aware of his body and what was happening with his cock way before it wanted to ejaculate. To illustrate this, I started to massage his cock with one hand and asked him to talk me through what he was feeling, but forbade him to climax and warned him to tell me if he felt he was getting anywhere near that point. Initially, he was not comfortable talking about what he was feeling in his body as I stimulated him – in fact, he didn't have the words to describe it. I prompted him along, to get him to tune in a bit to his cock and also to get him comfortable with chatting during a sexual act.

He started by saying that it felt okay, good even, that he was quite relaxed and comfortable with what I was doing. I changed the position of my hand and massaged his balls and the tops of his thighs. He liked this, but it was a new sensation for him – he didn't do it when he was masturbating and neither did his wife when she was giving him the occasional hand-job. I asked him to describe how the lubricant felt, then added some balm that gave a hot, tingling sensation. All the while my touch was gentle and not intended to bring him even near to the point of climax. I moved my hand to the shaft of his penis and did a couple of gentle strokes. I asked him to tell me if he felt like climaxing. He said he wouldn't last much longer if I continued the strokes, so I pulled back his foreskin and moved my thumb and forefinger tightly to the base of his cock and held it firmly there. The idea behind this move is that it halts the increasing blood flow that occurs when orgasm is imminent, while at the same time stopping the arousal. I explained to Peter that it was really important to use this technique well before orgasm was on the way, or he would steam past the point of no return.

As with everything, practice makes perfect, so I asked Peter to take over and let me watch him masturbate, using the squeeze technique. He started a little too enthusiastically and had to squeeze within seconds, but he got the hang of it. I then suggested he switched sensations, moved his hand in a different direction or altered his body position so that less of his cock was available for stimulation. He moved on to his side, with his legs slightly bent up towards his tummy, and continued stroking himself. All the while, there was no kissing between us and he hadn't yet touched me: I was still wearing the red ensemble I'd had on when we had first got on to the bed. This was one of those meetings that was turning out to be something very different from what I'd expected.

We continued with this stop/start/squeeze/alter sensation/change position set-up for some time. I wanted to prove to Peter that, with the right knowledge, he could help himself overcome his problem. He had managed to pull himself back from the brink of climax a few times now and I felt it was a good time for him to come as he was probably getting tired. Also, there was something else I wanted to show him that might help. I told him he was now going to allow himself to embrace the sensation of imminent climax and not hold back, that he was in control and was going to enjoy it, but I told him to try and prolong it by not going hell-for-leather straight off. I wanted him to see how long he could last with a bit of advice and practical tips.

He lasted about twenty seconds before squirting his thick cum on to his abdomen. I let him lie there, enjoying the aftershocks, then got some tissues and cleaned it up.

I handed him a glass of water and we stayed there silently for a while, until he was recovered and could talk coherently again. 'Right, so this is totally nothing like I expected,' he said, looking at me calmly.

'Me either, but it turns out this is what's needed, don't you agree?'

'Jesus, for sure. I really didn't think driving here today that only a few hours into it I'd've actually learned a few ways to help my problem. What we just did is probably the longest I've lasted touching myself without coming until I wanted to in years – that's a bloody good day's work! Is this what sex therapists would do?'

'Em, no, I don't think so.' I laughed. 'Definitely there would be no touching with a sex therapist. I think they talk about your problems and give you exercises to do at home, but I've never heard of one actually demonstrating the exercises. See, I'm unique!'

He grinned. 'But how did you learn all this stuff?'

'Well, I love reading, always have, and for me bodies are just bodies, it's what's inside that matters, and sex is such a basic need we all have. It's a shame to see people suffering in the bedroom when really the answer to any sexual problem is out there if you want to find it. Loads of couples suffer in silence with PE when it doesn't have to be that way at all. Speaking of which, I want to talk about how you're going to approach your wife about your plan to sort out your PE. Would you like to grab a shower while I make us a cuppa?'

As we sipped our tea, I suggested to Peter that, when he got home, he logged on to the Internet and ordered the most recommended self-help book on PE. When it arrived, he should sit his wife down and tell her that he'd got this book because it would help resolve the issues he'd been having. I advised him to ask his wife to read it with him, tell her how much he loved her and how much he hated letting her down in bed, and that he needed her help to sort it out – he had let it go on too long because he was embarrassed, but he really wanted them to be enjoying a great sex life together. I couldn't imagine any partner not responding positively to this. Only Peter knew the best setting in which to deliver this information but I suggested he didn't broach the subject in bed: it was preferable to start seeing the bedroom as a space for rest and sex – good sex – not associate it with lengthy chats about their sexual difficulties. I also suggested that he could practise what he was going to say to her – it would help him to gather his thoughts and get him used to hearing himself using the language he had avoided for so long.

Peter seemed satisfied with this and agreed that it wasn't as daunting as it had seemed only a few hours earlier. We'd spent almost four hours together by this stage and it was time for him to leave. As he got dressed, I asked him if he was still okay with what I had charged him. I was pleasantly surprised, given that we hadn't followed our original plan, when he said that he had had no problem with it because he had had value for money. That was a relief: I didn't fancy handing it back! He asked if it would be all right to call me if he had any questions or wanted to book me again for more practical help. I told him I'd be delighted to see him again, but that I hoped I wouldn't as that would mean he and his wife had sorted everything out. He gave me a peck on the cheek and off he went.

I shut the door behind him and sank on to the bed, marvelling at how my job could still surprise me. I wasn't in too much of a rush home because the children had a sitter with them so I decided to run a hot bath. As I relaxed into the bubbly water, I felt exhausted – I had used far more mental than physical energy, and it was more tiring than just having sex.

As I lay in the bath, I thought about how many couples must be affected by PE and how shit it must be if your man refuses to get help out of shame or embarrassment. It's something I've heard of among my own friends. I know one girl whose husband developed a problem with PE after their first child was born. She reckoned it started because, with a young baby who woke frequently at night, they'd ended up rushing sex in order to climax before the baby inter-rupted them. It got to the stage when he didn't even make it to penetration – he would come almost the instant he became erect. She had begged him to go to his GP or to a sex therapist, but he had refused point-blank to do anything about it. He insisted that it would resolve itself in time and that she was making a fuss over nothing. That was eight years ago and it still hasn't been resolved. How ridiculous and wasteful is that?

If I had a boyfriend with PE, would I want him to do what Peter had just done and discuss it with an escort? No. I wouldn't want a partner who visited sex workers: I would rather resolve bedroom issues with someone I loved through open, supportive communication and compromise. The majority of sexual problems boil down to lack of communication. I had met them all in the course of my work: the guys who wouldn't talk with their partner about what they wanted in bed for fear of being judged and rejected; the men who did pluck up the courage to talk to their partners openly but the partner ignored the conversation and did nothing to address the situation; the men who blamed it on something else entirely – like love-making – and buried their heads in the sand about the real causes; and the men who forwent a sex life with their wives rather than disappoint them.

I've met quite a lot of men who did raise the issue with their wives, only to have their request for co-operation ignored. Some told me they believed their wives subsequently turned a blind eye to their nights out, and that there was an unspoken agreement that the man could play away. Whenever I heard this, I always found it incredible: that wouldn't be my style at all. But I began to notice a common thread in the stories: each of the men mentioned that their wives seemed happy with their lot – kids, nice house, car and the various materialistic trappings of modern society – and didn't seem to mind the lack of a fulfilling sexual relationship. It was easy for those men to take lovers or visit escorts because their wives didn't ask awkward questions. Bloody money, I thought, it rots everything.

I'd love to think I helped Peter, that he went home and sorted it out with his wife: life without a healthy expression of sexuality seems so empty and soul-destroying. It's sad but true that some people's sexual self rarely gets an airing. Peter was a genuinely nice man and wanted to be in a loving, stable relationship with his wife, so I hope that's how things have turned out for him. He never called me again, which I take as a good omen!

26. An Unpleasant Encounter

The appointment with Peter was so unexpected and went so well that I felt good about my work and myself afterwards. I should have remembered that pride comes before a fall, because just three days later I had a client from the other end of the spectrum. Any sense of contentment with my work evaporated afterwards, and I was left feeling guilty and a bit seedy.

It was a working Saturday for me: the children were with their father for the weekend, so I had a client and a hotel booked for three p.m. He was new, so I'd be pocketing four hundred euro for my ninety minutes' work. It was badly needed because I had some bills due to be paid the following week. By two o'clock I was preened and ready for the meeting. I was just dropping my work phone into my bag when it started ringing. It was the new client, and he couldn't make it. Something had come up, unforeseen, so sorry, blah blah blah. He'd call back next week to arrange a new appointment. I was as nice as pie to him on the phone, of course, but when I hung up I let out a string of curses. Damn! Damn! Damn! I'd really needed that bit of work and now I was dressed up with nothing to do. On top of that, I'd turned down a get-together with some old school-friends because I had to see a client and get those bills paid. I was fed up.

Not one to be deterred so easily, I logged on to my computer and went scouting for a last-minute client. Saturday afternoon is the best time of the week for meeting guys online and a shag can be arranged within minutes. There are so many sites to choose from that it can get a bit confusing remembering usernames, passwords and exactly what details I was sticking to; I didn't want inadvertently to give away any more information than was strictly necessary. I'd narrowed it down to two sites that supplied my type of man: bored, horny and with a bit of cash to spare on treating themselves to a girl. It had proven handy on those occasions when I'd had a late cancellation and needed a replacement in a hurry.

After about ten minutes online I hooked up with a local guy who could see me within the hour. All I really needed to know was that he was married or attached, understood safe sex, had no problem with my fee and didn't want anything too outrageous. Quinn seemed all right, but then he started asking me stupid questions via MSN instant messenger: what did I look like and would I text him some pictures of my pussy? If he was a seasoned client he would never have asked for pictures – he either wanted an appointment or he didn't. He was irritating the hell out of me but, unfortunately, he'd got me by the short and curlies because I needed a client. Rather than tell him to fuck off, which was what I normally did, I agreed to text him one picture.

My pussy pic obviously passed muster because he agreed to a meeting, but said he'd only got thirty minutes to spare so he wanted a discount. With much effing and blinding at my computer screen, I said I'd do thirty minutes for 150 euro. He agreed. Good – I was ready to go and 150 was better than nothing. My work phone rang. One final thing: Quinn couldn't make it to the hotel and needed me to come to his workplace instead.

'Don't be so fucking stupid, that's way too risky,' I snapped, my patience really wearing thin now.

'But I can't get out of the office. I'm the only one here,' he pleaded.

'Well, where do you work? Is there a bed there or somewhere suitable?' This was a nightmare – he sounded like a complete asshole.

'I'm in a car-sales garage,' he said.

'Ah, please, you must be joking. What are you saying, that you'll close up shop while I do you in the office?'

'There'll be no need to shut up shop. I haven't had one customer in all day,' he said.

'So you've been on sex sites out of boredom, is that it?'

'Yep, you have it in one, and I'm bursting with frustration!'

'Fuck it, I'll do it. I'll be in to you in about twenty minutes,' I said, feeling a little rush of adrenalin. I had been thinking about my planned meeting with the client who'd cancelled and thinking about sex had made me horny – that was all it took sometimes. And any money was better than what I'd earn sitting at home all dolled up and no place to go. In hindsight, it was an impulsive decision made on my state of arousal and the need for money. I can see now that I was starting to get a bit complacent. Also, living, breathing and doing paid sex for nine months was making me forget that this was still a completely unacceptable way to earn a crust and that complacency could be a slippery slope to ruin.

I hung up and threw my phone into my bag. Damn, I'd forgotten about the bloody hotel for the original client. Should I cancel it or hope that I got another client that evening? I rang the hotel and cancelled the room, whereupon they informed me that fifty euro would be taken from my credit card for the inconvenience. That was one-third of the money I was about to make already spent. I was getting angrier by the minute; I couldn't afford 'inconveniences'. The guy I was about to see was seriously pissing me off now.

In a moment of inspiration, I decided to do a 'come and run'. Clients had told me of girls making them come as quickly as possible just to get them out of the door. I'd always thought this was really mean, but I was now about to use the tactic myself. I stripped off my underwear and flung it on the couch. I was still logged into the sex site, so I logged off quickly and shut down the computer – it wouldn't do to have a break-in and a thief getting his hands on my business details. I was wearing a tight V-necked T-shirt and jeans. Thank God for Lycra – my boobs still had enough support without my bra. I put on my raincoat and was out of the door by three thirty.

I knew the business park on the outskirts of town where Quinn worked, but got a little lost in the maze of shop fronts. It was 4:02 on the clock when I pulled up outside his showroom. I took one condom out of my bag and put it into my coat pocket, then checked the clock on the dashboard again: 4:03. I was going to time myself.

I walked confidently past the shiny new cars and through the main reception area, where I spotted a door with a 'Staff only' sign in black lettering. I went straight in and found him at his desk, eyes glued to the computer. I locked the door behind me.

'Hi there, cash please,' I said, in a fake friendly voice.

He got the cash out of the desk drawer and handed it to me. I put it in the back pocket of my jeans. He'd already told me he was frustrated, and if he'd been on sex sites all day, he wouldn't last long. Taking the condom from my pocket, I put it on the pile of newspapers on the floor beside his desk, then threw my coat beside it. I walked up to him as he ogled my breasts through my T-shirt. He was sitting in a reclining swivel office chair. I took his hand, pushed it under my top and placed it on my breast. With my other hand I felt Quinn's cock through his pants. He was hard within seconds. Everything was going to plan.

'Lie back,' I ordered.

He rested his head back and the chair moved with him. He lifted his butt further out of the seat, to free his cock. I took it out and massaged it. He was huge, I'd give him that, but otherwise it was hard to find anything physically attractive about him. He tried to kiss me, but I pulled away, saying, 'I don't kiss clients.' He didn't push it.

I stood back, took off my jeans and, with one leg between his, raised the other on to his desk so my pussy was right in front of his face. Whipping the condom out of its wrapper, I had it on him before he had a chance to say anything. I knelt on the cold lino with my ass to him and ordered him to fuck me. He still had his trousers on, so he pulled them down a bit and knelt behind me. I wasn't wet and I'd no lube with me so it was a tight fit, but that was all the better to get him there quickly. He did a couple of short pumps, then gasped as he came. I grinned to myself: it was over. *Touché*.

He pulled out of me. I didn't look round, just stood up and quickly pulled on my jeans and jacket. He was sitting in the chair with the condom still on his cock, looking like he'd been struck on the head.

'Thanks for the booking,' I said dismissively. I strode across the room, unlocked the door and walked out.

As I put the key in the ignition, I looked at the clock: 4:09. Seven minutes from start to finish. Fuck him, he annoyed me and bollox to a man who thinks your pussy has to be viewed before he confirms a visit. He wasn't browsing a Laura Ashley catalogue choosing wall-paper, he was getting laid at work by a hooker while his missus was at home with his offspring. He might think twice before he started bartering down a working girl's fee again. I couldn't help smiling with satisfaction, though: that little tryst had ended up costing him 21.42 euro per minute.

I felt vindicated until the next day, when I started to feel guilty. I had treated him badly and I didn't like myself for it. It wasn't his fault that my original client had cancelled, but I had taken out my anger and frustration on him. Sure, I hoped he would treat escorts better in future, but still, he was a paying client and he deserved my respect. I vowed never to do another 'come and run'. I haven't.

27. The Men Who Pay for Sex

Prior to working in the sex industry, I had certain ideas about what it would be like and what kind of men would seek out and pay a girl for sex. Those notions had imploded over the first ten months I'd been working – virtually everything I'd thought had been incorrect. This had been the most fascinating aspect of my work – to be able to find out the truth behind the sensationalist headlines. Of course, I had plotted my path voluntarily into the sex industry to suit myself, so I wasn't typical. The number of women who join the oldest profession involuntarily – either as a result of drug addiction or people trafficking – must be very high. At least, that's what the media tell us. I have huge sympathy for these women because it must be a hellish existence for them. I have been lucky enough to be able to plan it carefully and control it well, so I haven't had the bad experiences we sometimes hear about. I've met a wide variety of very nice men who were normal and ordinary and told me typical stories of what went on in their relationships that they had been unable to discuss openly with their partners.

So who are those men? Do you know any of them? The answer, most definitely, is yes. My clients have come from almost every stratum in society, from labourers to university professors. They have all been either married or attached, and not all are unhappy. They are husbands, fathers, sons, brothers and brothers-in-law. As selling sex is illegal in Ireland, there are no figures to tell us the percentage of Irish men who have availed themselves of or who do avail themselves of escorts, but from my own experience and research I'd reckon it to be high. In countries where it is legal, such as New Zealand, statistics show that on average 70 per cent of men have used or would use an escort; it's probably safe to say that that figure is true of Ireland, too. Women might balk at the idea, but men are using escort services, out of desire or necessity, every day of the week.

At first, to me, my clients were just 'men', but as time went on I started to see patterns and began to slot each one into a personal category. It was often an amusing way to pass the time when I was with a boring, bog-standard client. I'd think about his 'type' and give him a category. The most populated category was 'Unhappily Married', often a direct side-effect of the recession. In this case, the couple got married in the boom or before, had a great time when money was reliable and were knocked for six by the crash, which had wiped out everything they'd thought they had. Even if they hadn't committed to dodgy investments, this couple were saddled with an enormous mortgage and their nice life had disappeared, replaced by stress and money worries. This had led to unhappiness, arguments and, in the end, they had forgotten why they ever fell in love in the first place and felt they'd make a much better job of things without the dead-weight of their spouse to pull them down.

I heard this scenario, with a few tweaks and variations, over and over again. It made me so sad because I couldn't help wondering whether they could have made it if they hadn't been ridden over roughshod by events beyond their control. Those men were either afraid to confront things with their partner, so lived a half-life with her and found solace with me, or else they had confronted things and decided they couldn't afford to separate, so agreed to live together and allow discreet extramarital sex.

The latter approach may sound crazy, but it's a product of another problem: divorce, Irish-style. Unlike other countries, divorce in Ireland is a very long-drawn-out affair. A couple can only apply for a divorce when they've been separated for four out of the previous five years. If it's an amicable split, you might have it all done and dusted within a few years after that, but if it's not, you can be going through the courts for anything up to ten years. That has been exacerbated by the country's economic doldrums: negative equity can mean couples are trapped under the same roof, unable to sell up and move on. I hadn't thought it all out like that before I set up in business, but I had inadvertently tapped into a huge group in society who were unhappy and badly in need of an outlet for all that stress and frustrated desire. Several of my clients visited me for some relaxation. Sex with an 'Unhappily Married' was usually hardly worth the effort.

One of my clients, Ray, was typical in this regard. He was based in Donegal, but travelled regularly in his job. Whenever he stayed over in my area, I visited him at his hotel. Ray and his wife had admitted to each other that they had no marriage and behaved more like a brother and sister together. They had one child, whom they both adored, and neither was prepared to leave their home and miss out on any part of their child's life. As a result, they had come to an arrangement that both of them were free to see people for the purposes of sex only. Relationships were not allowed as this might jeopardize their arrangement. For example, if a third party fell in love, not knowing that Ray and his wife wouldn't leave the family home, this might be a recipe for disaster.

While Ray admitted that their arrangement was very far from perfect, it was better than never having sex at all. He started by engaging in one-night stands, but that soon lost its appeal as the sex became superficial. He really wanted a connection with someone, and that was why he contacted me. He wanted to have regular sex with the same person, but with the security that I wouldn't get emotionally involved with him. I gave him that guarantee and we embarked on regular meetings that were satisfying for both of us. This type of client was really looking for a relationship. He wasn't a sleazebag who wanted to fuck any woman he could, he was a hurt and lonely person who would like to sort out his home life and commit to a new, happy relationship. Again, I saw this quite a bit.

The second category I encountered frequently were the 'Fearful Catholics'. Unfortunately, the legacy of Holy Catholic Ireland is very much alive and well. These men were brought up in a violently repressed environment, which made them believe their libido, desires and fantasies were shamefully wrong and sinful. The lucky among them seek out a woman who will treat them as a sexual being and accept them as they are, without judgement. As they are cautious of their own sexuality, and often of intimacy with women, they find it easier to engage an escort and pay for what they want. Sex with these men is usually downright dirty as they unburden years of fantasy in a short time.

A category related to this was 'Students' – men who came to me looking for tuition in sex because they had zero confidence in that area. Stephen is a good example. He contacted me saying that a friend of his had given him my number. 'Have I seen your friend?' I asked. I didn't mind occasionally if my number was passed on, but the client must have my permission before doing so.

'I don't think you have, but my mate knows my personal situation. We were out for a few beers last night and he said he had found the number of a lady who may be able to help me.'

I was wondering if he knew I was an escort and therefore charged. Maybe he thought his friend had passed on the number of someone who was interested in NSA. 'You are aware of what type of service this is?' I said.

'Well, I've a fair idea, but I'd like you to explain what you do and how it all works. I haven't done this before.'

I started to go through the basics, but he didn't seem too enthusiastic. 'Maybe you can tell me about your own situation and why you called me,' I suggested.

Stephen explained that he was fifty years old and single, had never been married and had had very limited sexual experience. He didn't fit my criteria but I agreed to see him after he told me his circumstances. He had a successful career in security and was well-mannered and genuine. I couldn't figure out why he'd had such restricted experience with women. He explained that he had a medical condition that had afflicted him from the age of fifteen and required multiple trips to the toilet when not controlled properly. Back then, there was less help available, so from fifteen to his early twenties he was very isolated and missed out on a lot of formative stuff, including dating. He'd had the problem under control for a number of years now, but hadn't been able to overcome his initial shyness and self-consciousness. He would have loved to get married and have children, but it hadn't happened. He was due for early retirement soon and wasn't relishing the thought of the years ahead on his own. He had mentioned this to a friend, who suggested Internet dating, but the whole idea made him very nervous. He was fine when it came to talking to women, but out of his depth when it came to taking it further and terrified that his lack of experience would scare women off. If he was going to attempt any kind of dating, he wanted a bit of help, to get reacquainted with the feel of a woman and to remind himself that he was still in 'good working order', as he put it.

We met, and I was able to put his mind at ease on all points. I was particularly struck, though, that his friend had put him in touch with me out of concern and the desire to help.

The next common category I'll call the 'Middle-class Liberals'. These accounted for a sizeable number of my clients. They were Irish men who were well educated and well travelled; more European Irish than plain old Irish. They lived in Dublin and other prosperous cities, and enjoyed paying for the good things in life. For them, sex was like fine wine or premium olive oil – they wanted to taste the best because they deserved it. These clients were good conversationalists and we'd chat easily about the economic mess and compare it to how other European countries had dealt with the global crash. When I met one I'd offer him an instant coffee, apologizing that it wasn't a soya decaf latte, and he'd know what I meant. Sex with those guys was usually a bit more interesting because they were good company – engaging conversation is a great form of foreplay for me.

Then there was the 'Young Family Man' – not so many of those due to my high fee, but still enough for me to recognize them. This guy had had the big wedding in the boom years, followed by the house in the commuter belt. He and his wife were high achievers, big earners with ambitions. When the 'having it all' mentality took hold, they decided to have two children, which they did in quick succession. The recession hit them and their big mortgage hard and they'd had the conversation about the missus giving up work because her job barely covered the cost of childcare. They'd gone straight from 'smug marrieds' to 'confused couple' and the first thing to suffer was their sex life. His wife would be faced with a huge adjustment from kick-ass career woman to stay-at-home mother, and she'd be using up every scrap of her energy just to get through the day. He still needed a little TLC, which was why he'd started looking up escort sites and wondering if it was for him. Invariably, he'd never been to an escort before, so I'd get a shy phone call from him asking very basic questions. His opportunities were rare because his wife knew his diary inside out, but eventually she'd take the kids to her parents' for the weekend or let him out for a round of golf, and that was when he'd make an appointment with me. He'd have my fee counted out beforehand and put in a separate pocket or part of his wallet. His wife knew the household budget to a cent, so it might have taken him some weeks to siphon off the cash without her knowing.

'Young Family Man' was a gentleman, paid promptly and was easy to please. Sex with him was usually fast and exciting – he was horny and still had youth and testosterone on his side. He was, however, the most likely to feel guilty, because he still loved his wife; the only reason he was with me was because his needs weren't being met and life seemed like one long drag. In spite of the guilt, he was also the most likely to make another booking when he realized that there was an outlet from his humdrum reality. He'd thought his days of fun were over, so his guilt could dissipate quickly when he remembered how much he liked switching off. Sadly for him, it would be another few months at least before he could afford to visit me again. In the meantime, he'd be content with a few saucy texts to keep him going.

The married men may have trouble sneaking off for a liaison, but the self-employed have much greater flexibility. Many of my clients fell into this category. Mr Self-employed managed his own diary and could easily slip out for a few hours during the daytime without anyone noticing. He also had more control over his finances and could hide a few euro here and there without anyone questioning it. Let's face it, if you're a PAYE worker and your salary is lodged to the joint account you share with your wife, of course she's going to cop a large sum being randomly withdrawn from it – unless she turns a blind eye.

The final category was 'Manual Labour Man'. He worked in construction, on the ground, and was a bit of a wheeler-dealer. This category made up the smallest percentage of my clients – especially after the construction industry took such a massive hit in the recession. These guys were the most likely to whinge about my rates and haggle for a discount. Even so, when it came to stumping up the cash, their wallets were stuffed with it. A few years ago, twenty-euro notes were considered small change and relegated to jeans pockets; only the fifty-euro notes and higher made it into the back section of a wallet. Now it's a few fifties and several twenties. Sex with these men was usually a bit rough and ready: they were straight into it, without much caressing or kissing – a little bit wham-bam, thank you, ma'am. One thing I really liked about them was that they were the most likely to compliment me on my recession-busting choice of work. They were the clients from whom I got comments like, 'Fair play to you for doing this, it takes some balls,' or 'Jesus, I admire you for doing this work. Sure we've all got to earn a crust, isn't that right?' That's right.

28. What the Men Want

I was curious as to what would be requested when I set up as an escort: would men want very off-the-wall stuff, or just a decent missionary-position screw? After months of meeting men for sex, I can say that 80 per cent want normal, common-or-garden sex that everyone's having at home. I'd estimate about 15 per cent want more left-of-field stuff, like prostate massage, S&M and rimming. A tiny minority requested things I'd either never heard of or didn't feel able to do, such as the sock-fetish guy wanting to sniff my socks while wanking, or practices involving defecation. They were always very polite and understanding when I declined. There is one thing, though, that 100 per cent have asked for: anal penetration. It doesn't always happen in our meetings, but they've all wanted to know that I'd be up for it, if requested.

Men are universally intrigued by anal sex. The majority have never tried it because their wives won't attempt it, or they've tried it once but quickly abandoned it when their wife complained it was too painful. Most don't realize there's a very particular technique to it. I don't think it's rocket science to understand why the ass is so appealing: it's a taboo area. Plus the anal area and surrounding perineum are filled with nerve endings, which make them extremely sensitive in both male and female bodies. In fact, once both parties know what they're doing, anal sex can be extremely pleasurable. The reverse holds true if you don't know what you're at: it can be very painful for the woman and a complete turn-off.

As ever, I've done my homework on this, so I find anal sex very enjoyable and was happy to perform it with clients. The woman needs to be very aroused to start with and both parties should be extremely aware of hygiene. A condom must always be used, as well as tons of lube, and any condom used in or near the anus should never, ever go near the vagina – change condoms as necessary. So, here's the trick to great anal sex: listen up, men and women!

The man must do *exactly* as the woman says, be very controlled and *never* thrust before she says she is ready. The anus is not under voluntary control – that is, the woman cannot relax her sphincter muscles and make herself open up, so patience is required for it to work. The man places the head of his cock at the entrance to the anus and waits until the muscles relax of their own accord, which takes five to ten seconds. The man will feel the anus opening and the woman will feel she can take more of his cock inside her. She tells the man when to go further inside her. He must do this very, *very* slowly and gently because there is a second band of muscles about an inch or so inside the rectum that must also relax before full penetration can be achieved. The man will feel this band of muscles and must stop again. He must wait for the woman to tell him to progress once this second band of muscles has relaxed, which she will feel. Then penetration can be achieved. Anal sex can be excruciating if the guy thrusts or moves deeper before these muscles relax and can cause internal damage to the woman, so remember, *slow and steady*. Guys, listen to the woman and follow what she says, or it could be your first and last opportunity to try anal sex.

While many women might laugh (or be appalled) at the very idea, anal sex can be extremely arousing for a woman; she is giving her partner something he has probably fantasized about. It feels great, too, and with practice, you'll be able to manage a vibrator in your pussy while your man, or you, stimulates your clitoris as well. When all three areas are receiving attention simultaneously, the climax is mind-blowing. When you come, the man can feel your ass muscles grasp his cock and that is sure to make him come, too.

As I said, I've been asked for anal by every single client I've ever seen, but it doesn't always happen because you can't fit everything into a session. Even the fact that I enjoy anal sex seemed to be enough for some men. It made them think I was quite naughty and they liked that. It's rare to meet a client who opts for anal sex in preference to vaginal penetration; anal is an adjunct to the main course for the majority. I had one client who had never tried anal before, but was dying to give it a go. He contacted me with that intention. Tom hadn't seen a working girl before, but had considered it many times, always baling out at the last minute. He told me that was because he feared being found out, so when he saw my ad highlighting discretion, he thought I might appreciate his cautious approach. I spent a while explaining my service, reassuring him that I went to extreme lengths to avoid exposure. I then explained that, with regard to anal sex, he would have to do exactly what I said at all times. He assured me that he was so obsessed with it he had read up on it and knew exactly what was involved. By the end of the phone call he was hard and couldn't wait to meet up. We made an arrangement for the following day.

I was used to anal sex after vaginal sex, when I was usually well aroused. On this occasion, however, it would be straight anal, with no vaginal penetration, and I was a little concerned that my body wouldn't be relaxed enough for it. I needn't have worried. To be fair to him, he spent ages making sure I was well ready with a combination of his fingers and tongue. I guess it must have been true that he had read lots about it as he knew I needed to be very aroused for it to be successful. We had anal sex in the missionary position, with my pelvis tilted upwards so he had a full view of my pussy and of me rubbing my clit. Tom didn't disappoint: he was great, and after a while of slow, deep penetration, I started rubbing my clit faster and faster until it got frantic and I gasped with the most intense orgasm. He was so horny, with his cock up my ass and watching me come, that after a couple more thrusts he roared, filled my ass with his load, then lay on top of me with his cock still inside, unable to speak for what seemed like ages.

Once he had caught his breath, I asked him if he had enjoyed it – was I worth the money? He'd enjoyed it so much that we started arranging our next meeting there and then. He told me his wife would never try anal sex or anything other than the missionary position. He knew she wasn't interested in him sexually and felt that she recoiled from him whenever he made approaches. He got laid on his birthday, Christmas and on holidays, but he knew even that much was a chore for his wife and she made him feel like he was pressuring her into it, which in turn made him feel like shit. He had sat his wife down and explained that he needed to express his sexual self and wanted to express it with her exclusively. He had shared some of his fantasies, but she was horrified, and he had felt like a deviant for even wanting to be more sexually explorative. He said it was the sheer frustration and isolation he felt that had forced him to look at paying for sex. He admitted to feeling guilty initially for even contemplating it, but now that he had done it, he felt a huge sense of relief that he could express himself without judgement or consequence.

We put a date in the diary for the following week and I asked him what he'd like to do on that occasion. He asked for something else that a lot of my clients wanted to try and were curious about: prostate massage. Tom was one of my early clients, so at that stage I hadn't done it before, but when he asked if I was familiar with it, I said, 'Of course I am. I did a weekend course in Spain on it.' (There is a place in Spain that is renowned for teaching tantric sexual practices and sensual prostate massage.)

'Oh, brilliant,' he said, beaming. 'Would you be happy to do it to me? I'd love to try it – it's supposed to be amazing.'

'Yes, no problem,' I said. 'I enjoy it. It's very satisfying and arousing for me to watch. I'll look forward to it.'

When I got home, I started researching prostate massage online so I could appear to be the expert I'd claimed to be. When I Googled it, I was bombarded by a huge choice of sites – obviously it was far more popular than I had thought, so I was glad he had turned me on to it: I'd be ready when other clients asked. Prostate massage is carried out by inserting a well-lubed finger or fingers into the rectum. The prostate is a hard, round mass about two inches inside, at the front of the rectum. The site warned me that it should only be performed when the man is very relaxed because, as with women and anal sex, a man's anal muscles are not under voluntary control. The recommended technique is to place a finger at the entrance to the anus and wait for the muscles to relax, whereupon the anus will open and sort of suck in the finger. Feedback and communication are important: most men will never have had anything up their ass before, so the new sensation will take a while to get used to.

Once you've located the prostate, you move your finger very gently, in a sort of beckoning motion, to stimulate it. Combined with either perineal massage or a hand-job, this type of massage promises to bring about an amazing orgasm, one that feels very different from a regular orgasm and with far more ejaculate. It takes a while for this to happen, so patience is needed, but I can tell you that your man will be unbelievably grateful if you try it on him. It goes without saying that scrupulous personal hygiene is required; in my line of work, I wear gloves. The masseuse must also be careful that nails are short because the lining of the rectum is very delicate and can easily be torn.

One interesting aspect of my research on prostate massage was the discovery that it has a medical application. It is used to treat a benign but uncomfortable condition called chronic prostatitis. Emptying the prostate of its fluid clears out any lingering bugs that may cause irritation. Interestingly, it is done under general anaesthetic because it is considered too uncomfortable to be carried out while the patient is awake. In some cultures, the emptying of the prostate without orgasm is seen as cleansing and detoxifying.

By the time I was due to see Tom the following week, I felt like an expert and was eager to do it. I was glad he was my first PM client because his willingness to experiment made it all run smoothly. From what I'd read it could take a bit of practice, but it worked a treat with him. I made sure I had everything planned, with extra long-lasting lube, gloves and wipes. I rehearsed in my head how I would position myself and where I'd place the necessary accoutrements. We shared several saucy texts in the run-up to our meeting, I knew he was ready, willing and able, and I got a kick out of the thought of making this happen for him. We met as arranged and I started off by kissing his neck and back. This moved on to touching each other everywhere – I needed to climax before I went near his prostate: if I didn't, I knew I'd be all jittery and impatient with him and that wouldn't be good. He obliged and watched as I let my fingers work their magic. It didn't take long, with him sucking my nipples.

I asked if he was ready and lined up my accessories. Sitting on my hunkers, I got him to bend and spread his legs. With my well-lubed hands I gave him a mini hand-job. I paced it slow enough and with a loose enough grip that I knew he wouldn't come; I didn't want him to, of course, and neither did he. I proceeded to massage his balls and slowly work around to his perineum and anus, paying particular attention to the perineum: massaging there also stimulates the prostate. His gasps let me know I was doing everything spot-on, and when he started naturally arching his bottom towards me, I knew we were ready to proceed further. He confirmed he was ready and I donned a pair of gloves over my well-filed fingernails, then squidged a blob of lube on to the fingertips. Very gently I began to insert my index finger into him. I knew what to expect and felt his muscles tighten, only to relax again in a few moments. I proceeded further with my finger on the upper wall of his rectum waiting to feel the hard lump that would indicate to me that I was on target and had located his prostate. To my relief, it was exactly where I had read it would be. I glided over it very, very gently at first, letting him get used to the new sensation. When he gave me the go-ahead, I made a beckoning motion with my finger, slowly but consistently, keeping my eyes locked on his face so that I could read his response.

'How does this feel?' I asked, needing some feedback.

'Fabulous,' he replied, 'but touch my cock as well.'

I massaged his hard cock with one hand while I continued my fingertip motion on his prostate. It wasn't long before he was approaching climax. I focused on keeping my hands working simultaneously and not losing my rhythm. 'Tell me when you're about to come,' I said, wanting to see if his ejaculate was any different from usual. Seconds later he panted that he was coming and I watched his cock squirt out what seemed a huge amount of cum over several seconds. With my finger in his ass I could feel the intensity of his contractions, and also see how far his cum had shot out. I was delighted with myself!

I'm well up on sexual practices, but sometimes I was asked to do stuff that was a definite no-no for me. That was the case with men who liked 'ball-breaking'. Yep, there are men out there who love having their balls kicked, beaten and battered – the harder the better. Amazingly, it's not a rare fetish, which is hard to believe if you ever see it in action. I did toy with the idea of it because the guy who first asked me to do it was willing to pay way over the odds, but I wasn't at all comfortable with the idea of inflicting pain and entering into an area of sexual expression that I could neither understand nor feel secure about. What if I hit the guy too hard or not hard enough? Would he get aggressive? What if he was loud and had to roar each time he was hit, alerting people to our activities? Also, I couldn't figure out if the ball-breaking thing was the sexual high and if ejaculation eventually happened after a prolonged beating, or if it was a prelude to penetration. Either way, I based my service on my being in control at all times, and I wouldn't have felt like that if I was engaging in 'ball-breaking'. I explained to the guy why I wouldn't do it and pointed him in the direction of some girls who advertised online that they provided this service.

What about dirty talk? I can tell you that every single client talked dirty to me – absolutely 100 per cent. It's all in the heat of the moment, it's part of sex, and I learned to enjoy it. It means a guy is absorbed in whatever we're doing and it gives me a sense of job satisfaction. Okay, so technically not job satisfaction *per se*, but I love hearing how aroused I'm making him feel. What about sex talk for women? I think women are often a bit apprehensive about this and it can feel foreign to begin with. Start off gently with something like 'I love the feeling I get in my panties when we kiss. It makes me tingle . . . and I wonder what it does to you . . . and as I start to wonder, I imagine your cock getting hard . . . and I start to feel myself getting wet . . . and thinking how great it would feel to have your cock there . . . and . . . and . . . and . . .' You get the picture. See how your man responds, then take it up a notch. I was too lovey-dovey with my ex to talk dirty; it somehow felt disrespectful. That was long ago and now I know better. Every man is different in terms of what he wants to say or hear. We are all so PC in our everyday lives, abstaining from profanities, that sex provides a perfect chance to let go and say what you really want.

The idea of escorts not kissing clients was made famous by *Pretty Woman*, but it's based on truth: kissing is so intimate that sex workers rarely kiss clients. I'm no exception, although I do kiss some. The majority of men have asked my policy on kissing, but I really never know whether or not I'll kiss them until I've met them. Prior to every meeting I'd tell a new client that I wouldn't kiss on the lips. If that changed during the meeting, they didn't complain. My decision to kiss a client was not necessarily about his appearance, teeth or how aroused I was. It tended to come down to whether I found a man attractive in the 'brain' sense. If he was intelligent and stimulating company and we had enjoyed good pre-sex conversation, then I was more likely to want to kiss him during sex. Although there were also clients who were so good-looking I knew immediately I wanted to kiss them and didn't care if they couldn't string two words together! It's not an age thing: there were young guys I wouldn't have dreamed of snogging and older men with whom I enjoyed passionate erotic kissing. Surprisingly, with some clients I had the tender kissing I'd usually only expect where there was mutual fondness and special connection.

I can't explain exactly why kissing is so personal: I could give a blow-job to someone I didn't particularly like or find attractive but I couldn't kiss him.

29. A Boyfriend

It's an unwritten rule that if your washing-machine is going to lie down and die, it will do it on a cold Friday in November when you've a mountain of washing waiting to be done. I was frantically trying to find a plumber to come and fix it, but each one I called told me it was impossible. I was working my way through the *Golden Pages* when Ultan answered and said he could be at my place within the hour. Thank God!

When I opened the door to him, I don't think I looked at him properly, just mumbled that I was grateful he could come at short notice, showed him the problem and said, if he needed me, I'd be in the living room. I was up to my eyes on the phone and computer, doing chores that I had to get out of the way, but I was also taking work calls as I wanted to have next week planned. That way, I could relax for the weekend, knowing I would have money coming in.

Just as I was finishing my work calls, I heard a knock on the door. Shit, had he heard what I was discussing with clients?

'Hiya, Ultan. I hope you haven't been waiting there for me to finish on the phone?'

'Yep. I was waiting as you said you were making work calls and I didn't want to interrupt you, but your washing-machine is working again, so I'd like you to come and check it's okay for you.'

Christ! Had he made out what I was chatting about on the phone? I needed to suss him out.

In the kitchen I offered him a coffee, which he accepted, and made small-talk, trying to gauge him while pretending to give my washing-machine the once-over. I was trying to stay relaxed and calm, but I couldn't let him go until I knew for sure if he had overheard my conversations. He told me he was divorced, single and busy setting up his business in Ireland, having returned from the

States after the divorce. He asked what I did for a living and I said I was currently between careers, but had lots of little projects on the go to keep money trickling in.

'Yes, I noticed you're into the mind, body, spirit stuff,' he said.

'How did you work that out?' I asked, in a friendly way.

'Oh, when I was waiting for you to finish on the phone I flicked through a book you had on the hall table. Very interesting, actually. I was getting really stuck into it when you finished your phone call.'

Thank God. I breathed a sigh of relief. Unless he was unlike any other man I'd ever known, he couldn't have been listening to my conversation through a closed door and reading simultaneously. While my heart rate returned to normal, we continued chatting about the book as we shared an interest in this area. He was a great believer in mind power and had used this in his business in the past with real results. I offered to lend him the book and he accepted, saying he'd drop it back soon – he lived reasonably locally, so he'd be around. We discovered we had a few other things in common and ended up having a really nice chat. Before he left, he asked if we could perhaps continue our chat over a drink some evening.

'Yes, I'd like that,' I said, secretly delighted – he was very cute, intelligent and had impeccable manners, which I find irresistible in a man.

I got on with my weekend and had kind of forgotten about Ultan when he phoned a week later to arrange a date. We agreed to meet the following Friday and I realized I was excited and nervous all at once. By Thursday, I was more nervous than excited: I don't know what was more stressful – choosing an outfit or planning what answers to have ready in case he probed more about what I did for a living. I had to be so careful not to trip myself up and let slip anything that might sound odd or suspicious. It was mad that I could be nervous about a simple drinks date, considering my work, but it hit me that I really cared what this guy thought of me and wanted to make the right impression. So far, he was ticking all the right boxes.

Ultan knocked on my front door at the appointed time and greeted me with a kiss on the cheek. I got the faint scent of fresh aftershave, just the right amount – enough to make me want to smell it again. I had probably dressed too conservatively in a pair of well-cut black trousers, high heels and a black V-neck top. I wanted to feel ladylike and sophisticated, and nicely cut clothes always make me feel great. I had made a special effort with my hair and makeup, perfecting the 'nude' style of eye-shadow application. My hair was simply dried and some shine serum added, showing off its glossiness to maximum effect. A simple clutch bag finished off my outfit and I felt great – always a confidence booster.

On the drive to the pub, we agreed we were both a little peckish and decided to go for a bite to eat first. He drove us to a favourite restaurant of his, and as he opened the door for me to walk in, I prayed none of my clients would be there. I did a quick scan of the room, but there was no sign of anyone I knew. I relaxed into my chair, looking forward to the meal ahead. The conversation flowed, without one awkward silence. As the designated driver, Ultan was sticking to sparkling water and I decided it was safest to do the same. When he asked me about my job, I told him the story I usually used: I was continuing in my previous profession, which involved lots of meetings and computer work. He accepted it without any hint of suspicion.

We ended up having a lovely evening together, and when he dropped me home, I was tempted to invite him in for a coffee but thought better of it. I didn't want him to think I was too available or that an offer of coffee translated to an offer of a shag. Strange as it may sound, with a guy I genuinely like I can be quite reserved initially and set the bar pretty high. Yes, it takes a lot of self-restraint, especially if I really fancy the guy, like I fancied Ultan, but from past experiences and from everything I've heard over the years from my girlfriends, a good relationship rarely, if ever, evolves from sex on a first date. Some women say that's because he got what he wanted and then high-tailed it, but I think first-date sex suggests to a man that the woman doesn't place a high value on herself. It's not the sex that's the issue, it's more that it doesn't show discretion in her choices and physical boundaries. That's my theory anyway, so Ultan and I finished the night with a gentle kiss and I pulled away before he did, hoping it would leave him wanting more.

It took six more agonizingly frustrating dates with Ultan before I decided I had kept him waiting long enough and we made love. It was so worth it. He was tender, romantic, passionate, considerate, kind and generous. I liked him a lot, an awful lot, and I could tell he felt the same way about me. I even introduced him to my children and my ex-husband, and everyone thought he was lovely and that we were a good match.

Of course, this unexpected love affair threw up problems. I worked as an escort, having sex with men for money. Ultan didn't know this. I couldn't imagine the hurt it would cause him if he ever found out. I thought we could have a future together, but should I stop seeing him now out of fear that, one day, he might discover the truth about me? Or should I take the gamble on him never finding out? Or should I give up my business and pretend it never happened – close that chapter in my life and put a line under it? It was a tough one and it occupied my mind more and more as we grew closer. Sometimes I felt angry with myself: why the hell did I have to choose such an extreme way of making money when it had the potential to fuck up my life if those I cared for ever found out?

I suppose I was so desperately broke when I'd started that the thought of meeting someone decent had never even entered my head. My top priority was to get cash and keep the wolves from the door. Recently I'd toyed with the idea of telling Ultan, but knowing him as I now did, I didn't believe he could ever accept it. Let's face it, there can't be many men out there who would. I had separated my work sex life from my sex life with Ultan in that I rarely kissed clients any more. I saved kissing for Ultan. I treated work very much like a performance I clocked in and out of, but the truth was, of course, that would be very cold comfort for him if he ever uncovered my secret. He wouldn't be comforted to hear that I hadn't kissed a guy while I was fucking him for money.

That dilemma was actually part of a wider one. I'd done almost a year as an escort and the double life, the secrecy, the possibility of being 'outed', was becoming more stressful as time passed. The longer I did the work, the more time I had to think about the devastation it would cause my family, friends and Ultan if they ever found out. The burden of my secret grew heavier and heavier. One part of my brain was saying, 'Save what you love, give it up,' but the practical side – the bigger side – said, 'Don't be stupid, girl, you've still got to make money and your children always come first.'

I had thought the recession would be shorter and that by now new employment opportunities would have presented themselves, but that hadn't happened. The country had gone to hell in a handcart and it was every man and woman for themselves – survival of the most dogged. And the sad truth is, escorting was the easiest money I'd ever earned. What other job paid so well for so little? Except it wasn't little, was it? It was an overwhelming secret and to have to cover it up on a minute-by-minute basis was threatening my well-being.

I'd noticed, with some concern, that I could switch instantly from Mum to working mode. Initially I'd had to be so careful and double think everything I did, mentally tracing my steps before I met a client to ensure no one would suspect anything, pausing before I answered any questions to make sure I didn't trip myself up. It would be all too easy on a night out with girlfriends to make a joke of what I did or a comment on the sex industry that might arouse suspicion. I was used to it, but double thinking was mentally exhausting, remembering which hat I was wearing, so to speak. I'd forgotten all the lies I'd told family and friends by this stage – a sign of a very bad liar, apparently – which was also a concern. I longed to be just me again, without the lies, the alias, the multiple mobile phones, the passwords, the six email addresses, the locked suitcases and the cash dealing.

I was getting more and more stressed by the idea that the longer my double life went on, the greater was the chance of being caught out. I might unwittingly reveal the truth, or a client might recognize me somewhere and let the cat out of the bag – deliberately or naïvely. The fear of being revealed hung over me 24/7. Recently I'd had a nasty shock, which forcefully brought home to me what a dangerous game I was playing. I was in the bank, waiting to speak to my mortgage adviser. I was reading a book when I heard a man in front of me talking to his companion. I recognized his voice instantly – it was very distinct. My instinctive reaction was to keep my head buried in my book and not look at all until my name was called. Obviously it was the real one, but I jumped up and strode straight into the adviser's office, not stopping to find out if my client had seen me. If he had, then he would know my real identity. There was a good chance he wouldn't give a shit, but there are some odd-balls out there and you never know the strange goings-on in other people's minds.

Inside the office, I had to grip my handbag to hide the fact that my hands were shaking. I felt sweaty and nauseous – a typical shock response. Nonetheless, I got on with my business with the mortgage adviser, and as we were chatting, he told me things were worse for a lot of people and that the stress was tangible in many couples who came to see him. He also mentioned that one area of personal expenditure was non-existent these days: 'social life'. That was bad news for me, but increased marital stress was good. As for my own situation, he told me I was managing quite well, all things considered. The problem was that the damn mortgage lasted for another twenty years and my house was worth a third of what my husband and I had paid for it. My first thought on see-ing my client outside that office was, I'm giving it up, I'm done, but after I'd gone through the figures and seen the exorbitant repayments reaching twenty years into the future, I knew I had no option but to carry on.

When I came out of the bank, there was a thin layer of snow on the ground. It was falling heavily and seemed to be sticking. Bol-locks! Not what I needed right now. How was a client supposed to explain to his wife why he was going out in terrible weather? How was I supposed to travel in snow? I was seeing Ultan later and hoped he'd make it. Ultan. Ultan, me and my work – I just couldn't think my way around all the angles of that deadly triangle. For now, I had to put it out of my mind because I had to work.

30. An Overstimulated Market

It was a cold, icy December and I needed to work harder to ensure I had enough money to give the children a good Christmas. As they got older, they were more demanding of Santa, so it cost a little more every year. With that in mind, I'd decided to try renting an apartment again, to see if I could increase the number of clients that way. I'd had an apartment during the summer and it had worked out quite well: I'd seen one or two clients per day and made about three thousand euro in profit at the end of the month, after expenses such as rent and diesel were covered, plus childcare and summer camps. This time I was renting a place further to the south of the country, which meant a commute, but also opened up a whole new market and contact with new clients. I wanted to see if it was worth doing this in various towns and cities around the country.

So far, I'd had the apartment for a week and it wasn't working out well at all. My regular clients wanted to see me at our usual hotels, so I was forced to book the hotels as well as pay the month's rent on the apartment. The guy who had rung this morning was different, though. He was a trucker, driving through the area that afternoon, he said, so the apartment suited him well. He hadn't tried an escort before, so I did my usual chat and put him at ease. He was just plain horny and wanted a shag – it was straightforward. We arranged to meet at one thirty.

One thing I'd learned from the apartment rental was that the number of escorts working in the region had increased. When I'd suggested meeting at the apartment, a number of clients had said it was a well-known spot for sex workers and they'd rather the anonymity of the hotel. One guy told me he knew of at least two foreign girls working very close to me, both of whom charged a hell of a lot less than I did. It sounded like the recession was pushing more and more people into the business, which was not good for me. The only bonus was that, with the warning about other escorts in the area, I was ultra careful to cover my tracks. The block of apartments I was working from had been raided by gardaí within the past six months and was being watched.

I'd enough time before my afternoon client to do a bit of browsing, so I wandered down the town and went into an Internet café to see what I could learn about the scene there and also see if any southern town was not well serviced by escorts. I'd a feeling that particular town wasn't going to work out for me because I was getting the impression that the atmosphere was quite negative, unlike other towns I'd worked in. It was a buyer's market and I'd noticed that men in the area were far more *au fait* with the going rates, the lingo and how it operated. They were also a lot tighter than men elsewhere and wanted lots of discount. They were not familiar with the idea of a high-class escort like me, being more used to the impersonal conveyor-belt, the half-hour hand-job/shag deal. It had only been a week, but I was already pretty sure I wouldn't be working in that area again; closer to the west was far more lucrative and the men there seemed to have the readies available to them. Ah, well, nothing ventured, nothing gained.

An allocated parking space came with the apartment and I'd noticed that a Mercedes was always parked in the one beside mine. I hadn't paid much attention to it at first, but since I had become aware that the apartments were used by working girls, I'd started to be more observant. Several times I'd seen a man and woman parking or driving off in the Merc. They were foreign, but I couldn't place the language. The man was fit, well groomed, tall, muscular and always did the talking. He dressed casually in tight jeans and a sweater, with aviator-style sunglasses, even though there was no sun. The woman was small, tanned and had a beautifully petite figure. Her clothes, albeit skimpy for December, were perfectly co-ordinated and her long nails perfectly manicured. I couldn't put an age on her as she also wore oversized shades, but I guessed from her figure, skin and hair that she was no more than mid-twenties. I started to wonder if he was her pimp or minder and if she was one of the working girls my client had warned me about.

In my naïvety, it was a week or so before it occurred to me that the apartments and adjacent area were their 'patch' and they probably wouldn't take kindly to another girl taking clients away from them. After a moment of panic, I looked at it logically and reasoned that looking 'respectable' as I did, and driving a grubby, well-worn car, there was no way they could suspect I was earning my living in the same way as the perfect Barbie girl. I got out of my car in mismatched jeans, jumpers and fake Ugg boots, while she placed her perfectly polished heels on the ground and strutted in, drawing attention to herself by looking too well groomed for daytime in a town like that. I was also a few stone heavier than her and fifteen or even twenty years older. I comforted myself that even if her minder/pimp got wind that another girl was working from the same block of apartments, he'd never suspect the chubby mum who parked next to him. Indeed, I had never seen him so much as glance at me, even though we were only inches apart when we were parking. I was that invisible to him.

My client that afternoon was Vincent, a truck driver ten years younger than me. I gave him clear directions to the apartment, but when he wasn't there on time, I phoned him. His truck had broken down on the outskirts of the town and he was waiting for the AA to arrive and fix it. He still wanted to see me and reckoned he had plenty of time; he asked if I'd mind collecting him. I threw on a dress, high-heeled boots and a three-quarter-length coat, then sped off to Woodies DIY store car park, where he'd said he'd be waiting.

When I parked I spotted him straight away – he'd given a good description of himself and looked muscular, toned, young and fit. Yummy! I beeped the horn and he hopped into the passenger seat, apologizing for putting me to any trouble. There's an ease between people who have chatted about sex with each other and we talked comfortably about everyday stuff on the drive back into town. It's funny how you can chat about the weather and the state of the nation knowing that in no time you'll be fucking. He needed to stop at an ATM to get cash for me, so I pulled in at a garage. It was a bit weird being out like that in broad daylight with a client and I was anxious to get back to the apartment. I concocted a story to deliver in case I bumped into anyone I knew, which was quite possible: it was a big shopping town just under an hour from where I lived. Vincent got back into the car and off we went again. We chatted about his young kids, his wife and his job on the way to the apartment, but once in the door, it was down to business.

I ran the shower for him, and poured two glasses of sparkling water. It was a cold wet day, but I'd had the heating on since morning so the bedroom would be cosy. While he showered, I lit a scented candle, stripped off my dress and put on some music. Instinct told me that fast music would suit him best; I reckoned he'd be good.

Minutes after I'd started to run my hands over his body, he asked if he could kiss me and we began very slowly to tease each other with our lips. As I've said, I very occasionally broke my rule about not kissing clients. I could instantly spot a guy I'd want to kiss, and Vincent was my sort. He was the type of man I would be attracted to anyway, with expressive, smiling eyes and full lips. I nibbled and licked his lower lip, and he raised his hands to caress my nipples. Sensing my pleasure, he flicked his tongue over them, then sucked as much of my breast into his mouth as would fit. I pulled his head away and we kissed hard and fast. Fuck, this was good. This guy was so horny, he clearly wasn't getting any at home. I could feel his cock hard against my inner thigh as I straddled him. I didn't want it to end too quickly, so I suggested he lie down and let me look after him for a bit. I wanted to slow him down but keep him very aroused. I teased and caressed him, but he moaned that he wanted to be inside me.

Within seconds we were fucking, and it was hot, sweaty and deep. He was very vocal and I was loving that he was so turned on. Sometimes the chemistry is just there. We managed a simultaneous climax and collapsed in a sweaty heap on the bed.

We stayed like that for a while, not talking, lost in a comfortable post-coital silence. Then Vincent sat up, took a sip of water, leaned over and kissed me. Within moments we were kissing passionately and frantically again, stirring up all the arousal that was still lingering in both of us. I was amazed to feel him grow hard again – quite the little powerhouse of testosterone. He grabbed a condom from the bedside table and put it on, then entered me slowly and with purpose. This time, he moved deliberately and made every thrust count. We fucked slowly, with intent, for what seemed ages. Then he brought his cock to the bare entrance of my pussy and waited, knowing by now I loved the anticipation of what was coming. He thrust hard and deep into me. I screamed and bit down on his shoulder with the pleasure and pain of it – I love very deep thrusting. I came again and without clit stimulation, which happens rarely for me. It was a beautiful, deep, intense climax that left me satisfied and sleepy. He was so knackered he didn't have the energy to fuck any more, so I finished him off with a hand-job.

We were both well satisfied when his time ended. He joked afterwards that I should be paying him, seeing as I'd enjoyed it so much. He checked his phone, then asked if I could drop him back up to his truck as the AA man had reckoned he'd be there shortly. I warned him I'd have to throw on my non-work clothes to do it as I was heading straight to pick up my children. He laughed and muttered something about not caring what I looked like – he liked me anyway and he'd enjoyed himself.

I pulled on jeans and a sweater, checked myself in the mirror, spritzed on some perfume and grabbed my bag. He handed me my fee and I shoved it into my pocket, having forgotten to get it off him first. I did a final check that I'd left no traces of my work in the apartment, and two minutes later we were in my car, chuckling that I'd forgotten to add taxi fees to his bill. I brought him to where he'd left his truck and he thanked me for a good time. I smiled at him. 'Well, I hope we'll get to do it again some time.'

He shook his head. 'I don't think so.'

'Oh,' I said, hiding my surprise, 'I thought you enjoyed yourself.'

'Christ, I did, I did,' he said quickly. 'It's just that, well, your rates are a bit high and there's loads of other options about, if you get me.'

'You mean, you'll choose another escort next time?'

He smiled. 'I'm not saying better, but a different girl, yeah. I've a mate who goes to someone round here and she only charges 150 euro for the same.' He shrugged. 'You're one hot lady, but I'd like to see someone maybe once a month and I just couldn't afford four hundred a go.'

Damn the bloody recession! How would I keep my business going in an oversubscribed market? I had already differentiated my 'product' through guaranteeing discretion and safety, so what else could I do to convince customers to spend their money with me and not some other girl? If this kept up, I wouldn't be able to keep all the plates spinning for much longer.

31. A Decent Proposal

I hate Christmas. I hated it when money was available and I hate it even more now. I had thought I might get the odd gift from my regulars, an extra twenty or fifty slipped into my hand on top of my normal fee, but I was wrong. It was the complete opposite: everyone was strapped for cash and every client I talked to asked for IOUs, two for the price of one and blow-jobs as 'corporate gifts'. They'd be asking for loyalty cards next. It seemed they felt I should be playing Santa Claus for them rather than the other way round. On top of that, the snow had come down in earnest, the temperature had plummeted and the roads were impassable in some places, which meant cancellations. And my ex hadn't confirmed his plans for the holidays, so I couldn't work again until the kids were back at school in January. Bless him, when was he going to realize that, apart from being entitled to have a life, all I actually did with my free time was work to pay bills? He was looking for sympathy because he was finding it tough, too, but his understanding of being cash-strapped hadn't stretched to telling me he'd cancelled the maintenance direct debit. How did he think I managed to keep the roof over our heads? The obvious answer was that he didn't consider me at all.

Lately, I couldn't help wondering just how many people had taken extreme measures in dealing with their money issues, especially at this time of year. I couldn't be the only one who'd chosen to do this work. In fact, I knew I wasn't. One client had told me his physiotherapist now allowed him to masturbate at the end of his back massage for an extra few quid. She didn't partake, but she allowed him to relieve himself in her presence. I also knew of a beauty therapist in an upmarket spa who would give male clients a 'happy ending' for an extra fifty euro cash, if requested. That was fifty euro for ten minutes' work, so it was good money, but she was taking a huge risk – she'd lose her job if she was found out. It's a proven statistic that all vice crimes increase during a recession, but I wondered how many women or men like me – middle class, educated, previously in professional employment and never before involved in an illegal activity – had come up with alternative, atypical ways of keeping the show on the road. I reckon this issue will be discussed in years to come, when the doom and gloom is all over and people admit how they managed.

Right now, though, I'd enough to think about with the number of cancellations I was getting. The weather, the season, the family obligations – it was all I was hearing, excuses. It was a few days before Christmas Eve, and I was close to giving up and starting the holiday season early. I was outside, trying to defrost a frozen car, when my work phone beeped. I grabbed it out of my pocket: a text from a regular, William. Thank God! He was local and didn't have to come up with too many excuses to get away from home because his wife rarely asked what he was up to. I rang him immediately and we agreed to meet at our usual spot, a large commercial hotel on the outskirts of our nearest big town, which was easy for me to get to even if the snow continued.

'Just one thing I want to ask,' he said suddenly, as I was about to hang up. 'I'm sure you're the same yourself, but is there any chance, with it being almost Christmas, that you could give me a few quid off? My young fella is looking for one of those new Xbox yokes and they cost an arm and a leg.'

Shit! I'd known it was too good to be true. I was badly in need of the money, though, so I decided to compromise rather than lose the booking. 'God, yeah, I know, it's hard for everyone, William, but I'm in exactly the same position myself. I've three to get Santy for so I do understand. I'm willing to drop it a bit as a favour, but I'm sure you can appreciate I can't do this again.'

'Ah, you're a pet, thanks a million, I'll have two hundred in cash for you, okay?'

'Jesus, I can't drop it that much – that's almost half-price!'

'I know, I'm so sorry, and I'm embarrassed even having to ask you, but it's all I have at the minute and the missus is watching the money like a hawk because of Christmas. Tell you what, how about we say two hundred for forty-five minutes? Would you do it for that?'

I'd no choice really, had I? 'Yeah, okay, William, but just this once. As the sign in the shops says, "Please don't ask for credit as a refusal may offend."'

He laughed. 'Gotcha, and thanks. See you later – should be eight. Is that all right?'

'Grand, see you there.'

My ex was taking the kids for the night, returning them to me for the holiday period, so I spent the afternoon doing a few chores around the house, then waved the kids off at six. I got myself ready and left myself plenty of time to get to the hotel on the icy roads. I was there by seven forty and went in to get the room ready. William had been a regular for a few months and he was an easy client. He usually wanted straightforward sex or a decent hand-job with plenty of fondling of my body. He was a nice enough guy and always made a bit of an effort to spruce himself up.

At eight o'clock exactly there was a knock at the door and I let him in.

I wasn't such a fool as to give him a full session when we'd agreed on forty-five minutes, so I put my personal mobile phone on the bedside locker because it had a huge clock as its screensaver. It was on silent and I positioned it where I could see it clearly. We got down to work and I glanced at it occasionally, to keep an eye on the time. We were about twenty minutes into it and I was just about to put his sheathed cock into my mouth when I saw the phone flashing. It was an incoming call and I could see the name – my ex was trying to call me. I knew instantly that something had happened because he never called me unless there was a problem.

I apologized briskly and reached over to grab my phone. William looked at me questioningly, but I put a finger over my lips to signal to him to keep quiet.

'Hey, what's up?' I said, into the phone.

'Everything's okay, but there's been a small mishap and we're in Casualty.'

Panic rose in my throat. 'Jesus, what's happened, who's hurt?' I got the bare details from him. By then I'd moved off the bed and was pacing round the room. William had the sensitivity to get out of bed quietly, take his clothes into the bathroom and reappear dressed and ready to go. I agreed to go straight to the hospital to meet my family and hung up. The youngest boy had been bouncing on the beds when he took a tumble and got a nasty cut on his forehead.

William had obviously overheard what was going on and knew our session was most definitely over. 'Listen, I'll leave you to deal with that,' he said kindly. 'I'll let myself out. Hope the lad's okay, and mind yourself.'

I pretty much ignored him, just glancing up to say goodbye. I was almost dressed, but I couldn't go into the hospital in what I was wearing. I remembered there was a scarf in my car and an old outdoor jacket in the boot – they would have to do. I grabbed the condoms and other sex stuff and shoved them into the drawer. I was booked into the hotel for the night, so I'd have to come back later and tidy the room properly, but now I needed to be with my son. I grabbed some tissues on the way out, and in the lift down to Reception I wiped off most of my makeup. Then I took off my earrings, necklace and bling ring and threw them into my handbag.

I rushed out to the car and donned my old coat and scarf. I looked perfectly normal now, not like an escort at all. The hospital was about fifteen minutes away and I drove dangerously fast in the icy conditions.

When you have kids, you get used to panicked trips to Casualty, but this time I was far more stressed and upset. Usually I didn't have my personal phone beside me when I was with a client. It was pure fluke I'd had it in view that time. What if it had been a normal session and the phone had been out of sight? My ex would have asked all sorts of questions about why I wasn't there when one of the kids needed me. More importantly, what if it had been a serious accident and I, their mother, wasn't there? I felt physically sick at the thought of any of my children needing me and not being able to contact me – especially if I was shagging some stranger for money.

I arrived at the hospital, flung the car into a parking bay and dashed through the double doors into A&E. My little troupe were huddled together in chairs, with the injured one cuddled on his father's lap, a nasty-looking cut on the side of his forehead. He reached out his arms to me and I lifted him up; I think I needed the hug more than he did. While we waited for him to be called to see the doctor, the children gave me dramatic reconstructions of the accident, saying how cool the fall was, that he'd looked like Spiderman flying through the air until the locker got in the way and collided with his head. 'Spiderman' was laughing, so I stopped worrying that the injury was anything more than superficial.

At last, my boy's name was called and I went in with him while my ex waited with the others. I was ushered to a treatment room, where the doctor introduced himself and started to go through the details on the chart, to confirm name, address, etc. He asked my name and relationship to my son and I had to pause – even in that situation I had to think before I gave my name and address. After a few minutes, it became obvious that I hadn't been there when the accident had occurred and therefore couldn't give the doctor the information he needed so I swapped places with my ex. As I was waiting for them to emerge from the treatment room, I wondered about the hotel: should I go back just to check out, or should I make some calls and try to get some work done? Somehow I wasn't up for work, still shaky at the idea of being uncontactable in an emergency. I was feeling a bit paranoid, too, wondering if all the bored-looking people in chairs were sizing me up and figuring out how I earned my money. *Do I look suspicious? Do I look like an escort?* The paranoia had been creeping up on me because of Ultan and it was particularly bad that night because everything had happened too quickly: I'd gone from bed with a client to A&E in twenty minutes. I was a bit disoriented.

Finally, they returned, my boy's wound glued together, and we were free to leave. My ex asked if I wanted to take Spiderman back to mine to keep a close eye on him. I felt the tug at my heartstrings, but the hotel room was waiting for me. I told him I was happy he would take good care of him and that it was only a superficial injury, nothing he couldn't handle. I said I'd keep my mobile switched on all night, just in case, and that he could call me any time. I kissed the little ones goodbye and told them not to behave like monkeys for the rest of the weekend.

I sat into my car and breathed a sigh of relief. It was all I could do not to break down in tears. Thank God I'd had my phone with me earlier; thank God I'd happened to have an old jacket and casual scarf in my car; thank God my ex didn't notice anything unusual about me or my scattered behaviour; thank God William had had the cop-on to stay quiet while I was on the phone and quietly leave; thank God my boy's injury was nothing serious. That was too many happy coincidences for comfort. It could have been so different. I knew it was possible for anyone to be out of reach for a variety of reasons, but the thing that freaked me was that if I had been out of reach, it would be very hard to explain the reason. Not exactly model mother behaviour.

I drove slowly back to the hotel and wearily took the lift up to my room. In my rush I'd left my work phone on the desk. There were a few missed calls, but nothing of significance. There was also a text from William, saying he hoped everything was okay and to give him a shout later. I supposed he wanted his appointment. There was nothing wrong with that, but I wasn't in any humour to entertain people. I texted back that my boy was okay, that I was back at the hotel and exhausted. He replied immediately: he'd been in the hotel bar since I left and wanted to pop up to run something by me – he understood that I probably wasn't in the mood for work. This was unusual and intriguing. I told him he could come up.

A few minutes later, we were sitting on the bed and William told me what was on his mind. He'd had to let his full-time PA go earlier in the year because he couldn't afford to keep her on. However, he still needed someone for a few hours per day and, having known me for several months, considered me to be professional, punctual, efficient, well organized and excellent at communicating in person, by phone and email. He was wondering if I'd be willing to do a few hours for him every day. There wasn't any generous package on offer, no private pension, health insurance or share options, but I could work from home and more or less choose hours to suit me.

I was stunned by the offer and it sounded good – but how much would a few hours' admin work pay me? As it happened, William told me, his work was of a delicate nature, involving legal proceedings and details of alleged medico-legal negligence. I would have access to witness statements, medical histories, witnesses' personal details and some unsavoury stuff. He needed someone very reliable, very discreet and very trustworthy who could keep quiet about any information they had access to, and who would do some research on the correct way for certain procedures to be carried out so he could ascertain if someone had been negligent or not. I had told him bits and pieces about my past professional employment during our meetings over the previous months, so he knew I was able to do the job. I'd inadvertently proven to him that I met all his criteria in terms of being the right person for the role. And he would pay me thirty euro an hour, starting with ten hours a week, if I was interested.

I sat there, open-mouthed, staring at him. This was out of the blue and I didn't know what to think. I didn't know what William did for a living – he had once mentioned that he worked in a law-related field but hadn't expanded and I hadn't asked. He had always struck me as a quiet, reserved man who didn't give away much about himself.

'What about when we're asked how we knew each other, though? Will I have to keep this job secret as well?' I asked.

'Easy. We can just say you replied to a job offer online. Anyway, you'd mostly just be passing what you'd researched to me so you wouldn't be dealing with anyone else.'

'And I'd have to tell you my real identity. I'm not sure I want you to know who I really am.'

'Well, we both have something to hide – my wife would lose her reason if she found out I visit escorts, so you keep my secret and I'll keep yours. Quits, yes?'

'What do you mean "visit escorts"? Are you seeing more than one? And I suppose you think I'll throw in the odd free shag every now and then. Well, that's not going to happen. If we're seriously considering this, it has to be on a completely clean slate, no reference whatsoever to our previous relationship. I'm really fucking serious about that. I can't have it that I'd be treated like some piece of shit at work just because you know what I do.'

'Well, I'm sorry to have to tell you but, yes, I see plenty of girls. I have a fondness for you because you look and act classy and – don't get me wrong – you're worth every cent of what you charge . . . but I can't afford you any more, especially when I know girls who will provide a full service for a hundred euro.'

'A hundred euro?' I squeaked. 'You can't be serious! They must be skanky. How could it be worth anyone's time to do it for a hundred euro? Are they druggies or what?'

'Well, I'm sure some of them have social problems, but I've found a few who are lovely, work at it full-time, are single and don't have children, so are available pretty much 24/7. They don't have pimps either, so at least I know they're getting all their money. I suppose when you're working at it full-time with no restrictions or time limits, the hundred euros start to add up. The recession is even affecting the rates sex workers are charging – everyone's lowering their prices and the competition's getting fierce in certain towns. Most importantly, the two I've found insist on safe sex. Why would I pay you what you charge when I can get it a lot cheaper? Anyway, your brains are wasted at this – and I saw how you reacted when you had to go to the hospital. You're a mother trying to provide for her family and that's where your head is, I reckon.'

Well, he'd read me right there. Yes, I wanted to be at home with my kids and, yes, I'd been finding the work harder to cope with lately. If I was to believe what he was telling me, there was no way I could compete with the women he'd described. They'd put me out of business soon, no matter what. I looked at him. My brain was scrambling for the angles, the downsides, the cons, but his offer seemed to be the break I needed.

'So if I'm basically just researching stuff, I could work from home most days?'

'You can work wherever you like so long as you get me the information I need. I hardly think you're going to doss when I've seen how hard you work and what you're prepared to do to pay your way and raise your kids. And you'd have no contract, so I'd only pay you for work completed once a week. It would have to be pretty hush-hush – I don't want anyone knowing I employ you because I prefer to keep my business life private. Look, don't say anything now – you've had a rough night and I've surprised you with all this. Just have a think about it and give me a shout in a few days to let me know your answer, okay?'

He gave me a quick peck on the cheek and left.

I was exhausted, but my head was spinning with ideas. I removed the remainder of my makeup, had a hot bath, filled out an order for breakfast in bed and put my personal phone on the bedside table in case my son needed me. Tomorrow I'd work out the pros and cons and revise my business plan. That would clarify where I was at, and where I wanted to be.

32. Year-end

I woke up to a knock at the door. 'Room service.' I hopped out of bed and let the waiter in. He laid the tray on the table and handed me the chit. I signed my real name without thinking. I always booked hotel rooms in my real name but it felt so damn good not to have to think about what name I was using that day, and brought back my chat with William the previous night. If I took up his offer, it would put an end to my double life. I could go back to having one name, one mobile number and one email account. I wouldn't have to watch myself all the time in case I let something slip. I could anticipate a future with Ultan without living in terror of being found out and rejected. I poured the coffee and sipped it slowly. I phoned the children and was relieved to hear that Spiderman was in high spirits. Last night's dash to the hospital had crystallized all the doubts I'd been feeling of late. I had to face the fact that my work was becoming unsafe and uncertain, which meant I had to review my options and see what was viable, realistic, achievable and would keep me solvent.

Although I had become more stressed out by my life as an escort, I didn't regret it. It had served me well in more ways than one: I'd earned good money, I'd met some interesting men, I'd broadened my outlook on sex and the sex industry, and I'd learned more about humanity and sexuality than any book could ever teach me. But if it had reached the stage where I was no longer comfortable doing the work because the fear of being caught outweighed the financial benefits, it was time for an honest reassessment. Plus, if what William had told me was right, even sex workers were struggling and having to lower their prices. That wasn't an option for me with my financial commitments.

I showered, dressed and wrapped up warmly to walk across the street to an Internet café. I didn't have to be out of the hotel until midday and could book a late check-out if I wanted to, so I was in no rush. If I had a call to squeeze in a client I'd have to take it to make up for last night's lost earnings, but he'd be one of my very last. That thought would get me through the session.

I chose a corner seat to avoid prying eyes and Googled 'sex dating in Ireland'. There are adult dating sites to cater for all likes, fetishes, orientations and marital states. Looking at the number of them, I was sure it had increased since I'd first started looking up this stuff a year ago. Anyone anywhere in Ireland could arrange NSA sex within any given hour, if they were so inclined. No-strings was not my thing, so I looked up the classifieds on the major Irish buy / sell / exchange sites and, yep, William was spot on! There were hundreds of 'massage services' advertised. I also noticed several ads for 'older ladies', women in my age group who were advertising their experienced services. So I was just one of several women in their forties who had turned to sex work in the recession. However, no one was advertising my particular type of service for attached gentlemen. I scanned the prices and rates and saw that I was in the minority with what I charged. The average rate was a hundred euro per hour and, yes, there were 'special rates, fifty euro, full service, all inclusive'! That hadn't been how the land lay last year, when I was considering this work. It was so blatant now, totally in your face, ridiculously easily available and affordable. It had told me all I needed to know: this work was no longer as lucrative as it had been when I started.

I headed back to the hotel to mull over my options. I made myself a pot of tea and sat down with a pen and paper to write down my choices, with the pros and cons of each. I could diversify into fetishes as there was definitely more money in it, especially the more extreme stuff like infantophilia – men who enjoyed dressing up as infants. I dismissed that because there were so many factors I'd have to consider: always being the dominant one; whether I'd be able to participate in degradation stuff, like water sports and pooing on someone; finding a very secure and discreet base from which to work; the small size of the market, given that a relatively small percentage of the population enjoyed taboo or extreme fetishes. To make it work, I'd have to be prepared to go very niche and move to a high-density population area. It wasn't viable.

Second option: continue what I was doing, but lower my rates a bit. That would mean I'd need to see more clients to maintain the same income. If I were seeing larger numbers of men, I couldn't use hotels any more: I'd have to get a place of my own. I didn't like that idea because it would be easier for people to notice something suspicious. I absolutely couldn't risk a nosy neighbour coming over all good citizen and making a phone call to the gardaí.

Third option: recruit a few ladies like myself to do the shagging, take care of the organizational side, maintain a thorough screening process and take 50 per cent of 'my girls'' takings. But then I'd be a madam, which was despicable: controlling other people, being responsible for their well-being, and feeling shit for taking a cut of their earnings. There was also the increased burden of accountability: if I was organizing sex for sale, I might end up in jail. Out of the question.

My work phone beeped. It was another regular, Xavier, whom I'd known for quite some time, long enough for us to feel more like friends than punter and escort. He had been one of my first clients and what I considered an easy one. We got on well and had had conversations about our lives, so he knew why I'd started this work and how I managed my business.

'Hello there, how are things?' he said chirpily.

'Shite, to be honest,' I replied frankly. 'The usual fucking money worries.'

'I thought you had it all sorted, a nice little earner. What's changed?'

'The recession, that's what. It's got fucking worse!'

He laughed grimly. 'Tell me about it. I take it the lads don't have the money you're asking for any more?'

'Got it in one. I still get loads of calls, but when we get on to my rates, far more of them say it's out of their league at the minute.'

'So you're spending more time on the phone and getting fewer bookings at your usual rates?'

'Yeah, and it's a pain because the initial phone calls are the most time-consuming part of it.'

'What you want is not to have to deal with calls, and still see clients who have no problems paying you?'

'Exactly. Any brainwaves to help me out?'

'Well, maybe I have. Why don't you contact your good regulars, guys like me, and let them know you're changing how you operate your business. Tell them you won't be taking on any new clients, and from now on you'll only see a select few. As whoever has been such a good client, you'd like to offer him a regular ongoing appointment.'

'How exactly will that work for me? I'm not with you.'

'Tell them you're offering them a one-off opportunity to be kept on your books, so to speak, and reduce your rate to make it affordable for them to stick to a regular ongoing appointment. Some are bound to take you up on it. I mean, you told me yourself that some of your clients said they'd been looking for someone like you for literally years and are happy to keep coming back for more. They're hardly going to give you up that easily. Plus it'll make them feel like they're getting an exclusive deal – to be one of your few clients and at a lower rate per visit.'

I raised my eyes to the ceiling and thanked God for sending me William and Xavier. I couldn't believe that the answers to my dilemma were coming from my clients!

'That's a bloody good idea, Xavier,' I said. 'That could actually work really well for me. If I saw just four clients a month at two hundred euros each, that'd be eight hundred altogether. I could even see them all on one weekend, which would leave me with my other free weekend to myself. My ex has the kids every other weekend, which means I'd have one full weekend off a month and actually get some time to myself. Jesus Christ, you're a feckin' genius. I hope you're not going to charge me now for consultation fees.' I laughed.

'Nah, it's all free to you! But any chance you could squeeze me in, so to speak, in the next hour?'

'Sure, no problem, and would you like to be the first to avail yourself of my new exclusive service, sir?'

He sighed. 'Well, speaking of family stuff, I'm afraid an ongoing arrangement with you is out of the question, not a hope in hell now.'

'How come? What's been happening to you?'

'The missus has lost her job, so it's just me earning now. Thought I'd push the boat out and book you one last time before we were poverty-stricken.'

'Ah, shite, that's awful. Well, I'll make sure you enjoy today. I'll see you in half an hour. You know where I am.'

'Eh, reduced rate for a great client?'

'Fuck it, why not? Someone's gotta pay the fat man in the red suit, eh?'

'What are ye on about now?'

'Santy, ye gobshite. See you in a bit.'

I was chuckling to myself as I hung up. I sat there, thinking over what he'd just said. His idea might work. If I wasn't doing all the admin and phone calls that went along with new business, I could easily take up Xavier's suggestion. I started jotting down figures on the page in front of me: I'd be getting eight hundred a month from escorting if I could secure just four regular clients for a monthly appointment; wages from William would give me another twelve hundred a month; children's allowance was another few hundred. Between that and the maintenance that was now coming irregularly from my ex, I would have enough to cover the mortgage and house-hold bills, and even a bit left over for treats. And all going well, I'd even have a weekend off. I sat back in the chair and exhaled. Christ, this might be the best plan I'd ever had.

I suddenly remembered that Xavier was on his way for his parting shag. I grabbed the room phone and dialled Reception to ask for a two o'clock check-out. They told me it wasn't possible – fully booked tonight and Housekeeping were anxious to get into my room. Damn! Xavier was my last chance to make some money this weekend.

There was a rap at the door and I opened it to find Xavier standing there, a big smile of anticipation on his face. 'God, I'm so sorry, but I forgot to arrange late check-out and have to be out of here pronto.'

'So this is you making it special for my last visit, is it?'

I giggled. 'I'm sorry. If you've any more bright ideas, I'm all ears.'

He cocked his head to the side. 'What about your car?'

I looked at him in disbelief. 'Em, it's minus two out there!'

'It'll be grand,' he cajoled me. 'You've a big winter coat – just wear that with nothing else on so you're all ready. God, I haven't done it in a car in years. It's getting me going just thinking about it. Do you know anywhere quiet we could go?'

'I do, as it happens. You run down to the car park and wait while I check out.'

I stripped naked, then threw on a fresh red lace thong and bra set, my coat, knee-high boots and woolly scarf. I hoped to God I wouldn't trip on the way out or the whole hotel would get a look at my almost-bare arse. I was feeling up for it myself now – spontaneity was making me giddy and flushed. I stuffed a few condoms into my coat pocket, picked up my bags and shot down to Reception.

Outside, I phoned Xavier and told him which car was mine. He had already spotted me getting into it, so he was hot on my tail. I blasted up the heater and crawled along – the roads were slick with ice and unpredictable. My slow pace was giving the interior more time to heat up, and the windows were steaming up – a bit of privacy, at least. It was still snowing on and off and there was a good covering everywhere I looked. I was taking us to a quiet little wooded area nearby. When I pulled in, I was pleased to see no other cars parked there.

Xavier parked a little away from me and climbed into the passenger seat of my car. It was awkward, uncomfortable and cold, but strangely nice. It was actually good to feel like a teenager again! I slipped a condom on to his cock and moved over to straddle him.

It wasn't working – I couldn't get a decent rhythm and neither could he. Today my car just wasn't big enough for comfy sex. It had been fine with my Czech mate but Xavier had a more imposing physique.

He was getting frustrated. 'How about we just run over there behind that tree and I fuck you on the bare cold ground with the snow falling around us?'

'Oh, quite the exhibitionist, aren't we?' I laughed. 'Feck it, let's go for it.'

We had a great fuck in the snow and I kept my promise to make his last appointment a good one. Afterwards, he handed me two hundred euro and I thanked him for his suggestion about the monthly regulars.

'But you'll make time for me if I get the odd chance to see you, won't you?' he said.

'For you,' I smiled at him, 'any time.'

After he'd gone, I sat there in the snowy silence, thinking how utterly mad the last year had been. I'd embarked on a 'career' I'd never have thought possible; I'd shagged about 120 men in twelve months; I'd had some of the best sex of my life; I'd kept the house going through a very rough time; and now two punters had shown me a new path that might lead me to a very good life. What were the chances? I took out my piece of paper again, with my scribbled pros and cons, and made up my mind. I would accept William's offer and I would do as Xavier suggested and offer an exclusive 'contract' to my four best regulars. There was no doubt I could make it work financially, but the big bonus was that weekend off every month and the time I'd save by not having to take calls and send hundreds of emails. I decided that, first, I'd talk to William to finalize the job with him. Then I'd draw up a list of the clients who would be most likely to accept the proposed new working arrangement.

It could all wait until tomorrow, though, when I'd had a good night's sleep.

Epilogue: Just a Normal Woman

It's more than sixteen months since I saw my first client and six months since that December morning when I decided to take up William's offer and try to follow a new life. It has been a hugely interesting exercise for me to write this book, bringing my escort work to the forefront of my mind again when I had relegated it to the back, behind the more pressing issues of day-to-day living. I've had to revisit that past, my motives, enjoyments and regrets, and it hasn't all been easy. But it has given me a new perspective on it and a new distance from it, which is helpful and important for me. It's a good time to review and sum up the key things I've learned from that whole strange experience.

I still see a few regulars, and the occasional new client when things are a bit tight. Birthdays, holidays and school expenses put too much strain on my regular income, so a few extra clients every now and then get me through the tight spots and stop me going further into debt. As part of the review process, I had a full Well Woman and STD check-up, which set me back a few hundred euro – hardly encouraging people to have a sexual-health MOT, is it? I couldn't scrape up the money from my weekly budget so I saw a client to earn it – yes, the irony is striking, but there you are: escort work is still the fastest way I know to get my hands on cash. Thankfully, I'm 100 per cent healthy. I've always been incredibly careful not to engage in unsafe sex acts, but there was always a niggle of doubt that perhaps some aberrant bug had made its way into my body. The check-up laid that anxiety to rest. This confirmed to me, yet again, that safe sex is the only way to go because, quite simply, it works.

I enjoy my part-time work, and if it wasn't for the fact that the sex industry is taboo, I'd love to be more open about it. But the fact is, it's utterly unacceptable. I dread my children ever finding out, especially at a young age. If they find out when they're older, I can only hope that they'll understand and won't judge me harshly. I hope I'm raising them to be the type of people who don't rush to criticize or condemn in the absence of the full facts. I hope they're confident and proud individuals. Proud of their bodies, too, and not plagued by the insecurities that are pandemic in the twenty-first century. Even though I only work as an escort occasionally now, the secrecy is still a huge burden and I don't know if it will ever lighten. The more time that passes from when I worked full time as an escort, you'd think I'd be less paranoid, but it's still there, 110 per cent, making me think and rethink my responses in everyday conversations. I make a dinner reservation and have to double check what name I'm giving; I go to fill out a form in the bank and have to remind myself of my real name. I've spent so long talking in my work persona that my working name comes to my mind when I'm being introduced to someone new. I haven't let it slip yet, but I always feel like I'm one handshake away from it. I'm also way, way too comfortable talking about bodies and sex and have to bite my tongue constantly. How could I explain why I've such a good working knowledge of sexuality without sounding like I'm obsessed with it?

I suppose the first question people might want to ask me is, Do you regret it? I believe I did what I had to do at the time and it got me through a financial shit storm. I considered all the alternatives before resorting to sex work, but if there was only me to think of, I'd have no regrets. Of course, the regrets will be in the millions should I ever be exposed. I've made a running-away plan, but I don't go there in my mind because it's too horrifying a place. I can barely touch on it before I recoil at visions of my distraught parents and my children being slagged at school. I feel physically sick at the thought of those I love ever finding out and severing all ties with me.

It was a multi-faceted experience: on the one hand, it was a revelation in terms of what I discovered about the sex industry, the clients and my own sexuality, but on the other hand, I wonder if I'll ever be happy with a typical monogamous, 'vanilla' sex life again. That worries me. Will one partner ever hold my interest long term? I want the love, stability and certainty that come with a healthy exclusive relationship, but will my mind wander to sexual pastures new? Maybe I'll prove to be a great long-term sexual partner in that I've loads of ideas for how to keep things alive in the bedroom. Who knows? Ultan and I split up some time ago. He didn't want to take on a ready-made family but did want children of his own, and I'm done with making babies. Strange that it was the thing I'm most proud of, my children, that came between us in the end. I worried all through that time that my shameful dark secret would break us up.

I've moved on financially, too. Let's just say that I've more money coming in through various other entrepreneurial pursuits, so a couple of clients now and again are sufficient. I'm no longer under the pressure to do escorting as my main source of income.

This book is the biggest risk I've ever taken, but I'm hoping it will prove worth it. I don't want fifteen minutes of infamy. My hope is that it will buy me some time to get myself more financially secure, maybe retrain in a different area where there may be better employment opportunities than in my previous field. One can never predict how these things will go, of course. It's hard for me to imagine my book becoming an overnight success and making me a fortune. If that happens, there's a chance some sections of the media will make it their mission to hunt me down. While my story seems straightforward and not at all sensational to me, I'm sure it might sound fantastical to others. That's the chance I've taken. I want to have and enjoy the success, but without the devastation of being outed.

My family raised me to be independent, which has been a blessing and a curse. I'm so independent that none of my family is close enough to me to suspect what I've been doing. On the other hand, I've probably been overly independent in the past and perhaps didn't ask for help when I could have done with it. My friends and family were all busy, too, and dealing with the economic crash, so I didn't want to ask them for money: they might have had to refuse because they didn't have it themselves. It may seem odd that my ex-husband has never cottoned on to anything, but I suppose that highlights how little thought he gives to where his children's food and clothing come from. I believe he doesn't think about it at all, and that to me is plain sad.

If my daughter came to me in years to come and confided that she worked in the sex industry, how would I react? Well, I'd be an awful hypocrite if I were to be anything other than concerned but supportive. If she could make a good living by working at the high end of any subsector of the industry, be it movies, toy sales or erotic fiction, I don't think I'd object, as long as she hadn't ended up in it out of desperation. However, I hope that I'm providing her with sufficient education to have alternative career choices in her future life.

If either of my sons ever told me they had visited an escort, the only thing that would concern me is why they were telling me such a thing. I'm their mother – 'sex life' and 'mother' don't usually appear in the same sentence.

Working as an escort has been life-changing, but I won't know if that change has been for better or worse just yet. I hope to God my gamble pays off. If I were found out, people would assume I was the stereotypical prostitute, and would wonder how I could stoop so low. That sort of patronizing, unimaginative response would be very upsetting and would ultimately paint me into a corner I'd probably never emerge from. I don't think the world – certainly not my world – is ready for the escort who enjoys what she does and makes it work well for her. Most people either couldn't believe it or wouldn't want it to be true because it would challenge their notions of women and female sexuality. That's a whole other story!

The experience has changed me in some ways. I've learned that the sex industry attracts ordinary men, and the service is largely supplied by ordinary women, like me. I want to emphasize that I know there is a much darker side to the industry. I know women are trafficked, led into prostitution by men who claim to love them or who threaten them, and that some women fall into prostitution because their minds are so clouded by drugs and addiction that they can think of nothing other than securing their next fix. This is all true, but it doesn't apply to me. Mine is just one story in a country that has four million sexual stories to tell.

I have been intelligent, well organized and well prepared in my work. I have also, I imagine, been lucky. Some men made me feel wary and uncomfortable, and those encounters might have ended differently. I've managed to navigate my way through everything, but I know that, at times, plain old luck was involved. The kind of prostitution we see vilified in the media deserves to be rooted out and stopped. No woman should be forced to do anything she doesn't want to do. It's just a shame that the kind of work I did is tarred with the same brush. It would benefit us all, I reckon, to take a wider, more mature approach to the issue of the sex industry. Again, that's a whole other story!

For me personally, what has working as an escort meant? Well, I've laid my own hang-ups to rest by recognizing a basic truth about men: they love women who are confident in themselves, regardless of shape or size. They want a normal woman who is laidback, enthusiastic and sexually open. Women believe that men want the waif-like, picture-perfect girls of the catwalks and glossy magazines, but I think men understand that this image is unattainable – and the truth is they don't care because they want the real deal. From my experience, the client's satisfaction is as dependent on the conversation that takes place as it is on the sex. Now when I'm with female friends and they're talking about their pot bellies, bingo wings or thick ankles, I have to bite my lip to stop myself telling them they have it all wrong. I can't exactly explain that I'm basing my opinion on extensive first-hand experience! I only wish I could because I could save them a lot of self-loathing and heartache.

I'm a mother, an ex-wife, a daughter, a friend and a sex worker. At the start, I was afraid the last would undermine all the rest, but that hasn't been the case. I'm no 'fallen woman'. My sexuality doesn't tally with most people's idea of women, but then, that's just me. I'm not representative of all women, I'm just doing my own thing in my own way. In the end, that's what life's about, isn't it? Ploughing your own furrow and all that. I faced the challenges and I made the choices to get me through them. You might disagree with my methods, but I don't think anyone could criticize my motives. Regardless of what people may think of me, I'm a normal woman, just like any other.